To. Ken + Sara

Thank you so much for your work over so many years.

[signature]

Joho!

To the memory of my father, Willem Andreas Boesak,
and in dedication to continue to strive for his unfulfilled dreams

Published by Joho Publishers (Pty) Ltd
LIPCO Chambers, Village Walk, Parklands, Cape Town
First published 2009

Publication © Joho Publishers 2009
Text © Allan Aubrey Boesak
Cover photo © Images24
Photographs © Greg English
and Oryx Media

All necesarry steps were followed to contact all the relevant copyright owners.
If there has been an oversight, please contact the publishers.

Editor: Bronwyn McLennan
Proofreading: Language Mechanics
Indexing: Language Mechanics
Typesetting: Joho Publishers
Cover design: Flame Design

Set in 11.5 pt on 18 pt Adobe Garamond
Reproduction by Joho Publishers
Printed and bound by Paarl Print, Cape Town.

ISBN 978-0-9802754-8-3

Running With Horses

Reflections of an accidental politician

Allan Boesak

Joho Publishers

Cape Town

Also by Allan Boesak

COMING IN OUT OF THE WILDERNESS –
A Comparative Study of the ethics of Malcolm X and Martin Luther King, Jr.

OM HET ZWART TE ZEGGEN –
een bundel opstellen over centrale themas in de zwarte theologie. (Ed.)

FAREWELL TO INNOCENCE –
A Socio-ethical study of Black theology and Black power.

THE FINGER OF GOD –
Sermons on Faith and socio-political Responsibility.

WALKING ON THORNS –
The Call to Christian Obedience.

BLACK AND REFORMED –
Apartheid, Liberation and the Calvinist Tradition.

IF THIS IS TREASON, I AM GUILTY

WHEN PRAYER MAKES NEWS – Coeditor with Charles Villa-Vicencio
reflections on the call for a day of prayer for the end to unjust rule.

MACHTIGEN HEEFT HIJ VAN DE TROON GESTOTEN

GERECHTIGKEIT ERHÖHT EIN VOLK

LIVET VAERD

COMFORT AND PROTEST –
The Apocalypse of John from a South African Perspective.

SHADOWS OF THE LIGHT –
biblical reflections in a time of trial.

THE FIRE WITHIN –
Sermons from the Edge of Exile.

DIE VLUG VAN GODS VERBEELDING –
Bybelverhale van die Onderkant.

THE TENDERNESS OF CONSCIENCE –
African Renaissance and the Spirituality of Politics.

TOT STERWENS TOE

Contents

PART FOUR: COMING HOME?

Preface

The idea for this book began as a seed in the mind of my friend Danny Titus, who was bothered by the fact that much of what I had to say during the struggle for liberation in South Africa remains unrecorded. In those days, only three of my books were able to find a publisher in South Africa. All of the others were published abroad. Translated into at least seven languages, they could be read by people across the world, but South Africans had no ready access to these writings. They were brought piecemeal into the country. Of the many speeches and sermons I made in front of countless audiences at meetings, rallies, marches, church services and ecumenical gatherings here and abroad, some, but not nearly all, survived. That is partly my own fault. I almost never speak from written texts, and those in the know will understand how difficult it is to find the time to sit and write it all down after delivery. Others simply did not survive the years, were forfeited to the security police in their searches over time or perished in the fire that lay our home in ashes some years ago. Some old-fashioned tape recordings did survive, though, and some of the words saved on these were published.

It was pointed out to me not only that these speeches and writings might be important for history's sake, but that so much contained in them remains relevant to the debates we are engaged in today. The idea to simply gather them all into one publication, did not appeal to me, as I am sure it would not have appealed to readers. But, reading through those speeches, I did rediscover the historical importance if not of the speeches themselves then of the time in which they were made – how they captured the contexts of our unfolding politics, and how they reflected our thinking and actions. We were, after all, making history. And Danny Titus was right: there is great value in reclaiming history. Also, there is a generation growing up that needs more than the facts they find in the prescribed history books. So, this is what I came up with: a book of reflections on my 30 years as theologian and political activist, which would include selected speeches and writings from crucial and decisive turning points – for the country as well as for me personally – representing the journey of a whole generation at some of the most exciting moments in our country's recent history.

This is not an autobiography. I am not sure that I am much taken by the genre, and some have suggested that I am too young for such a venture – so much still must happen. Is it vanity that makes me agree with them? Make-believe? Both, probably. In any case, this book is the result.

The four parts of the book cover those important periods, beginning with 1976, when for the first time I stood on a public platform to make a political speech. I recall the moment as crossing an important divide: from now on I would not just confine myself to 'church matters'; I would put my theology to the test in the field of politics. I would seek earnest answers to the challenges posed to the church and theology, as well as politics, by Aunt Meraai Arendse, Steve Biko and the children of Soweto. Christians became involved in politics, Argentinean liberation theologian and friend José Miguez Bonino wrote, even though at first it was a strange new world for us. 'We must move into that arena, we decided, crudely ambiguous and dirty though it may be, to courageously assume our position as believers, and dare to name God, to confess God from within the womb of politics, from within the very heart of commitment.' After 30 years I still believe that, despite being a sadder and, hopefully, wiser man. Much may have changed in 30 years, and I have learnt to draw the distinction between politics with a capital 'P' and party politics, yet, in the words of yet another liberation theologian, Rubem Alves of Brazil, 'What drives us is not the belief in the possibility of a perfect society, but rather the belief in the non-necessity of this imperfect order.'

The historic moments that followed 1976 are axiomatic: the 1979 address before the South African Council of Churches and the call for mass civil disobedience and the beginning of the long, drawn-out period of confrontation with the apartheid government; the period (1980–1983) leading up to the launch of the UDF, including the growing role of the churches in political activism and the consequences of that phase of the struggle (from 1983 to 1990). These are dealt with in Parts 1 to 3 of this book. The fourth and final part deals with the post-1994 period, one that for me, even as I write, is far from over. Every part starts with a chapter of theological and political reflection that will provide context for the addresses and writings from that period and hopefully open insights into the spiritual, intellectual and political journey the reader is invited to take with me.

There are things that seem to be unique to my generation, and yet continue to plague South Africans as we wrestle with becoming a nation. One of these is the persistent matter of race and identity, and the reader meets this in the very first chapter. My thinking on these matters has been irrevocably shaped by the philosophy of Black Consciousness. So I speak of 'black' in terms of the way we used it: meaning 'black African', 'coloured', and 'Indian' people. The reader will notice the quotation marks, and for some they may even prove bothersome. They need some explanation from me. My generation, in that most formative of times (the late sixties and seventies), learnt to overcome the consciousness of race and ethnicity like no generation before – or since, it now seems. I speak much of Black Consciousness in these reflections, and with good reason, I think. It represented an extraordinary transformative period in the life of a whole generation at one of those genuine turning points in history. It taught us to understand the political significance of South Africa's emphasis on race, racial identity and colour consciousness as an indispensable tool in the continued oppression of South Africa's oppressed people; the arrangements of power relations, and the acceptance of a sub-humanness quite crucial to South Africa's political and economic realities. The division of the oppressed groups in South Africa into Bantus, Coloureds and Indians was not at all accidental, nor natural. The Black Consciousness generation identified, exposed and rejected those evil purposes, overcame those divisions and understood the nature of the foundations of non-racialism. It began with the destruction of our own inferiority, the affirmation of our own humanity in the celebration of our blackness, and the embracing of our power as children of God and heirs of history.

Against the overwhelming, ever-present apartheid realities, we asserted our own understanding of our identity. Of necessity, the tags of racial inferiority and subjugation – of the inevitability of our human, social, political and economic stagnation because of the colour of our skin – had to be resisted and destroyed. We succeeded. And so, apartheid's colour-coded designations of us were replaced: we refused to be called 'Bantus', 'Coloureds' or 'Indians'. We were black South Africans.

Black Consciousness did something else for us. It de-emphasised the negative connotations racial classification brought and instead emphasised the solidarity of the oppressed. It absolutely stood upon the equality of humankind. Our emphasis on our blackness was in response to the dehumanisation of black personhood and to confounding white racialist understandings of those of us 'more favoured' by apartheid as a

10

result of the twisted imaginings of the apartheid mindset. Our solidarity embraced that which we, according to apartheid, should have despised. Instead of striving toward whiteness and all the symbolic political, economic and social ramifications of 'being better', 'moving upward', becoming 'more acceptable', we celebrated our blackness, affecting that all-important reversal so crucial to all oppressed people. We gave life to Fanon: we took off the white masks and took pride in our black faces. We lived Biko: from now on, our minds would be our own.

With that, Black Consciousness relieved us from the perpetual burden apartheid's race-based thinking had foisted on us: the worry that being of mixed descent somehow made one 'less'. Those who remember Mrs Marijke de Klerk's insulting description of coloured people as 'oorskietmensies' in the early nineties will know immediately what I mean. Listening to conversations now and occasionally peeping into internet discussions, this concern seems to have returned and occupies quite disturbingly – to me at least – the minds of a younger generation. With us this embrace of our ancestry had less to do with 'not worrying what white people think', and far more to do with our own self-perception, sense of worth and our place in the South African nation. Such was the confidence instilled in me by Black Consciousness that in 1973 I wrote an open letter published in the Christian Institute's *Pro Veritate* to a very dear Afrikaner friend explaining to him what was happening to us and rejoicing in my hybrid ancestry and heritage, embracing the richness of it all. I wrote this letter in Afrikaans, and the language is in fact very much like the lyrical, poetic language Thabo Mbeki would employ in his rightly celebrated 'I Am an African' speech so many years later. I wish that pride and confidence would return and find its place within the marvellous and fascinating tapestry of our non-racial African oneness, such as Thabo Mbeki dreamt of.

When the ANC returned from exile, they acted as if those political and philosophical battles were not fought, or won. Worse: as if they were of no consequence. Before we knew it, we were once again saddled with the racial terminology of apartheid. We were once again Coloureds, Whites, Indians. But something had changed: now only black people were 'Africans'. The rest of us suddenly had to prove that we were Africans. Before we knew it, we had to prove that we were in the struggle. Suddenly there were layers of suffering during apartheid, and hence layers of reward. Suddenly we had less right to speak and less of a claim on our history. Suddenly there was real anger among us, racial anger, and not just anger caused by that convenient and ubiquitous 'scarcity of resources'. But this makes this issue much more than just a coloured one, since all of us have been inflicted with these new contradictions, which are fundamental to our self-created dilemmas with race. We will now, all of us, have to deal with this if we want to honestly re-embrace our non-racial ideal.

In an angry, blunt letter to a KwaZulu-Natal Sunday paper recently, a coloured person who hates what the new racial stratification is doing to all of us writes about how history is being twisted, forgotten and faded in the right places in order to justify the new brand of discrimination. How come, he asks, we so soon forgot what really happened, for example in the resistance to the Tri-Cameral Parliament and the Bantustan governments? For those coloured elections, he reminds his readers, only 50% of the 'coloured' people who were eligible to vote even registered, even though it was a criminal offence not to register. Only 18,1% of the registered voters cast a vote. The 'ANC's apartheid wing' (so he calls the coloured Labour Party) received only 11,2% of the vote. Altogether this would be less than 6% of the coloured people who were registered voters. He then makes the point that exposes the twisted post-1994 logic that has so many so angry: 'Now weigh this with the fact that in 1963 in the Transkei elections most of the voters registered to vote and the percentage poll in the main electoral districts averaged 70%'. And yet, in many ways the role coloured people have played in the struggle for decades is being denied or diminished. His response to this, amongst other very persuasive reasons, such as the failure of the Constitution in racial matters, is a decision not to vote at all in the 2009 elections. Others turn away in their droves, looking for another political home. Some form new organisations to protect and further 'coloured interests'. I think their complaints are justified, but their solution to the problem is wrong.

This is part of the reason the younger generation find themselves living once again with a sense of alienation my generation had truly overcome. My friend, Anglican priest Courtney Sampson, has found a way to describe this. He speaks of the 'mostly-pre-slightly-post-1994 generation' (people like me and him, in other words), for whom this issue matters greatly. Hence our discomfort with the easy usage of racial terms, and the return of the 'coloured' label. It represents so much of the apartheid times and mindset that we shudder. We, unlike those who play politics with ethnicity, seem to be afraid of the consequences of such politics. But for our children, the 'slightly-pre-mostly-post-1994 generation', this does not seem to be an issue. But there is something worse: it seems the reason it is not an issue is because this generation, confronted by the changes in our political language and the meaning of words, accepted the divide in the black population without reflecting on what that means for the ideal of non-racialism. What this means is that the racial divide in our nation as a whole is accepted as if this were the 'natural' order of things. Hence this unfortunate and weird occurrence: a teacher from Mitchells Plain tells me that her school was invited to a celebration of Madiba's 90th birthday. They did not go, however, because the invitation was for 'all children black and white'. The coloured children did not feel themselves included in this invitation. This is a sad state of affairs.

This is the generation that will feel 'odd' at seeing the word 'coloured' written between quotation marks. Does this mean that we are not real? they ask. That we don't exist, that we are less than others? This last one is a stinger. It refers to the bitter but now popular maxim, 'During apartheid we were not white enough, now we are not black enough.' It means that once again our human worth, and our worth as South Africans, is measured by the colour of our skin. We are back where we started, doomed to fight battles we as a people have already fought and won. Once again a large section of our nation feels itself, as Sampson puts it, 'a people in parenthesis': we feel obliged to add something onto our South African-ness, onto our very African-ness, to explain who we are, where we fit in. It is, I suppose, the recognition of the ambiguity we feel now, one of the more painful uncertainties of our unfulfilled liberation, our incomplete revolution, our failed nationhood.

It is sadder still: these are the people who are the children of the Khoikhoi and the San, the very first nations of South Africa, the originators, so science tells us now, of the human race. The one, brief, shining moment in the legacy of Thabo Mbeki, when he spoke of being African, wove us all together into the rich and varied tapestry of our common ancestry, has been spoken and forgotten, set aside to be ridiculed by the persistent, pernicious tenacity of our obsession with race and pigmentation in South Africa. It remains one of the most puzzling and saddening aspects of Mbeki's legacy: why he did not care enough to make this wonderful, unifying insight the cornerstone of his reign, the foundation of all his policies. As a nation we have not understood as yet that our secondary identity, however we describe ourselves, whatever the composition of the cultural contribution we make to the wealth of our being South African together, makes sense only within the wider existence of our primary identity, that of being African. We have not yet discovered our true soul, hence we have no idea what we have set out to save when we engaged in the battle against racism. Does this book provide answers to these perplexing questions? I honestly do not know, though I would hope it does, at least in some measure.

Although autobiographical moments cannot be avoided, they are not my intention; my aim here rather is to invite the reader on a historical and intellectual journey through these years of reflection and action. What were those historical and political contexts we have had to work in? What were the circumstances, thoughts and convictions that moved us, and how did a whole generation respond to the realities of oppression, struggle and dreams of liberation? I hope readers will understand the dangers and the excitements of our times, discover the relevance and power of ideas, and come to believe that there are values, truly eternal and universal, that never die and without which no society can live. I hope readers will also learn to be alert to the important lessons my generation has learnt and to avoid the mistakes we made; that readers will understand why we grappled with issues, look at our new situation and their responsibilities in it, and connect the dots. Above all, I hope that all of us might come to believe together that the dream of freedom, equality and non-racialism is never the dream of one generation only.

Something about the title of this book. 'Running with Horses' comes from the biblical book of Jeremiah, my favourite prophet of all. In Chapter 12, Jeremiah rages against what he perceives to be a great injustice visited upon the world. Why, he asks, do the unjust remain prosperous, and the just get such a raw deal? Jeremiah's fights with his God are legendary. He is the boldest of them all, challenging God as no other prophet before him or since. His dilemma is that most troubling dilemma of monotheism: appealing to God against God. That, however, is a theological conundrum which we cannot address here. Our interest here is the way God handles the matter. In wonderful, metaphoric imagery, God tells him that what he complains about is by far not the worst that could happen. The difficulties, perplexities and contradictions will continue to pile up. And even though personally things will get a lot tougher, the bigger issues are those of the people he serves as a young, reluctant prophet. The challenges he faces are the challenges of the people. Get real, God seems to say. There is a lot more at stake here than your own personal problems. And the race had not yet begun: till now you have been running merely with foot soldiers. What will you do when you have to run against horses? I think Jeremiah would have understood our South African situation very well indeed. And he would have passed on God's advice straight to us: this is about much more than your personal lament. South Africa's democracy is only 15 years old. Our problems now seem daunting but the real challenges still lie ahead. Our race with horses is still to come.

I joined the Congress of the People after this book had been finished. The inevitable question this new situation raises now is whether the subtitle of the book still applies. Am I still an "accidental politician"? I believe so. I wrote this book not as a party politician but as someone who feels passionately about South Africa and for whom participation in our democratic life is an absolute necessity for the very argument this book makes. For very good reasons, personal as well as professional, I had thought that my role in public life was over. I had made my contribution as best I could. I was ready to indulge my longing for a quieter life in academia and as a preacher. But politically and otherwise South Africa had come to a cross roads. Can one feel this strongly about the things that matter in our political life, be as critical, as insistent that we as South Africans should claim ownership of our democracy and then decline when called upon by the people? It is probably true that I would not have given in had the pressure not been so immense. Not a day goes by that I do not wonder about the turns my life had taken. And it is probably true that the party politician's mantle rests uneasily on my shoulders. It is an ambivalence I shall have to live with and in many places in this book the reader will see why. But it is equally true that I have never found it possible to turn away from the calls for justice and the fulfilment of humanity. That is a reality too compelling, too fundamental to my faith, too much part of my being to ignore.

I am grateful to so many people who helped to make this book possible. Curtiss De Young of Minneapolis in the United States, Nico Koopman and Courtney Sampson especially, who took such intense personal interest in this book, read the entire manuscript and came back with enormously valuable suggestions. The many persons who over the years listened to the addresses and read the pieces especially in the final part of the book and responded with gracious criticism. It is trite, I know, but I have to say it: they have been very helpful, but the mistakes are all mine.

I am a public speaker, and I revel in the live interaction with a responsive audience. It never is the same, of course, but I hope some of that excitement comes through in the written word. My publishers were not only enthusiastic and supportive but provided me with all the assistance I needed, going far beyond the call of duty. I love writing, but every author knows that is not enough. They provided me also with something I have sorely missed: a personal relationship that enhances the joy of writing to dimensions without measure. My wife, as always, is my strength in all things; sounding board, truest friend and most loving critic. Her love is measureless. My daughters mean more to me than they will ever know, and great is my joy when I see ideas take shape in their minds that will make their life worthwhile and help them to build, and stand guard, on the ramparts that stand between our future and the ever-present dangers to democracy.

PART ONE

Not A Single Inch: Faith And Politics

1

Sources of Resistance and Defiance:
Radical Christianity and a Theology of Refusal

now Mandela univ.

The remaking of a coloured preacher

I was standing on a table on the lawn in front of the cafeteria on the campus of the University of the Western Cape (UWC). The student crowd was restless, not yet angry as they would be a few months later, but restless. Curious about this young theologian only some of them knew, expectant, wondering what I would say. But I was the choice of the student leadership, so that must have been an endorsement of sorts. Just back from my academic studies in the Netherlands, having emerged with a doctorate after six years and landing in South Africa at the beginning of July 1976, I was, for most of them, an unknown entity. It was a month or so after the Soweto uprising. The country was beginning to feel the aftershocks of that momentous event (or the warning trembles of what was yet to come), but at that moment we really had no clue where it would lead us. I was not exactly sure why they had asked me to speak – that was before my call as campus minister late 1976 when the campus became 'home'– or what they had expected of me. The request simply was to speak on 'the meaning of Soweto for us'.

RU entered c.UW in 1966 Ten years earlier.

21

Even that early on Soweto needed no further explication. In the minds of these young people Soweto was already no longer a place, a township 'up in Johannesburg'. Nor was it something that 'happened'. Soweto was a condition, a symbol, a compelling call upon the suppressed anger, waiting for that anger to become public. Soweto was an exclamation mark on a page full of question marks. It was the end of one history and the beginning of another. Soweto was the haunting question so powerfully symbolised by the Hector Peterson picture: do I have that courage, that commitment? That Hector Peterson himself, like most probably all of the Soweto students, had no idea that things that day would end up in that terrible massacre, was not exactly the point. Soweto had become more than itself. That day became the unfolding of the words of Steve Biko, 'Courage is contagious.' And while the world would focus on that picture alone, these young people, accepting the symbol, were never fixated; they knew: he was one of many. They saw what the picture did not show and what South Africa was so slow to realise: the millions of young people from Soweto and Mamelodi, from Uitenhage and Lingelilhe, from Cradock and KwaMashu, from Langa and Athlone and Bonteheuwel running behind him. For that was what was coming.

That 'us' was the students on the campus of the university created and meant for coloureds, a proper 'bush college,' as we called all those apartheid black universities, a place where the apartheid government hoped 'good coloureds' would be produced. Domesticated, manageable. Above all, manageable. Educated to the limited extent of their coloured capabilities, predestined by the limited capabilities of their white teachers, readied to play their role in the upliftment of 'their people', ready to fit into the separate, coloured political, social and economic slot the government had reserved for them. They would be, in the juvenile but deadly imagination of the apartheid ideologues, the perfect counterpoint to that most dangerous of phenomena, the 'educated black', in apartheid parlance, 'die geleerde hotnot'. History all over the colonised world and in slavery-shaped societies like the United States has shown that an educated, enlightened, sophisticated and self-owned black mind is a highly dangerous thing. I grab at a few random names from among the hundreds: W.E.B. Du Bois, Bishop Nathaniel Paul, Franz Fanon, Sol Plaatje, A.B. Xuma, Charlotte Maxeke, Pixley ka Isaka Seme, Abdullah Abdurahman, Mahatma Gandhi, Kwame Nkrumah, Eduardo Mondlane, Martin Luther King Jr., Jawaharlal Nehru, Edgar Maurice and Ben Kies.

But this was the curious logic of the apartheid mind: the idea that a black person, when educated in the 'right' ideological environment, could first be moulded to accept her or his condition of oppression and second indoctrinate others and propagate the ideology of the oppressor with the legitimacy and status of her or his education. The educated black person provided much-needed credibility for the oppressive system, in all its manifestations, in the minds of the oppressed as well as in the world. At the same time the system could claim that it was just: it was offering the other races what it was offering whites – education – albeit not at the same level – that would be self-defeating. But best of all, it salved the consciences of the white population. And in the broader scheme of things this was not unimportant.

They were doing what God had called them to do: bringing development and enlightenment to the 'inferior races', equipping them to help their own people, while their education simultaneously taught them how wrong and futile it was to compete with the whites, or to strive to be equal with them. As these truths dawned on us, we needed no vigorous persuasion to understand when Steve Biko told us, 'The strongest ally of the oppressor is the mind of the oppressed.' In these expectations the apartheid architects were deeply disappointed. The experiment with UWC and the 'coloureds' did not work.

These students in front of me, these were the privileged ones – more privileged than most of their age group who would never enter the gates of a university, more privileged than their compatriots at the other bush colleges, because even if they had come from the gutters of coloured education, they were still better off than those who were doomed to the pits of Bantu education. The government, in its cleverly and carefully concocted divide-and-rule strategy, had made the coloureds the target of a special strategy. The Western Cape, considered by apartheid planners as a 'natural home' for coloured people, where they 'historically belonged', was declared a coloured preferential area. This meant that coloured people could own homes in designated areas, could hold certain jobs, and had privilege of movement without the hated 'pass' Africans were obliged by law to carry. This was a logical development of apartheid's political and socio-economic ethnotocracy, as if coloured people lived only here; the Eastern and Northern Cape, Free State, Transvaal (now Gauteng) did not seem to exist. The 'homeland' idea could not work here. But the Western Cape was special: it was what apartheid planners considered a 'natural home' for coloured people, where they 'historically' belonged. Yet white landownership (all those wonderful wine farms!) was too vast and too precious, white economic interests too wide, their cultural and historical roots too deep, and the Cape too beautiful and rich to share evenly. So although coloureds were to be accommodated here, they had to be kept separate. Hence the dispossession of many coloured families, and the birth of one of the most convoluted manifestations of apartheid.

The policy served the regime remarkably well. Not only did it make good political sense from the ruling party's point of view, but it was an absolutely necessary cog in the apartheid wheel. For coloured people in the Western Cape, it created that contrived sense of privilege and political, social and economic distance on the racial ladder without which apartheid could not have survived, even though the sense of it escaped thinking people. For whites, the psychological effect was not just a bonus; it was calculated. Coloureds came to believe that their better position was deserved, because they were 'better' than blacks. The system, insidious as it was, reinforced that attitude in any way it could. Over the decades coloured people were slowly but surely sucked into that apartheid mindset, beginning to believe that this was, also for them, the best way.

In numerous ways they felt themselves closer to white people, and there were always those whites, especially from the Afrikaner community, who assured coloureds that they were really family; those who earnestly took the government to task for 'taking apartheid too far', 'alienating the coloureds' by not giving them equal rights to the whites or, more correctly, by taking away those few political rights they used to have before the apartheid machine bulldozed them ruthlessly into the pit of white racial superiority. They meant well, I suppose, these whites, and one perhaps should not doubt the sincerity of some of them, but white–coloured rapprochement was not the remedy for our ills and not the solution to the country's problems. It was not what we wanted; it was not what the country needed. The future of South Africa would only be secured if it was built on the solid foundations of non-racialism. This is not perfect 20/20 hindsight: the most consistent and honourable strain in the politics emanating from these communities in the Cape had always been non-racialism. Around this ideal they had built all their strivings and activism. It kept them honest. It kept them sane.

But for now the apartheid juggernaut had made them coloureds and their relatively better position called for meek and grateful acceptance. The ultimate price, for there is always a price to be paid, in the form of allegiance not just to white people but also to apartheid, would be exacted with the zeal and precision of the merchant of Venice. The government in particular, and white people in general, were quite proud of their political generosity, and expected the gratitude they thought was their due. Many coloured people were impatient, not with the fundamental flaw in the politics of separateness and division, but due to the fact that they felt the whites would not go far enough in their acceptance of coloured people as part of 'white civilisation'. From the times of colonisation and slavery there were undeniable ties of blood and kinship, language and culture, and white denial of this fact was painful. That the colour code proved so strong was an insult not understood and difficult to forgive. Not only the Group Areas Act, but also the Mixed Marriages Act and the Immorality Act, which forbade marriages and sexual relations 'across the colour bar', drew blood from wounds too deep to describe adequately. The bottom line was written in tears: *not good enough.* Which meant not white enough.

That this part of the population was the result of the mixture of the races – from white colonists to South African black Africans – did not seem to penetrate their consciousness. Nor, more importantly, did they consider that they were the descendants of the Khoikhoi and the San, whose footsteps first imprinted the sand of the Kalahari, the beaches of Table Bay and the valleys of the southern Cape. The momentous, enormous meaning of it all – that was as nothing then. If they thought of it at all, they thought of it with a sense of shame. The weight of their blackness weighed them down, and the longing for whiteness, or at least white acceptance, was their everlasting burden. The only family picture on the wall would often be the picture of the 'Scottish' grandfather. Through some obscure psychological sleight of hand, they de-linked their ancient ancestry, the colonial past and their slave history from the shallow pretensions of apartheid and, like the whites, believed they could re-invent themselves. The sham of it all seemed to completely escape them.

There is no doubt that this psychological game played by white South Africa had done enormous damage to these communities. It made them susceptible to the political flattery of 'you people really belong with us'. It lured them into the trap of eternal patience: 'almost', 'just a matter of time', 'we're working on it'; 'it is the inevitable logic of our policies'. It made them vulnerable to the temptations of expediency: the 'real fight', or the 'interim goal', or the 'first step' is 'coloured rights'. It opened them to bribery: 'coloured wages' (blacks of course should earn less), a coloured university, Coloured Management Committees (whites had proper municipalities), a Coloured Representative Council (whites had Parliament), and finally a 'coloured parliament', one of an unequal, fraudulent and unholy trinity under white tutelage.

So, forgetting their history and forsaking their ancestry, compromising their very existence and sacrificing their dignity, submitting to the enslavement of their minds and playing with their children's future, they spoke of 'our people', meaning coloured people, our coloured rights, our coloured future – until such time as white people judged it expedient to make them white. And slowly but surely the poison of racism seeped its insidious way into their thinking, their way of speaking, their way of life. In their desire to bow to those above, they trampled on those beneath. The devastation to the soul was incremental, but real. They soaked up the coarse, internal subtleties of racism even though the bitter ironies could surely not have escaped them: not just white, coloured and black, but amongst them were 'slightly coloured' and 'darkie coloureds'; the texture of the hair, the straightness of the nose, the thickness of the lips became the marks of stature and class, the determinant of human value. They could never be best, apartheid's pigmentocracy told them, but they could be better than …

This existential paradox caused immense internal tensions, communal and personal. Most knew what was right, but the road to freedom is long and narrow. The power of the dominant white culture was tangible in every sphere of life, the temptations were terribly real, dissent always came with a price, assent with the prizes. The choice between instant gratification and long-term gain is never easy. Standing for justice always means standing in lonely places. The charming and disarming argument of 'our little place in the sun' fails to acknowledge that behind the pretense of humble expectations often lies the hidden desire to own the sun.

The whips of Egypt's slave drivers and the fleshpots of the Pharaoh are always far more real and immediate than the promises of a God one cannot see, the depths of a Red Sea one cannot fathom, the dream of freedom impossible to grasp while in chains. Real, too, is the vastness of an unknown wilderness one cannot even begin to calculate, where hunger and loneliness lie in wait. Never mind a promised land full of people 'stronger than we, next to whom we look like grasshoppers' (Numbers 13), and who do not believe in your God. When does survival become betrayal and compromise mere foolishness? What happens to the spirituality of one's politics when one is seduced and reduced to 'entering and using' the system when one has admitted the system to be evil and in fact knows it to be irredeemable? It is a poisonous logic and the soul does not escape it. All this is not unique, as we know. It is a dilemma coloured people who chose to work with apartheid shared in equal measure with all those who participated in Bantustan politics.

It is certain that the majority in these communities did not fall into this trap, even though the apartheid government's sophisticated propaganda wanted the world, and in the process most of them, to believe that apartheid was widely accepted and supported. Parents often found themselves having to be apologists for a system they detested and hated as they were placed in the invidious situation of having to explain such an indefensible system as apartheid to their children, whom they did not want to hurt. Often, their hatred came through when they could no longer mask it. But there were many times when, in defence of the self-respect, pride and confidence they wanted to instill in their children, they were tempted to make apartheid sound palatable enough so as not to make them doubt their humanity and worth. Just as often the post-76 generation, in their impatience and anger, had little understanding for these very real dilemmas faced by a generation not brought up in the political traditions of defiance. They found it hard to accommodate the fact that for the previous generation politics, like life, required the gentleness of civility, understanding the wisdom of give and take, and polite debate. The post-76 generation's brand of resistance politics, literally turning the world inside out, must have been frightfully difficult for the older generation to understand and deal with. The post-76 generation was like nothing they had ever known.

For the vast majority of these communities, however, apartheid was an abhorrent, evil system that had to be resisted and destroyed, even within the narrow margins of resistance that colonialism and apartheid allowed. They clung to the politics of non-racialism that always was the most persistent strain of black politics in the Cape, and their resistance, against colonialism and apartheid, was built around that precious ideal.

The disdain shown to 'collaborators' in the political circles of the Cape was legendary. In the many creative ways oppressed peoples always seem to find, they exposed apartheid and racism for the lies they were. It was this majority who responded so vigorously to the non-racial, non-violent politics offered by the United Democratic Front and who at last proved the nakedness of the claims of the regime with regard to coloured support. It was a traumatic experience most whites, especially Afrikaners, still find hard to come to terms with.

It was understood that exposing the lie of apartheid and all which that concept represented was a non-negotiable point of departure. That held true, as a matter of course, for politics as well as for the church. And because they exposed the lie not only in those who oppressed, but also in those who collaborated with the oppressor, the political divide in these communities was deep and visceral. It was one of the things Nelson Mandela failed to understand when, in preparation for the 1994 elections, he insisted upon forcing untransformed 'coloured politics' into the politics of the liberation movement, believing that they would bring with them a constituency the ANC could not do without. He never understood how offensive that thinking was to us, and how much it cost us. He wanted us to deal with this within the framework of 'reconciliation', not understanding that it should have been dealt with within the context of non-racialism.

Those who gave themselves to apartheid never saw the lie, because they did not begin to understand the truth about apartheid or about themselves when they embraced it. They never saw, nor believed in, any potential or political future for themselves apart from white domination and white political patronage and the tortuous climb up the ladder of white privilege, under the watchful eye of white paternalism. They never could admit the lie, that apartheid was fundamentally and fatally flawed, that it could never last and that it never, in any shape or form, nor by any stretch of the imagination, could embody the dreams and aspirations of our people. They never saw the monumental insult apartheid in all its forms, reforms, mutations and contortions inflicted upon all oppressed people, including themselves, and how their meek acceptance of that insult weighed upon the rest of us. They believed, with a political simplemindedness that is almost unforgivable, that apartheid, because it rested on such brute power and the seemingly unshakeable belief white people had in their own superiority and invincibility, would last forever; that the choices apartheid offered were the only choices there were.

Believing these lies, they could not see the simplest truth that was constantly held before them: that since the time of colonisation, the oppressed people of South Africa had made their intentions clear; that they were ready to break the yoke of racial inferiority and oppression and economic exploitation no matter what the cost. And the students standing in front of me that mild winter's day, the spiritual children of the ideals and hopes fashioned in struggle long before their time – they were ready to hear what I had to say. They were also ready to take up the mantle of struggle.

Whatever else they knew about me or expected of me, they knew that the young black theologian on that table was no longer the naive, Dutch Reformed-trained coloured preacher who left the country six years ago. The speech, held without notes, confirmed that. Not everything I had to say was especially new, I thought. After all, they knew Steve Biko, and his thoughts had already taken hold on the campus. They had in their midst Adam Small who wrote so convincingly about 'Black Consciousness and White Nihilism'. Among them were many who had discovered the philosophy of Black Consciousness; others

10 yrs after Jim + Cecil Cone

were about to be introduced to it. So I spoke of Black Consciousness, black theology and black power. In 1974 I had published an article entitled 'The Courage to be Black', I had just written and published my dissertation on black theology and with the fiery rhetoric of Adam Small still echoing around that place, I had a lot to say that day. 'We do *not* live by the grace of whites,' Small had written, and the students remembered, 'so although protest shall play a role in our future actions, we must realise that protest is itself a form of begging. We shall not beg. The primary form of expression shall be the manifestation of our blackness. We do not exist for the benefit of whites. We *exist.'* It would be vitally important for 'coloured' people to understand this difference, I thought, even as they flooded the streets with their righteous protests. So too would they need to understand the difference between protesting as coloureds begging for a little recognition from white society and proud black people determined to get their country back. In that respect, all of us, even as we drew inspiration from the roots of radical Cape politics, knew ourselves to be fundamentally different from the previous generations. We were seeking new ways, and there was no time to tread carefully.

I had walked far since that day in 1963, when, 17 years old, I had first set foot on this campus. When I had left, I was a coloured who, like most of us, were at best pulling on the leash. The man in front of the students, an alumnus of this university, had been remade. He had seen not only something of the world; he had seen the coming of the Black Messiah.

The coming of the Black Messiah
And it was true. In the week I left Cape Town for Amsterdam to get to Kampen, that charming little university city on the banks of the Ijssel

river in Holland that would become my home for the next six years of my life, I went with my brother-in-law, Samuel Pick, to say goodbye to Johan Heyns. Heyns was professor of Theology at Stellenbosch University at the time. Since our first acquaintance as student and teacher at UWC, we had become rather friendly and Heyns, quite unlike my teachers at the Dutch Reformed Mission Church Theological Seminary at UWC, was very supportive of my ideal of further theological studies. He understood my hunger for learning. That day, Johan Heyns looked at my brother-in-law and said, 'Take a good look at this man, for as you see him now, you will never see him again.' He was right, but neither Johan nor I really knew how fundamental that change would be.

It is not that the Dutch taught me anything about apartheid. That, growing up black in South Africa did more than adequately. After my ordination in Paarl in February 1968,[23] a town in the relentless grip of removals forced upon the communities by the Group Areas Act, I was once again face to face with the same devastation that had destroyed our community in Somerset West, where I grew up.

Three weeks after being ordained as the youngest pastor ever in our church, I was sitting down, facing one of the elder women in our church, whose house was going to be appropriated. She was angry and bitter and was not going to hide it. Aunt Meraai Arendse was by all counts a formidable woman, like so many of the mothers in the black communities. She wasn't going to soft-soap or spare this young wet-behind-the-ears pastor. 'You don't have to talk to me about Jesus,' she said without smiling as she spoke with biblical indignation. 'I have known and loved Him long before you were born. What I want to know is this: What is God saying about this injustice? Why is God allowing this to happen? I am going to lose my home, the place we built ourselves and loved, where my children grew up. I am going to lose my memories. Who do they think they are?! And what is God thinking?' Then she said, 'I will be in church on Sunday. I want you to tell me about God and this injustice. Then you can talk to me about the love of Jesus after.'

I was silenced, and shaken. Not because I thought she was unreasonable or not believing or trusting enough, but because I was to find that nothing in my theological training over five years, nothing at all, had prepared me for this. The theology taught me by white Dutch Reformed missionaries was totally inadequate to deal with the crises of faith that grew out of poverty, socio-economic injustices and political oppression. For this devastation we had no words in our creeds, doctrines and theologies; or in the Bible. Or so they made me believe. That Sunday I preached, but I know even now how inadequate my words must have been. My theology was too impoverished, my understanding of the Bible too shallow, my faith too pietistic, a pie-in-the-sky-when-you-die attempt at comfort without the redemption of protest and anger. Of the God whose very name is justice, of the fiery prophets of social justice and of the Jesus who came to bring good news to the poor I knew nothing. That Sunday I preached my first 'political' sermon, as people called it. Aunt Meraai was kind, but I knew I had failed. This would continue to haunt me. I would not rest until I had found the words.

Of course, that I knew nothing was in a sense not completely true. Deep down, instinctively, almost, black Christians always *knew*. Just as my mother knew not how to think politically and somehow always knew about God as the God of the poor, the fatherless and the widow. She knew because the Bible told her so and because that was her daily experience. That was her mantra to her eight children after the death of my father, and her own explanation of the tenacity and purity of her faith when others would have long since given up. The truth of the Bible, no matter how hard it is being suppressed or misread or abused, has a way of revealing and asserting itself. And I had met Beyers Naudé for the first time in 1965. So I had known something about the theology of apartheid of which he had become so deeply suspicious. I had come to learn about his life and the Christian Institute, but I had not known at the level that would help me articulate theologically and politically what resistance to apartheid would mean. I could see the door, but I did not yet own the key to open it.

That is what the Dutch gave me. With their theological thoroughness, tendency for hard work and single-minded devotion to academic excellence, they turned my theological world upside-down. But they did another thing that would have a life-long impact on my theological thinking and political activities: they introduced me to the reformer John Calvin. In the Netherlands I met not the insipid, doctrinaire, anaemic Calvin of South African Dutch Reformed pre-ordained election theology, the Calvin who blessed racism and guaranteed the rightness of the theology of apartheid. The Calvin I met was the radical Calvin, the constructive revolutionary whose fiery sermons about poverty and wealth, and whose deeply moving writings on Holy Communion and Baptism, forever captured my mind and heart. The Calvin of the persuasively logical arguments about politics and civil responsibility as the way of Christian discipleship; the Calvin for whom the Lordship of Jesus Christ was the explosive driving force of our deepest spirituality: personal, heartfelt, and public. At last I understood what Reformed theology was all about.

I was in the land of Abraham Kuyper, the Dutch theologian and erudite scholar who also became prime minister of Holland. In South Africa I met him in the neo-Kuyperian racist ideological theology of the

Kuyper

Dutch Reformed Church, articulated so well by Andries Treurnicht. I
heard of him through the sterile, doctrinaire philosophy expounded
by the philosopher Dooyeweerd in Amsterdam and lapped up by the
so-called Bloemfontein school. *That* Kuyper offended me. But here
I met Kuyper the radical social thinker who fought ferociously for
the poor and the less privileged in Holland armed with his Bible, his
understanding of Reformed theology, and his accurate and devastating
analysis of 19th-century Dutch society. Here was the Kuyper of the
1891 Social Congress, the man who claimed that he was engaged in
politics for the sake of justice because there was 'not a single inch of
life' that did not fall under the Lordship of Jesus Christ. Here was the
Kuyper who proclaimed that in the struggle between rich and poor,
Jesus *never* takes his place with the wealthier, but always stands with the
poorer. 'Both the Christ,' he said, 'and also just as much the disciples
after him as the prophets before him, invariably took sides *against*
those who were powerful and living in luxury, and *for* the suffering and
oppressed.' No ifs, buts or howevers about it. The words burnt on the
pages. This was like nothing I had ever heard in those mind-control
sessions called Theology classes back home.

And as my knowledge grew, so did my anger. The anger born of my
experience under apartheid blended with the anger that comes from
knowledge. It was, I had found, a most potent and creative mix.

I was fortunate also to have as my mentor a man who was an
acknowledged expert on the theology of Dietrich Bonhoeffer, that
great theologian of the resistance against Hitler. I studied Bonhoeffer's
Ethics and his *Letters from Prison*. I was captivated by his struggle
against Hitler and the Nazis and his fight against church authorities.
I sat through the night reading and thinking about his faith that led
him finally to choose for the violent struggle against the Nazis and his

participation in the attempt on Hitler's life. I was challenged by this man's conviction that grace was never cheap, that reconciliation calls for sacrifice and that when Christ 'calls somebody, he calls them to die'. Dietrich Bonhoeffer, unlike so many of his academic followers, who theorised about his theology, his life and his death, was a true theologian: he chose justice, acted for justice and stood up for the voiceless and victimised. 'Open your mouth for the dumb' was one of his favourite texts from the book of Proverbs. 'Those who cannot speak up for Jews cannot sing Gregorian hymns,' he said. In other words, if you cannot fight for justice, you cannot truly worship God. For this faith and action, Dietrich Bonhoeffer was hung by the neck with piano wire by the Nazis. *no! that's dohman*

I was shaken: nothing would be the same for me again. I was a sponge: I soaked it all up. I began to understand then that theology was worthless if it did not help me to make choices for the poor, for justice, for peace. My faith in Jesus Christ took on new, unknown dimensions.

But even with all that I was not yet ready. Biko's incisive, relentless criticism of the black church still haunted me. The black church had not yet found a way to give him an answer. That was the thing about Steve Biko. His outlook, his understanding, his commitment, his work – it was all so comprehensive and so totally intelligent. And so completely honest. He was not interested in heaping abuse upon white people even though he was scathing in his criticism of them, especially white liberals. He was, first and foremost, speaking to us as black people, articulating that 'first truth, bitter as it may seem, that we have to acknowledge before we can start on any programme designed to change the status quo'. We shall have to recognise, Biko insisted, that 'all in all, the black man has become a shell, a shadow of a man, completely defeated, drowning in his own misery, a slave, an ox bearing the yoke of oppression with sheepish timidity'. We heard, understood and were staggered. It was harsh, but it was the *truth*. One of the wells this poison was seeping from incessantly, Biko argued, was the Christian church where black people 'were conniving at the irrelevant nature of Christianity ... at the irrelevant interpretation given to the Scriptures in a country teeming with injustice and fanatically committed to the practice of oppression, intolerance and blatant cruelty ...' Note: we were not told or taught or bamboozled, we *connived*. Our minds might have been colonised, but we were not innocent. We actively participated in our own oppression. We helped forge the chains of our slavery. The church, he charged, was 'completely lost' in a country where, because of racial bigotry in church and society alike, black people were 'made to feel the unwanted step-children of a God whose presence they cannot feel ...'

And he articulated it all from within his own deepest heart, and therefore from within ours as well. We heard him and we knew the deepest truth of it. My generation could not escape or deny it. He had taken our histories, beliefs and philosophies so thoroughly denied but not buried deeply enough, along with Africa's *negritude* as expressed by the likes of Leopold Senghor of Senegal, the anger of such voices as Franz Fanon and Amilcar Cabral, and forged it with the voices from the African Diaspora who spoke through the mouths of Eldridge Cleaver and Nikki Giovanni and Stokely Carmichael. So our Black Consciousness was uniquely our own, but woven through with the threads of our continental and trans-Atlantic interconnectedness.

When I went to the United States as visiting scholar in 1973, I understood all this so much better. Listening to and talking with James Cone, one of the most brilliant theologians I have ever known, father of modern black theology in the United States; and with Gayraud

Wilmore, elder statesman of the Presbyterian Church who opened my mind to the radical black Christianity of the United States, my life once again underwent tidal wave changes. I sat in historic black churches from New York's Harlem to Atlanta to California and in Albert Cleage's 'Shrine of the Black Madonna' in Detroit. I began to understand why Marxist scholar Eugene Genovese would later write of the religion of the slaves: 'The very religion that their slave masters sought to impose on them in the interests of social control carried an extraordinarily powerful message of liberation in this world as well as the next.'

Now I knew Jesus the Black Messiah. The Man from Nazareth, so completely claimed and owned by Western Christianity with his blond hair and blue eyes and European accents, was a Jesus who had neither set foot in nor knew Africa. The Jesus of Nicea, Chalcedon and the ancient creeds – Light from Light, begotten not made, of one substance with the Father – was beautiful, but so painfully remote, untouched and unmoved by human misery caused by injustice and inhumanity. Indeed, in the rendition of the European renaissance, this Jesus was too beautiful, too aloof, too aristocratic for the pain, filth and ugliness of slavery and degradation, too light for the darkness of our misery as black people. The Jesus of Constantinian Christianity, without the crown of thorns but with the crown of laurels, with his wounded hands holding the sword and the standard of the empire, in whose holy name we were caught and chained, disrobed and shamed, flayed and slaughtered, disowned, unnamed and unmade and finally baptised – that Jesus bore no resemblance at all to the Human Son.

But in the faith stories of the slaves, in the belief in freedom that never died, in the life-and-death struggles with God and the appeal upon God against God, we found Jesus, the son of Mary the single mother, the man who grew up, in the wonderful phrase of New Testament scholar

Andries van Aarde, 'fatherless in Galilee', though not in heaven. The Jesus with dust on his feet, the homeless One who, unlike the foxes and the birds of the air, had no place to lay his head – him we did recognise. Jesus who rose up in anger against the ruling elites in the palace and the synagogue, who took whip to hand to clean the temple because it was meant to be a house of prayer for all the nations. Jesus, the One who came not only to bring good news to the poor but shared food with the hungry; who covered the shame of prostitutes and outcasts with his healing love and the inclusiveness of his embrace; the One whose compassion for the sick made him stand by them in the uneven and unfair battles with illness. When he came to dine, those who were relegated to sit on the kitchen floor found a place at the table. This was the Jesus who knew that he first had to defy the law in order to make it human and save it from nullification. Those present at his trial spat on him, spoke of him as they did to his believers, called him everything but by his true name. *That* Man was us. This was the Jesus we knew. The Jesus who did not discreetly dab his nose at the grave of Lazarus, but wailed louder than the women, screamed his outrage and grief to the heavens in his protest to God against the power of death. The Jesus with the bleeding hands and feet, the welts of the whips visible on his naked back, sentenced as a rebel against the empire, a criminal, hanging from that cross, dying the most shameful death of all. The blood we saw was not blood purified by doctrine, sanctified by God's divine will and hence not real. It was blood flowing from wounds. He bled like we do. From punishment he did not deserve but against which he was defenceless. And because we met this Jesus, we could believe that when he rose from the grave the representatives of the power of Rome 'became like dead men'. We recognised in the stranger who joined us on the road to Emmaus to break bread with us and dispel our fear and uncertainty, in whose presence our hearts beat with the warmth of truth, the Man who was there among us all the time, touching and healing, restoring and remaking, bringing good news to the poor and sight to our collective blindness. We had met the Black Messiah.

And because we found him in the fields and in the kitchen and on the factory floor, among the poor and the discarded, the sick and the bereaved, we found him in the scriptures. And there he was everywhere: in the slaves in Egypt's bondage, in the silence of Elijah's cave away from the triumphal clamour and senseless violence of Mount Carmel, in Isaiah's suffering Servant, in the abused, silenced and humiliated women of the biblical stories, in Jeremiah's prison pit with the mud rising around his ankles, in Amos's lion roaring for justice, and on every page of the gospels. The 19th-century African hymn writer and catechist John Ntsikana's gospel as a 'fabulous ghost', which we thought we would never see, had found shape and embodiment in the Black Messiah.

Now I had the key. All I had to do was to find the courage to open the door.

We are all Luthuli's children

It is not as if the keynote address at the South African Council of Churches Annual Conference in 1979 fell out of thin air. In the theological discussions of the Christian Institute headed by Beyers Naudé the matter of civil disobedience had been a constant theme. Beyers himself, in his confrontation with the Dutch Reformed Church authorities, had to learn to resist authority on points of principle. More and more, young white men were faced with call-ups to the army and drafted into battles on the borders with just about every southern African neighbour. The so-called security laws of the land were becoming more and more draconian. The laws based on race we found more and more constricting. The reach of the apartheid regime was long and deep. In a truly perverse inversion of an old Reformed belief, they had sought since 1948 to overrun every area of life, every institution, every personal domain. When the 17th-century Reverend Thomas Case sought with unstoppable Puritan zeal to reform 'the benches of judgement, the universities, the cities, the countries, the inferior schools of learning, the Sabbath, the ordinances, the worship of God … [for] every plant that my Heavenly Father hath not planted shall be rooted up!', he did not know what South African racist Calvinists would make of it. In the face of such a totalitarian onslaught on freedom and individual responsibility, it was unavoidable that the Christian conscience would rebel.

The results of this misunderstood Calvinistic zeal were everywhere to be seen and felt. Churches could not avoid taking cognisance of it. On 12 September 1977 Steve Biko was brutally murdered after long periods of torture. The government tried a cover-up and the whole white establishment became complicit in one way or the other. It took some time for the truth to emerge. The organisations of the Black Consciousness movement were put under immense pressure: organisations as well as individuals were banned and activists imprisoned, put under house arrest or run underground.

On 19 October, the day all remaining black organisations were banned along with the newspaper *The World* and its talented editor Percy Qoboza and the Christian Institute (CI) – with banning orders for Beyers Naudé and the CI's Cape director, Theo Kotze – the struggle came home for me, literally. That day I had my first visit from the Security Police. At 4 am I had this weird, long but instructive conversation with a Captain Mostert about my 'misunderstanding' of Romans 13. Surely a 'learned' Dutch Reformed person should know that that scripture calls for unconditional obedience to government as a sacred Christian duty, because government is 'placed there by God'? He was also upset that I was apparently not grateful enough for what the government was trying to do 'for your people', the same line I would hear from P.W. Botha in my very first conversation with him years later, except that P.W. added that 'coloured people' had a 'special place' in his heart. I thought of this conversation again when I heard George W. Bush saying to the Cubans that he would be their best friend once Castro died.

But the most important point I took away from my conversation with Mostert was the value of the conviction of the Afrikaners that apartheid was God's will, that it could be justified by scripture and that they, and their policy, could be recognised as Christian. He spoke with political conviction but with religious fervour. Coming from a non-theologian, a security policeman, I found this enlightening indeed. His quite visceral hatred of Beyers Naudé was focused almost exclusively on that issue. Apartheid would not be complete, nor understood, I knew, if not in its twin dimensions: as a racist, political, socio-economic system and as a religious construct essential to those who believed in it. I would never forget that lesson. That morning many of my books were confiscated, as well as almost ten years' worth of correspondence between Oom Bey and myself. An indescribable loss. I never got them back.

But in 1978 my own church, the then Dutch Reformed Mission Church, for the first time took a strong position on apartheid. On theological grounds we declared apartheid a sin and a 'pseudo gospel'. Other apartheid practices such as detention without trial, the Mixed Marriages Act and other pieces of offensive legislation were similarly condemned. It was a new, welcome space, hard fought for, and we would not easily let go of it. Simultaneously, under the new leadership of Bishop Desmond Tutu, the South African Council of Churches claimed that space for itself and became more and more the voice of the voiceless masses of South Africa. We had all heard Biko, and we all knew we had to respond. We were facing a new generation of young black Christians: politically astute, sensitive to what they were being told, knowing the dilemmas of the black church, and articulate in their anger, critique and aspirations.

By the time I received the invitation from Desmond Tutu, I knew that there was a reason why I was asked to speak on 'The Black Church and the Future' (the full speech is provided in Chapter 2 of this book). I saw this invitation as an opportunity to speak on the meaning of a black church, our political responsibility and our call to participate in the struggle for liberation. My call for civil disobedience was meant as a specific counter-call to the armed struggle that after Soweto had such magic allure for so many of our youth.

My mind was besieged with questions. How could the churches move from making statements to joining in action? Could the black church devise new initiatives to give substance to its analysis and actions? Could it have a dialectical approach to the political situation in South Africa? Could it say no to apartheid, and at the same time say yes to those ideals towards which it was striving? Could it make people excited about direct mass action in the face of immense government repression? Could it get them on the streets, visibly demonstrating their rejection of apartheid? Could it make people believe again in the power of non-violent action and the Christian activism of Albert Luthuli?

I have learnt much from studying Gandhi and Martin Luther King Jr., but our country's own history of activism during the defiance campaigns in the 1950s was immensely inspirational. Here in South

Africa, after the cowardly brutality of Sharpeville and the loss of our innocence at Soweto, were we ready to give non-violent resistance another chance? After Sharpeville and Soweto we could not so easily repeat Martin Luther King's conviction that 'unearned suffering was redemptive'. And Gandhi's satyagraha (soul power) had no African sound. But we could, with Luthuli, speak the words of Peter in Acts 5: 29: 'We must obey God rather than any human authority.' But also, and this was perhaps a question that could only be answered in the thick of struggle, in the heat of battle, in the solitary fear of the torture chamber, eye to eye with guns and dogs and tear gas, would the memory of the convictions of Luthuli be strong enough, stronger than the romantic power of Fidel Castro, Che Guevara and the armed struggle? Four years later, these questions would return with even greater urgency. I thought the answer to all these questions could be yes. After all, we were all Luthuli's children.

At the conference there were a few proposals regarding civil disobedience, which showed that many in the churches have clearly been thinking about these matters, Reverend Douglas Bax of the Presbyterian Church in Southern Africa foremost among them. By 1981, the Presbyterian Church was demonstrating defiance to apartheid by giving its blessing to 'mixed marriages'. So I was definitely not the first to have thought about this. But there was an essential difference between those proposals and my call. Those proposals on civil disobedience, as I remember, dealt mostly with the individual's response to unjust laws, and the duty of the church to support such individuals, concerning call-up to the South African Defence Force, for example, or defying the Mixed Marriages Act, or the Illegal Assemblies Act. I understood the responsibility of the church to support an individual, the young man who took great risk, say, in refusing to go to the army and to participate in apartheid's illegal wars of aggression. Those were courageous acts worthy of support. My purpose, however, was broader. I was calling on the church to deliberately take calculated risks in calling for open, mass action, demonstrations on a large scale in the streets such as we had seen in the 1950s in our own country, in India under the leadership of Gandhi, and in the United States during their civil rights struggle. Giving responsible institutional support to an individual was one thing. But could the church also take responsibility for the thousands that would flood the streets if the call were heeded?

The difference was even more crucial than that. My call was not a fall-back on liberal theological thinking prevalent in the white theological discussions of most anti-apartheid churches. Mine was a call upon the black church to take responsibility for its own struggle, based on a radical black understanding of Christianity. It was a direct response to the call of Biko and the radicalised youth after Soweto. I was seeking the emergence of the black church as a spiritual and political force, a transformational reality in South Africa, learning to speak the language not just of protest but of liberation and finding the courage to act accordingly.

Between 1960 and 1976 almost all ecclesiastical initiatives against apartheid were conceived and driven by white Christians. Concerned white Christians, to be sure, but white Christians nonetheless: the white liberals in the churches, the Christian Institute, the civil rights organisations like the Black Sash. Everything was done for us, on our behalf. The Christian Institute itself, the famous 'Message to the People of South Africa', the various resolutions at various synods and assemblies. The time had come for black South African Christians to become the architects of their own destiny, the shapers of their own freedom, the first line of battle in their own struggle. Steve Biko and the children of Soweto had woken us up from sleep.

In the 1960s I remember listening to a smuggled-in tape of Martin Luther King Jr. Under cover of the midnight darkness I listened to the man whose voice was banned in South Africa, speaking of 'remaining awake through a great revolution', brilliantly playing on the story of Rip van Winkle who slept right through a revolution, awaking astounded to find the world completely changed: a sign that had borne a picture of King George III of England, now had a picture of George Washington, the first president of the United States. That was the black church in South Africa; the revolution had begun in Soweto and we should be not only awake but also in the lead.

Those of us who came to the struggle with our faith in Jesus Christ, who believed in the God of the Bible as a God of justice and liberation, who saw struggle as discipleship – we were all Luthuli's children.

If that speech on UWC's campus three years earlier was my first attempt at understanding and explaining South Africa's post-Soweto political landscape from our point of view, this address was a deliberate attempt at helping the ecumenical church to find its place in that landscape. There was nothing accidental about it, nothing innocent or per chance. Alwyn Schlebusch, Minister of Justice at the time and once Beyers Naudé's church council member in Potchefstroom, was right when he divined that there was a divide, and that the churches and the government were facing each other across that divide, and that confrontation was inevitable. It was a time for making choices.

2

The Black Church, Politics and the Future: Responding to Biko and the Children

Following the momentous events of 1976 and 1977, the South African Council of Churches (SACC), under the leadership of Bishop Desmond Tutu, increasingly took the lead in the non-violent resistance to apartheid. It also functioned increasingly as a unifying ecumenical force as well as a platform for the black churches, and in important ways helped to shape black leadership for black and multiracial churches. In this regard the SACC stood in sharp contrast to the white Reformed churches, which supported apartheid. The annual conferences became an important indicator of the progressive involvement of the churches in the struggle. The following address was delivered at the annual conference held in July 1979.

Of blackness, the gospel and faith

I was rather surprised when your General Secretary asked me to address you on this subject. It suggests that the need to speak of a black church is not confined to those in the traditional black churches alone; blacks in the so-called multiracial churches may no longer be excluded.

This is a happy development, because it means that in spite of so many problems and reverses, the real meaning and significance of Black Consciousness has not completely bypassed the Christian church.

Black theology teaches us that theology cannot be done in a void. It is always done within a particular situation. The situation of blackness in South Africa is the unavoidable context within which the theological reflections of black Christians take place. We have come to realise that persons are influenced by their social and economic environment, and that their thinking is influenced by the social conditions in which they live. We recognise that Christians living in different situations will have different understandings of life, as well as vastly different understandings of the gospel and its demands on their lives. This is basically why, for some, the gospel is an incomparable message of liberation, whereas others find in it justification for a system that exploits and oppresses.

Black theology is a black understanding of the gospel. This understanding is not confined to one group or denomination only, nor is it an automatic universal revelation to all black people. It is rather the result of a painful, soul-searching struggle of black Christians with God and with the meaning of God's Word for their lives today. These black Christians have wrestled with black history – a history of suffering, degradation and humiliation caused by white racism. They have taken seriously the cry of so many who, through the years, refused to believe that the gospel could corroborate the narrow, racist ideology that white Christians were postulating from black pulpits and that white theologians were giving respectability to in their learned books.

These black Christians were the ones who refused to accept an anaemic gospel of subservience and dejection – both in the blatant forms of a hundred years ago and in the subtler forms of the present. Somehow, they always knew that the God of the exodus and the covenant, the God of Jesus Christ, was different from the God whom whites were proclaiming. It was when they understood this that they walked out of the established, white-controlled churches to form their own churches. It was then that they rejected white theology and went in search of a God 'who walks with feet among you, who has hands to heal, a God who sees you – a God who loves and has compassion', to quote that great leader of one of the first African independent churches, Isaiah Shembe.

Those black Christians knew that the gospel of Jesus Christ does not deny the struggle for black humanity, and it was with this light from God's word that they went into the struggle, both within the church and outside it. And it is this understanding that today inspires many black Christians in their search for authentic humanity and a true Christian church.

Out of this struggle, more than two centuries old, emerged the black church, a broad movement of black Christians, joined in a black solidarity that transcends all barriers of denomination and ethnicity. It shares the same black experience, the same understanding of suffering and oppression, and the same common goal of liberation from all forms of oppression. It is a movement deeply imbued with the belief that the gospel of Jesus Christ proclaims the total liberation of all peoples, and that the God and Father of Jesus Christ is the God of the oppressed.

There is another point I wish to make. We must remember that in situations such as ours, blackness (a state of oppression) is not only a colour; it is a *condition*. And it is within this perspective that the role of white Christians should be seen. Certainly I do not refer to those whites who for so long have been leaders in the black churches. Nor do I refer to those who happen to be in control of churches where blacks are the majority. I speak of those white Christians who have understood their own guilt in the oppression of blacks in terms of corporate responsibility, who have genuinely repented and have been genuinely converted; those whites who have clearly committed themselves to the struggle for liberation and who, through their commitment, have taken upon themselves the *condition* of blackness in South Africa. In a real sense, they 'bear the marks of Christ'. They are part of the black church, not as lords and masters but as servants, not as 'liberals' but as brothers and sisters, for they have learnt not so much to 'do for' blacks, but to identify with what blacks are doing to secure their liberation.

This is the black church, and it is about this church that I shall be concerned here. Before I can begin to talk about the black church and the future, however, I shall have to look at our present situation.

Of struggle, consciousness and choices

What is the position of the black church in South Africa today? It is a church that has been uncertain of its identity. The black church in South Africa has not yet succeeded in attaining for itself an authentic identity. In many cases, white control is still a reality and that makes it difficult for black Christians to identify with the church. By 'white control' I do not mean only administrative control – although it is important who decides and really speaks for the church. I am also thinking of the predominantly white image of the black church: in style, in witness, in commitment.

The structures that black people have inherited are geared to the needs of those who have no sensitivity whatsoever to the black situation. It is no wonder, then, that the black church sometimes finds it hard to respond meaningfully to the people in the communities it serves who are in need of God's presence in their lives. A precondition for the authentic identity of the black church is the ability to identify with the community where it works and gives witness. The black church must identify with the past, present and future of the community it serves. The black church must become part of that community, so that it may understand the joys, sorrows, and aspirations of that community. And the church must not be afraid to identify with the struggle of the people. For the struggle in South Africa is not merely political; it is also moral. The struggle is not merely *against* an oppressive political and exploitative economic system; it is also a struggle *for* the authenticity of the gospel of Jesus Christ. The struggle is as much against a political philosophy and practice as it is against a pseudo-religious ideology.

Apartheid and all it stands for is not a system that places its fortunes on the political judgement of a people. It demands, with idolatrous authority, a subservience and obedience in all spheres of life that a Christian can give only to God. Of course, this in itself is not strange; apartheid shares this demand with all other totalitarian forms of government.

To identify with the struggle is to realise that the struggle for liberation and the attainment of black humanity are commensurate with the gospel of Jesus Christ. It does not mean that the Christian has to condone and justify everything in the course of the struggle. It does mean, however, that in the struggle the Christian has the duty to be the salt of the earth and the light of the world. One may legitimately ask, of course, if Christians can stand aside and allow the struggle for our liberation to be monopolised by those who do not believe in the Lord Jesus Christ, for we know that God will hear the cry the oppressed have sounded since the Psalms, 'How long, O Lord?'

None other than John Calvin reminded us of this when he wrote:

Tyrants and their cruelty cannot be endured without great

weariness and sorrow … Hence almost the whole world sound forth these words, How long, How long? When anyone disturbs the whole world by his ambition and avarice, or everywhere commits plunders, or oppresses miserable nations, when he distresses the innocent, all cry out, How long? And this cry, proceeding as it does from the feeling of nature and the dictate of justice, is at length heard by the Lord … [The oppressed] know that this confusion of order and justice is not to be endured. *And this feeling, is it not implanted in us by the Lord? It is then the same as though God heard himself, when God hears the cries and groaning of those who cannot bear injustice.*

Of course, Calvin is right. So, although acknowledging that the powers of the anti-Christ are at work in every situation, the black church knows full well that refusal to participate in this struggle constitutes an act of disobedience to God. We know also that where true human liberation takes place, it takes place because Christ is there.

In the heat of the struggle Christians today are called to be the light of the world. In the midst of the struggle we are called to be the embodiment of God's ideal for this broken world. Christians must be there to represent God's possibilities for authentic Christian love, meaningful reconciliation, and genuine peace.

In arguing thus, I cannot urge that the black church be absorbed by the world, or that the struggle dictate to the church. It remains true that only a critical differentiation between the church and the world – that is, adhering to the criteria of the gospel of its Lord – will enable the church to make a meaningful contribution in keeping God's options open to those who in the thick of battle, because of their tears, their fear, or their anger, often fail to recognise these options. It is not a Christian struggle I am pleading for, but a Christian presence in the struggle.

This decision is not one that will face us some time in the future. It is facing us now. The church is facing a tremendous challenge. In the last decade or two, there have been profound and rapid changes in the black community in South Africa. These are not so much changes in tangible political structures as changes in political consciousness, which reached a peak in 1976.

Not all young persons who were prominent at that time have left the church. Some of them have done so – in disappointment and disgust. Many, however, with their parents, are still in the church, but with a highly sensitised political consciousness and with probing, critical questions about the nature and the witness of the church. These are young people with experience far beyond their years, experience born of their active and personal engagement in the struggle for liberation and for their God-given humanity. It is my contention that the black church does not yet know how to deal with this new generation.

This new political consciousness and the reborn consciousness of black humanity have brought a new sense of responsibility in the black community. This new sense of responsibility and the active involvement of the black community in the struggle have taken away almost completely the traditional deference to the church. Church officials are no longer judged by their office and the authority it represents; to the contrary, their office and authority are now measured by their active participation in the struggle for liberation. I daresay that although this worries us no end, we have yet to come to terms with this change of attitude.

There is yet another matter, and that is the black church's dependency

in America
Prosperity movement

on an alien theology. This I regard as very serious. At the basis of so many maladies in the black church – our inadequate lifestyle, dependence on white resources, the very acceptance and rationalisation of the situation that makes us so dependent – lies our dependence on an alien theology.

For centuries the black church has been engaged in a struggle to speak truthfully. In this struggle, two theologies were fighting for supremacy within its ranks. On the one hand, there has been the theology we have inherited from Western Christianity: the theology of accommodation and acquiescence. It engendered an individualistic, other-worldly spirituality that had no interest in the realities of this world except to proclaim the existing order as the God-ordained order. This theology wanted blacks to accept slavery and, in modern times, their lowly position as second- and third-class citizens. Either through force of circumstance or through sheer hopelessness, blacks accepted this anaemic, heaven-orientated theology, still rampant in the black church today.

On the other hand, there was a theology of refusal: a theology that refused to accept that God was just another word for the status quo; a theology that understood that the God of the Bible is a God who takes sides with the oppressed and who calls persons to participate in the struggle for liberation and justice in the world. This was a theology that understood God's love for the lowly and therefore uttered a clear 'no!' against those who oppressed and dehumanised them – whether on slave farms or native reserves, whether in the aseptic and air-conditioned temples of banks and boardrooms or within those dark and awesome prison buildings where so many brothers and sisters have lost their souls … and their lives.

This theology of refusal has been the theology of great black leaders;

to name but a few: Denmark Vesey, Frederick Douglass, W.E.B. Du Bois, Martin Luther King Jr., Nehemiah Tile, Mangana Mokone and Albert Luthuli. This theology was expressed masterfully by Frederick Douglass:

> I love the religion of our blessed Saviour. I love that religion which comes from above, in the wisdom of God which is first pure, then peaceable, gentle ... without partiality and without hypocrisy ... I love that religion which is based upon that glorious principle of love to God and love to man, which makes its followers do unto others as they themselves would be done by others ... It is because I love this religion that I hate the slave-holding, woman-whipping, the mind-darkening, the soul-destroying religion that exists in America ... Loving the one I must hate the other; holding to one I must reject the other.

This is the theology the black church must make its own if it is to survive, if it is to become truly 'church'. We must come to understand that this faith is not a new, politicised faith, but rather the age-old gospel. It is the message of the Torah and the prophets. It is a message that unmasks the sinfulness of humanity, in personal life as well as in the existing social, political and economic structures. It is a message that judges, but it also speaks of hope, of conversion, of redemption. It is a message for the whole of life. And it is our task to bring this message to our people in such a way that it makes sense in the de facto situation.

Of confrontation, grace and reconciliation

In light of what has been stated above, a profound question emerges.

What about the future?

Basically, there are two alternatives facing our country. One is to continue with the present trend of modernising and modifying white *baasskap* ('dominance', 'supremacy') and eventually to end up with a civil war; the other is to bring about radical and fundamental change that would inspire the search for a truly new society.

At the same time, the black church has two choices. It can develop a policy of realpolitik and accommodation, urging the people to accept piecemeal concessions and thereby making it easy for itself, or it can stand firm, challenging the forces of the status quo and accepting the risks that come with it.

We should not deceive ourselves. This choice will not be easy. Now that all meaningful black organisations have been banned, the black church has become more important than before as a vehicle for expressing the legitimate aspirations of blacks. The government knows this. That is why the government is going to concentrate its repressive measures on the church more and more.

If the black church is going to be true to its Christ and its calling, I can see no way that confrontation between the black church and the white state can be avoided. The government may also, however, try to persuade the black church that real changes are indeed taking place, and that, for the sake of peace, the black church should accept them. I think that we must expect a time when government officials will more and more employ a kind of Christian language, using terms such as 'love', 'peace', and 'reconciliation' for the purpose of undermining the watchfulness of the church. And many blacks, the so-called privileged underprivileged, may discover that the government is extending more privileges to them, and they may try to pressure the black church.

The black church is called on to be wide awake, to remember to take as its criterion not the privileges of those who already have more than others, but the justice or injustice done to 'the least of these'. The black church must remember always that an evil system cannot be modified or reformed. It must be eradicated.

The second choice of course is the more difficult one. It will leave no room for compromise. It is bound to bring confrontation, not only with the government but also with those Christians, white and black alike, who shout 'peace! peace!' where there is no peace. It will make the black church even more vulnerable. The government will accuse the church of subversion, and some Christians may shout charges of lovelessness and intransigence. In the end, however, the church will have preserved its integrity. The black church, like Moses, is not called to negotiate with the Pharaoh. It is called simply to convey the Lord's command: Let my people go!

I want to suggest a few things the black church must do in order to equip itself for the future.

First of all, we must reaffirm our commitment to Jesus Christ. For the black church, Jesus Christ is Lord. He is Lord over all of life. This confession we must cling to at all costs. Our loyalty and obedience are to him alone. If the black church is to have any future at all, this is where we must be firm. Our allegiance is ultimately not to the laws of the state, or to the laws of self-preservation, but to the commands of the living God. Our loyalty is to Christ. Our criteria are the demands of his kingdom. We shall have to learn not to be dictated to by the demands of the status quo, however intimidating, or by the demands of any ideology, however tempting. Our faith in Jesus Christ and the liberating power of his gospel must form the basis upon which we offer ourselves as a humble servant in the world.

Secondly, we shall have to learn to resist the temptation of what that great theologian of the resistance, Dietrich Bonhoeffer, has called 'cheap grace'. Love, peace, reconciliation, justice are evangelical realities the black church dare not ignore. But there is a danger in our South African Christianity today. Christians are sometimes so desperate for something 'good' to happen in this quagmire of political hopelessness that often they cannot distinguish between subterfuge and authenticity. In such a situation, it is very tempting to see peace and reconciliation where there is none at all.

Oppression of black people in this country has been going on for 300 years. In the course of those years, humiliation and degradation have left their mark on the souls of millions. Self-hatred and dejection have become the hereditary burden of countless generations. Many have died; many more will die. Distrust, suspicion, hatred have become part of our lives. Therefore, reconciliation is essential. But it will be costly.

In the process of reconciling God with the world, confrontation with evil almost made Christ give up. But it was necessary. It was necessary to unmask human nature for what it really was. It was necessary to rip to shreds the flimsy garment of pseudo-innocence that human beings had wrapped around themselves to convince themselves that they were guiltless.

True reconciliation cannot take place without confrontation. Reconciliation is not feeling good; it is coming to grips with evil. In order to reconcile, Christ had to die. We must not deceive ourselves. Reconciliation does not mean holding hands and singing 'black and white together'. It means, rather, death and suffering, giving up one's life for the sake of the other. If white and black Christians fail to understand this, we shall not be truly reconciled.

So it is with peace. One is not at peace with God and one's neighbour because one has succeeded in closing one's eyes to the realities of evil. Neither is peace a situation where terrorism of the defenseless is acceptable because it is being done under the guise of the law. For in South Africa, Adam Small's question remains pertinent: 'Which law? Man's law, God's law, devil's law?' Peace is not simply the absence of war or an uneasy quiet in the townships. Peace is the active presence of justice. It is shalom, the well-being of all.

If our theology fails to make clear that Christian love is not a sentimental feeling, but an act of justice, doing what is right, our theology does not reflect the gospel fully. We must not be afraid to say that in the South African situation Christian love between white and black must be translated into terms of political, social and economic justice. By doing this, we help the Christian church to accept the challenge of veracity. Even though this process will be a very painful one, it will prove to be rewarding in the attempt to generate an authentic Christian community.

Thirdly, we must be prepared to meet the challenge the new situation will present. There will be the challenge to preach a relevant gospel to the black community. For many of our black youth throughout this land, the crucial question is whether the gospel is indeed the gospel of liberation and not merely a tool for the oppression of the poor. This is a challenge only the black church can meet.

There is also the challenge to find a way of participating meaningfully in the struggle. Words and statements will no longer suffice. With tragic inevitability, the violence inherent in the system of oppression in South Africa breeds violence and counter-violence. In addition, as peaceful protest is made increasingly impossible, the belief grows that violence is the only solution. I realise that the issue of violence is a touchy one, and this is not the place to discuss it. I want to say, however, that the unbelievable hypocrisy of white Christians on this matter is appalling, and it will take all our resources to undo the damage done to Christian integrity at this point.

Of refusal, suffering and prophetic witness

Although the debate is not yet closed, and although we may be faced with even more taxing situations, we must in the meantime refuse to be idle. The church must initiate and support meaningful pressure on the entrenched system, as a non-violent way of bringing about change. The church must initiate and support programmes of civil disobedience on a massive scale and challenge white Christians especially on this issue. It no longer suffices to make statements condemning unjust laws and then tomorrow to obey those laws as if nothing were amiss. The time has come for the black church to tell the government and its supporters: We cannot in all good conscience obey your unjust laws because non-cooperation with evil is as much a moral obligation as is cooperation with good. So we will teach our people what it means to obey God rather than man in South Africa. A new study on the investment problem will not suffice. But direct and forceful action will show multinational corporations how serious the church really is about the plight of our people.

To do all this in South Africa is to expect trouble. The repressive, intolerant nature of the present government cannot allow it. And yet the church has no other option. And when we do this we must prepare ourselves for even greater suffering. It is the Lord himself who warned us: 'A servant is not greater than his master.' For the black church this word of our Lord is especially true: 'He who wants to hold onto his life at all costs shall lose it. But he who loses his life for my sake, shall gain it.' If the black church can understand this, we shall not have to fear the future.

I pray that the black church in South Africa will, by the grace of God, be truly the church of Christ:

- in the midst of struggle and in the heat of the battle – be a servant church;
- in the midst of violence, oppression and hatred – be a prophetic church;
- in the midst of hopelessness and pain – be a hopeful church;
- in the midst of compromise – be a committed church;
- in the midst of bondage and fear – be a liberated church;
- in the midst of intimidation and silence – be a witnessing church;
- in the midst of suffering and death – be a liberating church;
- in the midst of failure and disappointment – be a believing church

To God, the only God, who saves us through Jesus Christ our Lord, be the glory, majesty, authority and power from all eternity, now and forever!

3

Divine Obedience:
An Open Letter to the Minister of Justice

The SACC conference of July 1979 stood out because of its bold stand on matters such as civil disobedience as an essential part of the growing resistance to apartheid. My speech and the resolution taken at the conference received extensive media attention. They also elicited strong condemnation from the then minister of justice, Alwyn Schlebusch. This chapter contains my response to Mr A Schlebusch.

24 August 1979

The Honourable A. Schlebusch
Minister of Justice
Union Buildings
Pretoria

Dear Sir,

A short while ago you thought it your duty to address the South African Council of Churches, as well as church leaders, very sharply and seriously over radio and television and in the press in connection with the SACC resolution on civil disobedience. Although the resolution was not taken as a direct result of my address, I did express my point of view openly on that occasion and I am one of those who support the SACC in this respect.

You are the minister of justice and it is in this capacity that you have issued your serious warning. I take your words seriously, hence my reaction, which I express to you respectfully and which I ask you to read as a personal declaration of faith.

Your warning has become almost routine in South Africa: the government continually says to pastors and churches that they must keep themselves 'out of politics' and confine themselves to their 'proper task': the preaching of the gospel.

However, on this very point an extremely important question emerges: What is the gospel of Jesus Christ that the churches have been called to preach? Surely it is the message of the salvation of God that has come to all peoples in Jesus Christ. It is the proclamation of the kingdom of God and of the lordship of Jesus Christ. But this salvation is the liberation, the making whole, of the whole person. It is not something meant for the 'inner life', the soul only. It is meant for the whole of human existence. This Jesus who is proclaimed by the church was certainly not a spiritual being with spiritual qualities estranged from the realities of our human existence. No, he was the Word become flesh, who took on complete human form, and his message of liberation is meant for persons in their *full humanity*.

Besides, the fact that the term 'kingdom' is such a political term must already say a great deal to us. For example, this fact brought Reformed Christians to believe (and rightly so) and profess with conviction throughout the centuries that this Lordship of Jesus Christ applies to all spheres of life. There is not one inch of life that is not claimed by the Lordship of Jesus Christ. This includes the political, social and economic spheres. The Lord rules over all these spheres, and the church and the Christian proclaim his sovereignty in all these spheres. Surely it is the holy duty and the calling of every Christian to participate in politics so that there also God's law and justice may prevail, and there also obedience to God and God's Word can be shown.

The Dutch Reformed Church professes this in its report 'Race Relations in the South African Situation in the Light of Scripture'. The report states plainly that in its proclamation the church must appeal to its members to apply the principles of the Kingdom of God in the social and political sphere. When the Word of God demands it, the church is compelled to fulfill its prophetic function vis-á-vis the state *even in spite of popular opinion.* The witness of the church with regard to the government is a part of its essential being in the world, says the report. This is sound Reformed thinking, and the Dutch Reformed Church accepts this because it wants to be Reformed. Why, then, are you refusing to grant other churches and Christians (also other Reformed Christians!) this witness and participation?

But there is still another problem. Through its spokesmen your government has often warned that those of us who serve in the church must 'keep out of politics'. Yet at the same time it is your own colleagues in the cabinet who want to involve the clergy in political dialogue!

The only conclusion that I can come to is that you do not really object in principle to the participation of the clergy in politics – as long as it happens on *your* terms and within the framework of *your* policy. This seems to me to be neither tenable nor honest. In addition, are you not denying your own history by holding to this viewpoint? Did not the Afrikaner clergy speak as leaders of their people, and did they not inspire their people in what you saw as a just struggle? Did not the churches of the Afrikaner, even in the Anglo-Boer War, stand right in the midst of the struggle? Why, then, do you reject today with a sort of political pietism that which yesterday and the day before you accepted and embraced with thankfulness to God?

But, Mr Minister, there is even more in your warning, which I cannot ignore. It has to do with the exceptionally difficult and sensitive issue of the Christian's obedience to the government.

It is important that you understand clearly that I have made my call for civil disobedience as a Christian, and that I was addressing the church. The context and basis of my call may thus not be alienated from my convictions as a Christian addressing other Christians upon that same basis.

It surprises me that some have tried to interpret this as a call for wanton violence. It is precisely an *alternative* to violence! And I turn to this alternative because I still find it difficult to accept violence as an unobjectionable solution. Or perhaps there are some who fear that should Christians in South Africa perform their duty in being more obedient to God than to humans, the idolised nature of this state will be exposed. Surely a state that accepts the supreme rule of Christ should not have to be afraid of this?

I believe I have done nothing more than to place myself squarely within the Reformed tradition as that tradition has always understood sacred scripture on these matters.

Essential to this is the following: It is my conviction that, for a Christian, obedience to the state or any earthly authority is always linked to our obedience to God. That is to say, obedience to human institutions (and to human beings) is always relative. The human institution can never have the same authority as God, and human laws must always be subordinate to the Word of God. This is how the Christian understands it. Even God does not expect blind servility; Christians cannot even think of giving unconditional obedience to an earthly government.

Our past experience has taught us that this is exactly the kind of obedience, blind and unquestioning, that your government expects. I want, however, to be honest with you: this I cannot give you. The believer in Christ not only has the right, but also the responsibility, should a government deviate from God's law, to be more obedient to God than to the government. The question is not really whether Christians have the courage to disobey the government, but whether we have the courage to set aside God's Word and not obey *God*.

Over the years, nearly all the Christian churches in this country have condemned the policies of your government as wrong and sinful. My own church, the Dutch Reformed Mission Church, last year at its synod condemned apartheid as being 'in conflict with the gospel of Jesus Christ', a policy that cannot stand up to the demands of the gospel. I heartily endorse this stand my church has taken. Your policy is injust; it denies black people their basic human rights, and it undermines their God-given human dignity. Too many of the laws you make are blatantly in conflict with the Word of God.

I have no doubt that your policies, and their execution, are a tremendous obstacle to reconciliation between the people of South Africa. There are laws that are more hurtful, or more draconian than others, and these especially have been condemned by the churches. Now the churches have reached a point where we have to say: If we condemn laws on the grounds of the Word of God, how then can we obey those laws?

In my view, Christians in South Africa today do not stand alone in this decision. Scripture knows of disobedience to earthly powers when these powers disregarded the Word of the living God. Daniel disobeyed the king's law when he refused to bow down before the graven image of Nebuchadnezzar (Dan. 3: 17–18), because he regarded the king's law as being in conflict with the demands of his God. Peter's refusal to obey the commands of the Sanhedrin not to give witness to Jesus has always been the classic example of disobedience to a worldly authority. To this day his answer still resounds like a bell in the church of Christ: 'We must obey God rather than men' (Acts 5: 29). There are other examples. Paul displayed nothing of a servile obedience when the magistrates of Philippi wanted to release him from prison after having confined him unlawfully (without a trial!): 'They gave us a public flogging, though we are Roman citizens and have not been found guilty; they threw us into prison, and are they now to smuggle us out privately? No, indeed!' (Acts 16: 37).

In the case of Peter and John, the Sanhedrin was the highest authority, not only in religious matters, but in everything that did not lie directly in the sphere of the Roman Procurator. In the case of Paul, the magistrates were the highest officials in the Roman colony of Philippi. For both Peter and Paul it was clear that occasions could arise where disobedience to unjust authority was the only honourable way for the Christians.

Furthermore, Luke 23: 6–12, Mark 15: 1–5 and John 18: 8–11 teach us that Jesus himself did not always demonstrate obedience to state authority. Before Herod, on one occasion, 'he answered him not a word'. Also before Pilate there were those moments when he chose to give reply neither to the questions of Pilate nor to the charges of the high priests and scribes. John tells us something else of great significance. He tells us that Jesus reminded Pilate of something that every bearer of authority must remember or be reminded of: 'You would have no authority over me at all,' Jesus replied, 'if it had not been granted you from above' (John 29: 11).

I am not arguing that there is 'proof' from these actions of Jesus, Peter and Paul that violent, revolutionary overthrow of a government is justifiable. That is a completely different issue. I am saying, rather, that blind obedience to civil authorities is alien to the Bible; and that, for the Christian, loyalty and obedience to God are first and foremost. May I also point out, parenthetically, that the issue on which everything hinges, and the lesson that South Africa has to learn, is that what is needed is not servile submissiveness of citizens to the state, but *rightful co-responsibility* for the affairs of the state? And this is precisely what your policy denies millions of South Africans.

This is not the place to present a full treatment of Romans 13. However, I would simply point out that the first verse of Romans 13, which is often taken as unconditional legitimisation of a government's contention that its authority can never be challenged by Christians, is in fact a very serious criticism of that very authority. A government wields authority because, and as long as, it reflects the authority of God. And the power of God is a liberating, creative, serving power. Thus Paul can refer to civil authority as 'God's servant to do you good' (13: 4). Thus, throughout the years, it has been taken for granted in Reformed thinking that a government has authority as long as there is evidence that it accepts responsibility for justice, for what is right.

Put another way, the definition of government in Romans 13 does not simply point out that civil authority exists. It also suggests that there is proper authority only where there is a clear distinction between good and evil, so that it is not important whether a government is 'Christian' or not, but really whether it is still truly *government* – that is, whether it understands the difference between good and evil. Where there is no justice and no understanding, the authority of the government is no longer derived from God, but is in conflict with God. Resistance to such a government is both demanded and justified.

Even Augustine, one of the respected fathers of the church, who was concerned particularly with protecting the state and who defended political authority with extraordinary energy, had this to say: 'Justice is the only thing that can give worth to a worldly power. What is worldly government if justice is lacking? It is nothing other than a bunch of plunderers.'

Calvin echoed this sentiment when he wrote to King Francis of France in the letter published as the prologue to his *Institutes*: 'For where the glory of God is not made the end of the government, it is not a legitimate sovereignty, but a usurpation.' And Calvin added, 'Where there is no vision, the people perish.' Calvin also stated clearly that 'worldly princes' lose all their power when they rise up against God. Christians should resist such power, not obey it.

When, precisely, do the actions of a government collide with the demands of the Word of God? In deciding this, the church should be led by the Word itself, knowing its demands for justice and peace, and also by the actual experience of the people. It is in the concrete situations of actual human experience that the Word of God shows itself alive and more powerful and sharper than any two-edged sword.

In making this decision, the church should look for criteria not among those who make the laws and who have political and economic power, nor among those who are favoured by unjust laws, but rather among those who are disadvantaged by these laws, who are hurt at the deepest level of their being: those who suffer, those who have no voice – the oppressed, the 'least of these my brothers and sisters'. And in the eyes of the least of the brothers and sisters of Christ in our country, your government and your policies stand condemned. I need not repeat these accusations; I simply want to draw your attention to them, and to the truth that is in them.

The untold suffering of men, women, and children, the bitterness of too many, the wounds caused by your policies through the years can never be forgotten, nor compensated for by the 'concessions' your government is apparently willing to make. The superficial adjustments to apartheid already initiated do not touch the root of the matter. It is as one of your colleagues has said: 'The fact that a black man is allowed to wear the *Springbok* emblem (as he participates in multiracial sports) does not give him political rights.' Indeed, and we may add: it does not give him his God-given humanity either.

You complain that the churches are 'against the government'. But it is because of your policies that so many churches and so many Christians find themselves against you. In this, we really have no choice, because the church of Christ in South Africa *must* obey God rather than you. I plead with you: stop your disastrous policies.

May I end with a personal word? I am not writing this letter in order to be brave or arrogant. I must honestly confess that I am afraid of you. You are the minister of justice. As such, you have at your disposal awesome powers such as only a fool would underestimate. The victims of these powers are sown across the path of the past and recent history of South Africa.

I, like any other South African, want to live a normal life with my wife and children. I want to serve the church without fear. I want a country where freedom is seen as the right of every citizen and not as a gift to be given or withheld by the government. I want, along with millions of our people, to have co-responsibility for government in our native land, with everything you want for yourself and your children. I, too, want peace, but authentic peace, which is the fruit of active justice for all. However, my longing for a 'normal' life must not undermine the service to which God has called me. That would be intolerable. And my service is also to you. That is why I write this letter. I shall surely stand guilty before God if I do not witness against this government.

I think the time has come for your government to make a choice: you are either the 'servant of God' of Romans 13, or you are the 'beast from the abyss' of Revelation 13. Unless and until the right choice becomes *evident* (through the wholehearted and fundamental change of your policy), Christians in South Africa shall be called upon, *for the sake of their faith*, to resist you as we would the beast of Revelation 13. For the Christian, obedience to God and God's word must be the first priority.

I am aware that the decision to resist the forces of government cannot be an easy one. That is why the synod of the D.R. Mission Church made this so clear last year: 'If a Christian is bound by his or her conscience to follow the way of criticism, which brings them into conflict with the state, then they should obey God more than humans. In this case, however, they must be prepared to accept suffering in the spirit of Christ and his apostles.'

Once again, this is not a matter of being brave. Rather, I should like to use this occasion to urge you to realise that peace and salvation, indeed, the future of South Africa, do not lie in more 'security laws', in more threats, or in an ever-growing defence budget. They lie, rather, in the recognition of the human dignity of all South Africans, in the pursuit of justice, and in respect for the God-given rights of all.

You as whites are not in a position to achieve this on your own. That is why the churches have pleaded for a national convention where the people could be represented by authentic, chosen leadership. We demand the right to have the vote, so that our citizenship in South Africa may become meaningful. Give us the right to express ourselves and our political will. We need to have the opportunity to participate fully and meaningfully in the political processes in South Africa. Is this not the fundamental thing you grant yourself?

I plead that you make use of the offer and the opportunity to have discussions. Honest negotiations with the intention genuinely to share together in South Africa is always better than to stand against each other as enemies.

I am using this letter as an open witness, and thus will make it available to the press.

I thank you for giving me your time.

May God give you wisdom in everything.

Sincerely,

Allan Boesak

PART TWO

Taking Politics To The Streets

4

The Road to Mitchells Plain:
The Birth of a Movement and the Dawn of an Era

Between the Charter and Soweto

What lies between 1949 and 1976, and between 1976 and 1983? A history of struggle, is the easy answer, and not only from an activist's point of view. I recall 1949, because from the inception of the African People's Organisation in 1902 and that of the African National Congress in 1912 the people's organisations adhered strictly to what they called 'a constitutional struggle'. This meant working within the existing laws, however restrictive these may have been, working with the whites who had political power, however condescending they may have been, petitioning Parliament, even though it was ultimately safeguarding only white interests, appealing to the Crown, even though the British Empire had no desire for justice and had betrayed its black subjects time and time again and, above all, *trusting* the basic fairness of Western democracy and its institutions.

But 1910 saw the formation of the Union of South Africa, an indescribable political betrayal, and in 1948 came the victory of the National Party at the polls and with it, the coming of apartheid. Yet even after this, in 1949, as Nelson Mandela reminded the court in his treason trial, the ANC remained determined to avoid violence. This did not mean passivity, however. At that time the decision was taken to embark on peaceful protest. These demonstrations were peaceful, but nonetheless unlawful. The movement had decided to place itself deliberately outside the law because it considered those laws to be unjust. The result was a sure sign of things to come and a telling give-away of what South Africa's democracy was really worth. More than 8 500 people went to prison. Mandela and his colleagues were convicted for organising the campaign even though discipline and non-violence were stressed throughout.

During the campaign, the apartheid government reacted by enacting the Public Safety Act and the Criminal Law Amendment Act. These decreed harsher penalties for protests against the apartheid laws. The Defiance Campaign, as it had become known, continued, and the tradition of non-violent resistance became firmly established. Of the spirit of that campaign, the faith-driven, sacrificial courage and the vision that inspired the people, much is known, and I speak of it in Chapter 16.

Then there was Kliptown, 1955: the gathering of that vast throng of South Africans, black and white, communists and socialists, as well as those who would not proclaim any particular ideology but knew about freedom; people of all faiths. They had come from every corner of the country and most of them after confrontation and detention. They understood why they wanted freedom, and why they were ready to die for it. They had the words of the Freedom Charter in their hearts and acted them out on the streets long before they were written on paper. They did not come to find a purpose; they knew their purpose, and they had brought their integrity and authenticity with them. They wrote an eternal chapter in South Africa's politics. The contrast between

Kliptown and the Union Buildings, in style, intention, purpose, and integrity, could not have been greater.

In between there were in 1957 the women and their decision to take their stand within the struggle. Strijdom. The Union Buildings. The march. The songs. The steadfastness. The courage. Facing the police, facing the whole white apartheid power structure. The words, like sledgehammers: 'Strijdom, wathint' a bafazi, way ithint'imbolodo uzo kufa!' 'Strijdom, now you have touched the women, you have struck a rock; you have dislodged a boulder, you will be crushed!' The women, all 20 000 of them, and the man they confronted, who privately admitted that 'the white man cannot retain his superiority by merit alone', saw that day for what it truly meant. And it was the women who showed him.

Nineteen-sixty was the *annus mirabilis,* the 'year of the miracle' when after most of Francophone Africa – Cameroon, Central African Republic, Chad, Congo (Brazzaville), Dahomey (Benin), Gabon, Ivory Coast, Madagascar, Mali, Mauritania, Niger, Senegal, Togo, Upper Volta (Burkina Faso) – became independent. Somalia and Nigeria would soon follow. Other African states would shout *Uhuru!* But freedom for South Africans would remain elusive. Our road was longer, and first we had to pass Sharpeville.

There was something extraordinary about Sharpeville. After all, it was not the first time that there was confrontation between government and black people on the streets. The ANC's Defiance Campaign, a carefully constructed series of nationwide protests planned to climax in June 1960, was pre-empted by its new rival, the Pan-African Congress (PAC). The PAC, formed in 1959 in protest against what it perceived as the ANC's 'submission' to 'multiracialism', called for a non-violent protest against the pass laws. The protest was centred in Sharpeville, the

PAC's stronghold in the eastern Witwatersrand. One cannot say that the ANC was upstaged, as it bounced back quickly, but it was certainly taken by surprise. As PAC members, responding to Robert Sobukwe's call, offered themselves for arrest at the Sharpeville police station on 21 March, the peaceful action turned into tragedy. The police fired live ammunition, the crowd turned to flee. One hundred and twenty-three were wounded, 69 killed, most of them shot in the back. So now we had a large-scale massacre, a split liberation movement, suspicions cast on the understanding of the Freedom Charter and its intentions, and despite the original intentions of Sobukwe, a renewed emphasis on ethnicity. And rivalry for the loyalty of the masses.

On 30 March young Philip Kgosana of the PAC led 30 000 people from Cape Town's black townships to Parliament, and ANC leader Albert Luthuli burnt his pass and called on people to stay away from work. The stay-away was nearly total. The Stock Exchange plummeted. For the first time the world really took note and condemned apartheid's harshness. The ANC had reasserted itself and its authority with the masses. Whites were terrified, the government panicked. It called a state of emergency and in the next few weeks detained more than 18 000 people. On 8 April it banned the ANC and the PAC.

What followed was the decision of the ANC to embrace the armed struggle, the formation of uMkhonto weSizwe, and exile for most of the leadership and a host of others. Much of the struggle activities were driven underground. The people were scattered – 'like sheep without a shepherd' is the biblical phrase – bereft of their leaders but not of their dreams, sobered by the realisation of white South Africa's preparedness to use violence to secure white superiority, but buoyed by their ability to resist; shorn of their belief in white people's democracy but reaffirmed in their faith, their hopes shaken but not crumbled, their vision blurred but not surrendered. They were driven underground but not trampled to the ground.

White South Africa was relieved, but not secured. The government fortified the gates of apartheid with new draconian legislation and unprecedented military preparedness. They called it vigilance and security, but it was the nurturing of a greater paranoia and a deeper fear: of what black people might do now, of what they had done and what else they could do. For it really was the crossing of that fatal threshold: the predetermined murder of the innocent, and the premeditated killing of the dream of freedom in order to preserve might, power and privilege.

Although they did not know it then, white South Africa had changed forever. The hand they had lifted against the black people of this land would slay them. That strongest of pillars in white Afrikaner life, the Dutch Reformed Church (DRC), would turn away from the blood on the dusty streets of Sharpeville to look toward heaven, but the windows of heaven would be closed that day. At the conference called by the World Council of Churches and held in Cottesloe near Johannesburg, the churches, shamed by Sharpeville, would accept the Cottesloe Declaration condemning the killings but also apartheid's policies. The voice of an angry Verwoerd drowned out the voice of God and the DRC lost one more part of its soul. The Declaration was rejected, the DRC representatives at the conference disowned, and Beyers Naudé was destined to step forward.

In the words of ANC president Dr Alfred Xuma to Jan Smuts in 1943, Sharpeville was a 'last, God-given opportunity' for both H.F. Verwoerd and the DRC. But, like Smuts, they were too blinded by power, rendered sightless by ideology and the dedication to white superiority to see it.

What else happened between 1949 and 1976? There were the treason trials, Mandela and his comrades were sent to Robben Island, followed by so many in the years that followed, and the island began to take on its mythical proportions. The women once again pretended to be submissive, but they were never forgetful. Albert Luthuli grew in stature and dignity, white people's fear of him never went away, and his death, to this day, left us all wondering. His people's love for him and his legacy sustained them in the lean years that followed. In the political vacuum Steve Biko arose and woke us up with the philosophy of Black Consciousness, reminding us of who we were. New laws were spawned. The detentions and bannings continued. Steve Biko died, naked and alone, in the back of that Land Rover. The apartheid establishment, as they always did, lied about him, his life and his death.

They came and went, the Strijdoms, the Verwoerds, the Vorsters, the Bothas. They made the laws and locked their doors. They lied to the world and to themselves, and locked their doors. They built the most modern, strongest army on the continent, and locked their doors. They were taught by the best and the brightest of the CIA and the British Military Intelligence, bought the most sophisticated devices and trained themselves in terror and torture. And they locked their doors. The fear did not go away. And they killed the children. The world that had been lulled to sleep awoke and screamed in shame, and the people, the patient and determined Sizwe, arose again. The guilty powerful did not look at the blood on the streets, but at the walls, on which were written the words they knew, for they had read them before: *Mene, mene, tekel ufarsin.* In the short and better-known version: 'You have been weighed and found wanting.'

But other words remained and resounded in other hearts, the words spoken before Sharpeville and into the smoke-filled air after Sharpeville.

The words of the Freedom Charter:

> We, the people of South Africa, declare for all our country and the world to know: that South Africa belongs to all who live in it, black and white, and that no government can justly claim authority unless it is based on the will of the people ... that only a democratic state, based on the will of all the people can secure to all their birthright without distinction of colour, race, sex, or belief.

And then like a bell, clear and true:

> And therefore, we, the people of South Africa, *black and white, together, equals ...*

The words of Albert Luthuli:

> From the beginning our history has been one of descending unities, the breaking of tribal, racial and creedal barriers. The past cannot hope to have a life sustained by itself, wrenched from the whole. There remains before us the building of a new land, a home for all who are black, white, brown, from the ruins of the old narrow groups, a synthesis of the rich cultural strains we have inherited.

The words of Robert Sobukwe, that giant amongst our heroes, whose greatest characteristics were his incredible mind and his humility:

> We still have a mission, a nation to build; we have a God to glorify, a contribution to make towards the blessing of mankind.

I met Robert in early 1978 when he was literally on his deathbed. Lung cancer had ravished him. He had just read my *Farewell to Innocence* given to him by Theo Kotze, Cape Director of the Christian Institute, and he wanted to talk about black theology, Black Consciousness and my understanding of these. Theo took me to him. Had he not been kept under house arrest in Galeshewe township in Kimberley and virtually refused proper treatment, he might have been alive today. But his life, commitment and legacy are chiseled into the minds and hearts of those who came to understand and love this leader with the unique gifts. His truthfulness and integrity will long outlast the untruths told about him now, and his power will engulf the silences about him and like the stones cry out his monumental presence in the story of our nation's coming into being. He did not, as we are told, reject non-racialism. He rejected multiracialism because it meant racialism multiplied. The PAC, Sobukwe argued, recognised only one race – the human race. We talked about this in his hospital room in Cape Town and even though under the circumstances we could not argue conclusively, I will never forget it. The weakness of his political party today is no measure of the man and cannot be used to undo his greatness nor his permanent place in the firmament of our liberated skies.

The words of Beyers Naudé:

> [This] is not a choice between the church and the Institute. The choice goes much deeper: it is a choice between obedience in faith and subjection to the authority of the church. And by unconditional obedience to the latter, I would save face but lose my soul … Therefore I must go … God will not let you go until you have chosen! … To all Christians of all churches and peoples and races who sincerely seek and pray for this highest obedience to God comes his glorious assurance even for the unsure future: if God be for us, who can be against us?

And most of all, the words of Ingrid Jonker, beautiful tortured soul and poet without measure. She spoke of Sharpeville in the tones of one touched by a wounded and aching God. She wrote in Afrikaans, but those who spoke that language on the white side of the fence, their minds clouded by suppressed guilt and their hearts constricted by fear, did not hear nor understand her. Her words echoed in the wretched silence of their self-induced deafness. But when Nelson Mandela read that poem at the opening of the first democratic parliament in 1994, her words, so long ignored, almost forgotten, were reborn, reached out and embraced all of us, her enraptured audience, black and white. For the first time in the South African parliament, Afrikaans was heard as the language of all our people. And on that day Ingrid Jonker walked back out of that sea and into our hearts, never to be forgotten again:

> The child is not dead
> not at Langa not at Nyanga
> Not at Orlando not at Sharpeville
> not at the police station in Philippi
> where he lies with a bullet through his brain.
> The child is the shadow of the soldiers
> on guard with rifles *Saracens* and batons
> the child is present at all gatherings and law-giving
> the child who just wanted to play in the sun at Nyanga is everywhere.
> The child grown into a man treks all over Africa
> the child grown to a giant travels through the whole world
> without a pass.

Between pseudo-innocence and Tambo's agony

My early 1980s meeting with Oliver Tambo, president of the ANC in exile, had been planned weeks in advance. I was to be invited by Kenneth Kaunda, president of Zambia, and during my stay Tambo and I would meet for the first time. Like most of my generation I had great admiration for the man, not because I knew him but because of his reputation and his position as the man deemed worthy to succeed such giants as Dr Xuma and Chief Albert Luthuli. The propaganda of the apartheid regime told us one thing, but our reading of history through politically astute teachers told us another, although one's expectations were understandably clouded by what was hammered into one through the South African media.

He was shorter in stature than I expected: not much taller than me. A gentle, intelligent, soft-spoken man, careful in his choice of words, almost visibly weighing them as he spoke. Respectful, even to one as young as me. He carried with him an enormous dignity. I would come to admire this man even more as I learnt to know him better. We talked in general for a while with Kaunda acting as host – the real meeting would start with lunch. At the table Oliver Tambo, quite naturally, crossed himself, folded his hands and said, 'Shall we pray?' He did not wait for the theologian to pray; *he* prayed. And not just a quickie: 'For what we are about to receive …' It was, as I told friends later, 'a proper prayer'. For the country and our people and the struggle; for Zambia, giving praise to God for its people's courage and hospitality; for our families; and for 'this young man right here, destined for such great things'.

I was surprised. I did not know exactly what I expected, but certainly not this easy intimacy with God. After all, he should at least be a communist whose belief in God had long been eroded by the harshness of the Christian regime at home and his own dedication to Marxism. The notions of faith, prayer and God should have been completely foreign to him. Propaganda is insidious, and tenacious. I was, let's be honest, somewhat taken aback and strangely touched: it was a wonderful, deeply felt prayer and I was swept up in the sincerity of it. I was humbled: what was this great man expecting of me? Did he perhaps know more about me than I knew or suspected, and expected, of myself? Gone was the propaganda of the 'unbelieving communist', the 'tool of international Marxism bent on destroying our Christian values', the violent revolutionary who kills innocent people to satisfy some barbaric hunger for power. This was the *real* Tambo. Everything else about him made sense once this simple, basic fact was grasped.

But that was just the beginning. We talked for hours, and what I would learn that day would stay with me for the rest of my life. It also spoilt me a bit: from then on I have measured the ANC not just by its history but by this man, its leader. This made it hard for the ANC and for me. How fair is it that a whole organisation in all its different parts and manifestations should be personified by one, matchless man? He was like Luthuli, who wanted his faith to lead him 'into the thick of the struggle', hoping that it would influence 'for good the character of the resistance'.

Tambo wanted first to know everything about myself, and I told him. About my life, my convictions, my struggles with choices and my faith in Jesus Christ. About my fears and apprehensions, my longings for justice and my aspirations for our land and people. We talked about my dedication to non-violence: what I had learnt from Gandhi and Martin Luther King, what I believed to be the call of the Gospel. He listened, really listened, and I knew he understood.

But here's the strange thing: all of a sudden I missed my father with a pain that was almost physical. He had died when I was only six. My

mother was a heroine of the faith, a marvellous woman whose footprint
in the lives of her children will remain large and her memory for all of
us unsullied. But I understood then what she meant when she would
sometimes say to me, 'I wish your father were here.' She did not at all
feel herself inadequate, I think, or unequal to the task of bringing up
her children – eight of them, all on her own. But her inborn wisdom
withheld her from denying that a child needs both parents and that
sometimes, just sometimes, she found it hard to be both. She also
understood that my longing to speak to my father was no reflection on
her parenting or person. Those increasingly difficult political questions
could not be answered by one who was not a political animal. The
personal wrestling with life's demands, which came too early to a boy
whose boyhood was lost too soon, needed the guiding hand of a father.
My father was as dark as Oliver Tambo, as gentle, as wise. I could not
guess where, had he lived, his politics would have taken him. But I
hoped fervently he would have understood where mine had taken *me*.
How many times had I wondered what he would have thought of the
choices I'd made?

Kakamas, the small town on the banks of the Orange River in the
Groen Karoo where I was born, with its Dutch Reformed mission
school and its feudal relationships, and where the days of slavery, it
seemed to me, were touchable, a mere heartbeat away, just beyond those
black-burnt stone *koppies,* was a long way away from symbolically huge
Lusaka. How many times had I wondered about that, and wondered
too what he would have thought of the choices I had made if we could
have spoken?

Now here I was, for the first time in my life since becoming a man,
speaking to another man who could have been my father, *as if he were.*
Everything about him told me: trust him. It was a most amazing feeling,

almost devastating in its unexpectedness. So I spoke to him of things my mother did not know, and would not know for years.

And then Tambo spoke. About his life, the struggle, life in exile; about his faith in God and his belief in justice, peace and equality. About the ANC, its history and its battles, and about the choice for the military struggle after 1960. Years later I would see a film clip of Tambo speaking of that choice at the United Nations, but it was that conversation in Lusaka, in Kaunda's home, I would remember. He did not attempt to give me a history lesson and he did not pontificate; he spoke with quiet, utterly believable passion as if he had been there with every event, with every decision. At no moment, it seemed to me, did he see himself and his life as separate from the history of his movement. It was as if he had himself lived through every moment of history. He spoke as if he knew that while we would be seeing each other again, we would never again have the opportunity we'd had that day. Not once in that entire conversation did he try to convert me to the ANC point of view. He simply explained, trusting I would understand, just as he had understood my point of view.

In his moving trial testimony, Nelson Mandela had also explained why the ANC turned to the armed struggle. But Mandela wanted to be sure that the Court, and South Africa as a whole, understood clearly that the ANC's decision in this regard was a deliberate, calculated political decision after it had become clear that all else had failed and all channels of peaceful protest had been closed down, and that the government's only response to non-violent protest was violence. Mandela took the Court down the list:

> There had been violence in 1957 when the women of Zeerust were ordered to carry passes; there was violence in 1958 with the enforcement of cattle culling in Sekhukhuneland;

there was violence in 1959 when the people of Cato Manor protested against pass raids; there was violence in 1960 when the government attempted to impose Bantu authorities in Pondoland. Each disturbance ... showed that a government which uses force to maintain its rule teaches the oppressed to use force to oppose it.

Mandela's conclusion was chillingly logical: 'I came to the conclusion that as violence in this country is inevitable, it would be unrealistic to continue preaching peace and non-violence.' Everybody knew this to be true, but like all oppressive regimes the apartheid government saw its own incessant violence as necessary, lawful and righteous. This was the 'sword' of Romans 13 placed in its hands by God. The government's duty was towards the maintenance of white power and privilege, not to do justice and establish equality. For white South Africa, Mandela's words were the vindication of their fears and justification for their anger at the 'ungrateful Bantus', rather than the call to conscience and the revelation of bitter truth. But Mandela spoke for all of black South Africa when he said: 'I can only say that I felt morally obliged to do what I did.' They could identify with these words too: 'The lines were drawn.'

Tambo agreed with Mandela. With no one in the ANC, however, had I ever experienced what Oliver Tambo allowed me to see that day: not just the logic of the decision but the sheer agony of having to make that decision; the raw struggle with his faith, the agonising search of conscience that kept him awake at night. The pain when people died, his own personal reluctance to romanticise violence, his loathness to speak easily of the 'blood of the martyrs' watering the 'tree of freedom'. Oh, make no mistake: he knew the decision to be the right one under the circumstances, but he knew also how much he wanted things to be different.

It was his honest wrestling with the ethical dilemmas that come with such choices that reminded me so much of Dietrich Bonhoeffer. Like Bonhoeffer, Tambo, as a Christian, confronted with Marx's critique that religion is nothing but 'the opiate of the people', asked Bonhoeffer's question: 'Do we Christians have the strength to witness to the world that we are not daydreamers with castles in the clouds; that we simply accept things as they are; that our faith is indeed not an opiate that leaves us satisfied in the midst of an unjust world?' Like Bonhoeffer, Tambo chose another way. 'Instead, we protest all the more persistently and single-mindedly on this earth, precisely because we look for that which is above. We protest in word and deed!' And like Bonhoeffer, he found himself in a situation where he had no option, and no control over where those choices would take him.

Tambo too made that decision with wrenching difficulty. The difficulty was not making the right decision, but knowing that such decisions bring responsibility and with responsibility guilt. 'Everyone who acts responsibly,' Bonhoeffer wrote, 'becomes guilty.' There was no room for complacency and self-righteousness. Bonhoeffer's dilemma, I thought after that conversation, was Tambo's dilemma. In such a situation, one would incur guilt if one stood idly by, allowing others to die at the hands of the tyrant, content to be a spectator to violence. But in making that decision, would one incur guilt as well, even if one killed the instigators of massive genocide? Blood would be spilt. Lives would be taken. Bonhoeffer demanded that 'the last question asked by a human being who has a sense of responsibility should not be "How can I heroically extricate myself from this affair, but rather how are future generations to survive?"' And Tambo, like Bonhoeffer, knowing that his chosen way was not the way of Jesus of Nazareth, felt the guilt of disobedience, but still knew this to be the only way for him.

If white, Christian South Africa had the smallest bit of Tambo's conscience, if they had understood a scintilla of what the Gospel tells us, if they had dared to wrestle as much with God and their conscience as this man had, South Africa would have had a different history. But because they turned away from their responsibility to act justly and compassionately, they closed their eyes to their responsibility in guilt. Not only the guilt of having created apartheid and living off the human dignity of black people, or of legalised murder to maintain white superiority, privilege and wealth, but also the guilt of having forced others to take guilt upon themselves in order to seek the justice the Lord requires. The guilt they fled in facing the Truth Commission did not come close to the guilt they *knew*. If white South Africa had dared to share Tambo's agony this country would have been spared three-score years and more of apartheid. If they had understood their own responsibility, they would not have forced that awful responsibility on Mandela, Tambo and the liberation movements.

The conversation was a revelation. Tambo and I never again spoke of these things. But it was not necessary. I had joined the struggle and I would never choose for violence, but I would never feel that that choice was somehow 'less'. I had learnt, however, to avoid the trap of easy and convenient judgement, the self-righteous, hypocritical desire for clean hands, and the temptation to call neutrality and political opportunism 'responsibility'. Tambo's agony had left no room for the pseudo-innocence that leaves all responsibility behind.

apartheid as status confessionis

Between apartheid as racism and apartheid as heresy

By 1980 the anti-apartheid struggle already had a strong international profile with solidarity movements all over the world. The World Council of Churches (WCC) had inaugurated its Programme to Combat Racism (PCR) in 1979 and its support for liberation movements in southern Africa had caused havoc in WCC circles and in Western countries generally. The churches from the West, happy with vague statements against racism and 'prayerful support' for victims of racism (especially since they felt no guilt: they were talking about apartheid South Africa after all, not themselves!), had been shaken to the core by the WCC's determination to translate that support into actual political action.

The debates raged. The WCC was vilified for what was seen as its support for 'communism' and 'terrorism'. Overnight the churches of the West, whose very history since Emperor Constantine was steeped in violence and blood, became pacifist. Forgetting about their own history, their reading of the Bible and the glorification of violence in their theology and their hymnbooks, they demanded from churches in the countries they had colonized, oppressed and robbed of land and resources a non-violence they had never asked of themselves. Working with an amazingly de-historicised, hypocritical outlook on life, they set criteria for the oppressed peoples of the third world they had never set for themselves. Forgetting about the Western church's complicity in slavery, colonisation and racial oppression, with a pseudo-innocence that was stunning in its audacity and breathtaking in its scope, they condemned Christian participation in struggles for liberation, thereby condemning all of us to the death of complicity, passivity and indignity. For in the end, that is really what they wanted of us: meek acceptance of the world they had fashioned, while everything within us screamed that *that* world needed to be destroyed. It was astonishing how the voice of blood and kinship, of race and kind, of money and power, called louder than the voice of the Gospel, the voice of justice and equity, the voice of the poor and oppressed. It was an international repetition of what South African Christians had experienced through three centuries: whatever divided white Christians world-wide, and conversely what united blacks and whites *in Christ,* however significant both might have been, was not significant enough to break the bond of white solidarity and common white interest.

Most of the rich churches of the West would punish the WCC severely for taking this stance. They hit the WCC where it hurt by simply withdrawing their financial support and trying to cripple the WCC programmatically and structurally. It was truly the parting of the ways. New alliances were built in the ecumenical movement during the decisive decades of the seventies and eighties. But God, Desmond Tutu always says, is a God of surprises. In the midst of all this, Queen Juliana of the Netherlands not only shook the Dutch aristocracy and the European establishment but also exposed the hypocrisy of many Western churches. She personally made a contribution of 200 000 guilders to the PCR, including its Special Fund, which had been set aside expressly for the liberation movements. It was a lot of money for that time. But this donation was, of course, about more than money. It was a brave, supremely fine act of solidarity and justice. It was aristocratic in the best sense of that word.

It was the kind of act that went far beyond the Queen's personal intentions, I am sure. In addition to helping the PCR financially and giving the WCC much-needed public support, she helped to shore up the courage of those churches that had wavered, bending under the enormous pressure of the moneyed, conservative elites: those nominal Christians who went to church only on high days and holidays; the nobility for whom special pews in front were reserved for the rare occasions; those who never read their Bible but whose newspapers responded indignantly to the 'controversial' sermons of the brave preachers who dared speak of justice; those who didn't want to know about Jesus but insisted on knowing 'where our money goes'; those who, because they didn't know Jesus, were almost always wrong about where the church's money should go.

But she did another thing she never thought of. She pulled us all from the brink of distrust and enmity, just when we in the third world, enveloped in our struggles and battles, drowning in the blood of our revolutions, desperately searching for hope and light, thought that the churches of the West had abandoned us once again, leaving us to fight their legacies and the aftermaths of their betrayals on our own.

Her act reminded me of when I met Beyers Naudé, I thought. Just when I was so angry at the cruelty of apartheid, so disgusted with the hypocrisy of it all, so disillusioned by the deliberate abuse of both people and the Bible, so absolutely justified in my readiness to hate and write off all white people, Beyers Naudé came into my life. And all of a sudden, I had to face the fact that not *all* white people were the same. That if one of them could be like him, there must be more. That I had, in fact, no right to condemn all white people if there were some who were ready to stand with us in solidarity, to fight for justice and to pay the price. The ripple effect of Queen Juliana's decision did much to help save the ecumenical movement. We knew that she had had advisers, and that those advisers were not in government. They were in the churches.

Those wonderful men and women of the World Council understood the one dimension of apartheid better than most in the churches: the political, economic side. And they did exceedingly well in conscientising the churches to act politically and economically. But the other dimension, that of the claim apartheid laid upon the Gospel and the essentiality of it for Afrikaner Christian Nationalism, that we South Africans understood better. We also understood how making that dimension clear would help the churches of the world understand the depth of the evil we were facing, and the enormity of their sin in shirking their own responsibility.

The debates about racism in the seventies and the theological growth in the black churches helped us to see the issues in greater depth and detail than before. We began to see racism in less emotional terms. We began to speak of racism not just in individual, personal, that is to say attitudinal, terms but also in its historical, structural, systemic manifestations. We spoke of racism as sin because it denies the truth that all human beings are created in the image of God, people whose humanity is confirmed and made sacred by the incarnation of God through Jesus Christ. We are all human in the likeness of God, not in a physical sense, but in our unique, dynamic relation to God and hence to one another. The uniqueness of the other confirms the communality of both of us and turns both of us toward the divine. No wonder that when we in South Africa speak of ubuntu we recall an ancient African philosophical value, but simultaneously speak out of deep Christian conviction.

We called racism a form of idolatry in which the one dominant group assumed for itself a status higher than the other, and through political, military and economic power and socio-economic and psychological structuring, sought to play God in the lives of others. That in its denigration of human worth it was an assault upon the dignity and worthiness of God.

Most of all racism denied the liberating, humanising, reconciling work of Christ, who took on human form, thereby affirming human worth in the sight of God. This Jesus, so the Bible tells us and the church believes, broke 'the walls of partition and enmity [amongst human beings] and so [in his life and ministry, death and resurrection, hence literally in his body] became our peace'.

For that reason we called apartheid a pseudo-gospel and a heresy because it claimed salvific power – the power to be the 'ultimate and only solution' to the challenges facing our society. It claimed to be the will of God for South Africa and subjected God's will for justice, equity and reconciliation to the sinful desires and distortions of human beings. In the name of God, it legalised discrimination in all areas of life, exploited, dehumanised and oppressed people purely on the basis of skin colour, and laid down laws even on the permissibility of love, marriage and the bonds of family.

In its pigmentocratic madness, apartheid claimed that the most important thing about any person was not their being created in the image of God with inalienable rights but his or her racial identity. It meant that racial identity determined, with an overwhelming intensity, everything in a person's life. Despite the death of thousands of women, men and children, the ideology closed itself off from reality and criticism, believing in the self-proclaimed 'good intentions' of the system, or that the sacrilegious ends justified all means. Persons, stripped of their dignity, become non-persons, otherwise known as 'non-whites'. Dislodged from the image of God, they were not fit to be considered in terms of human emotions, pain, humiliation, dreams and aspirations, human degradation or fulfillment. They were the completed, and completely distorted, 'other', the product of the perverted, racially-obsessed imagination of the dominant group. And so we called apartheid a sin and its claim to be Christian a heresy and

a blasphemy

in S.Africa + Israel ...

a blasphemy.

These are the insights that grew from 1977, and these are what we took to the assembly of the World Alliance of Reformed Churches in Ottawa, Canada, in August 1982. And this is what led to the suspension of the two Afrikaans Reformed churches that were at that time members of the World Alliance: the DRC and the Netherdutch Reformed Church (Nederduits Hervormde Kerk). This is so important because of the impact these events had on world opinion and because of the political ramifications of the churches' actions in Ottawa.

Once the churches understood and accepted our argument, it became clear that the churches' political and theological analysis with regard to apartheid and the South African situation had enormous consequences the churches themselves could no longer escape or deny. The hysterical South African reaction helped to clarify international debate: it proved how right we as black South African Christians were in our emphases. Apartheid had long been declared a crime against humanity; now it was also regarded as a heresy and a blasphemy. Many more churches than before threw their considerable weight behind the struggle. The pressure on South Africa, its government and the churches supporting it became immense.

The churches also had to respond to other important issues. If we were not called upon to support violent revolution, how then should we seek justice for South Africa's oppressed people? Non-violent means of struggle chosen by the oppressed had a greater appeal than ever before. So, churches who had stood on the sidelines until then began to engage in actions of civil disobedience in their own countries on our behalf, supporting the economic, sports and cultural boycott, and taking action by enforcing disinvestment and sanctions. South Africa's exposure on the world stage increased, apartheid's harshness and its vulnerability became undeniable, and its bankruptcy all the clearer for the world to see.

The pressure worked both ways, though. The onus was now on black South Africans to provide those avenues for support for non-violent actions. And this could not be just tactical, either. Christians in South Africa would face enormous challenges in the decade to come and our own commitment to a non-violent, non-racial, democratic struggle would be severely tested. I was acutely aware of all this when in 1982, at 36 years of age, I stood on the stage in Ottawa, Canada, accepting the presidency of this World Reformed Communion, representing over 70 million Christians, the first third-world person, and the first African, to be so honoured.

Between Black Consciousness and non-racialism

Nothing, conventional wisdom tells us, is as unstoppable as an idea whose time has come. It is true, though something special stirs when it actually happens. I felt that special stirring when the idea of the United Democratic Front was born, budded and became a reality. I feel it still.

As international pressure grew and internal rumblings both above and underground could no longer be dealt with using suppression alone, the apartheid regime thought it had found a pro-active formula. In 1983, it came with its plan for a new constitution providing for a tri-cameral parliamentary system through which very limited power would be shared by a coloured House of Representatives and an Indian House of Delegates under white tutelage. Real Parliament and real power was to remain firmly in white hands. It was, in the eyes of supporters of this plan, a huge step forward, a significant sacrifice on their part, but a forward-looking move nonetheless. It was intended to appease the coloureds and Indians, give them democratic responsibility, hold out the promise of independence to blacks in their 'own' states, convince the world that apartheid was 'capable of reform', buy time for the fulfillment of the apartheid dream and shore up white support here and abroad.

For P.W. Botha, this was to be his lasting legacy, having brought the illusive justice to apartheid which H.F. Verwoerd and J.B. Vorster had not been able to realise. That is probably why P.W. Botha was so recalcitrant in recognising another 'rubicon' in 1985. As far as he was concerned, he had already crossed his! He had, in his view, already taken a great risk and succeeded in convincing white South Africa that this was the way to go. He had hoped for more recognition, more international reward than he was getting, and for more time to bring his plans to proper fruition. But as even more hard-line politicians like Andries Treurnicht and Jaap Marais constantly reminded him, he was putting unalloyed white rule in jeopardy, setting foot on a slippery slope on which white South Africa would not be able to turn back.

They were not completely wrong. 'The next step,' Jaap Marais prophesied, was 'negotiations with the terrorists!' This would not have come to pass, at least not so soon, if the UDF had not entered South Africa's history. The Tri-Cameral Parliament proposals and the infamous, so-called Koornhof Bills provided new stimulus to internal resistance. I was pleasantly surprised at the intensity of the reaction at grassroots level. People were, contrary to expectations, far from hopeless and apathetic. Repression since 1976 had clearly not broken the back of the resistance. There was sober assessment of the power of the apartheid regime, and how that power would be asserted to protect apartheid, but of giving up there was little sign, as far as I could determine. The plans of the government were immediately seen for what they were:

a political bribe aimed at entrenching the divide-and-rule strategy of the regime and strengthening South Africa's white power structures. They were also understood, correctly, as a tacit admission that apartheid as planned and implemented up to then, especially its coloured and Indian politics, had failed miserably. The exposure of the Bantustan fraud would follow. The people sensed victory at an important level, even though it would not be publicly conceded by those in power. There was a suppressed, angry energy, a longing for genuine freedom and a determined hopefulness. The past years of experimentation with Bantustans and coloured and Indian politics had not borne the fruits apartheid had hoped for.

People were seeking ways of articulation and political expression. The government had totally misjudged both the situation and the people; it was much too arrogant and self-assured, leaning far too heavily on the advice of its experts, especially its experts on the coloureds. It allowed itself to be misled by leaders of its own making, rather than listening to the leaders chosen by the people. Amichand Rajbansi, Allan Hendrickse and Mangosuthu Buthelezi had the government's ear and were elevated and revered: those of us who spoke the language of the people were reviled, ridiculed, hunted down and written off. The government could not see that the plans were fatally flawed because they had been ill-conceived, unilaterally planned and pushed through, and were, most of all, an unbearable insult to the oppressed people of South Africa. These were plans that considered only the white position, played on the basest political instincts of coloured and Indian people, as if black people did not matter, and did not care. As if these proposals were their highest aspirations, and the struggle of generations was of no account; as if greed, selfishness and forgetfulness were their most natural attributes. As if political analysis and understanding were completely foreign to their abilities.

Moreover, the apartheid government could not see that these plans presented black people with incontrovertible evidence of the widening cracks in the apartheid edifice, pried open the door to the secret fears of apartheid South Africa in the face of a new generation and laid bare its deepest weakness: the fact that the government desperately needed black cooperation in order to present itself as respectable, to respond to pressure and to survive. It was asking black people, without even thinking what it meant, to lend a hand in extending the life of their own long, drawn-out death. The people were ready to respond.

I was asked to make speeches at three important occasions during this time. The first was at the invitation of the Transvaal Indian Congress (TIC), at their conference in Johannesburg where the latest political developments were to be discussed (see Chapter 5). The second was at a conference in Durban organised by a Christian ecumenical organisation, Diaconia, under the leadership of Paddy Kearney (see Chapter 6). The third was the keynote address at the launch of the UDF (see Chapter 7).

It was clear that in all communities right across the country people were looking not only for answers, but for ways to respond. The speeches showed the levels at which I had been called upon to move in the months that were to follow: the ecclesial and the political. The political element would lead to the formation of the UDF. For the churches a choice against the government's proposals would lead to participation in politics in ways never experienced before, and to breaking points such as the call for sanctions and the call to pray for the fall of the apartheid regime in 1985. But for black South Africans, in the communities of faith and outside of them, a turning point in the struggle for freedom had arrived.

The choices we had to make had great political significance, but were also morally vital. What was, for us, the meaning of justice or of freedom? Does one always look for one's own interest in politics, and what are then the consequences for one's faith? By its actions the apartheid regime had forced us to look differently, or at least anew, at ourselves and the worth of our political convictions as well as our faith. It forced us to question with new intensity our own humanity in the light of the humanity of others, to reformulate our vision for ourselves and our country and its people. The government could no longer justify apartheid by itself. What did this mean for us? Sometimes political choices have redemptive value. The moment of truth of which my church spoke in 1982 had arrived for the politics of our era. In 1979, speaking before the churches, I talked of the theology of refusal. In 1983, at the TIC conference, it was time to speak of the *politics* of refusal.

My host for the day, Cassiem (Cas) Saloojee (now an ANC MP), met me at the airport. He was the one who convinced the organisers that I should be the main speaker for the day, and in turn, convinced me to accept. Again, for me, and I suppose even more so for the organisers, this was not an automatic choice. Cas Saloojee, a man of great integrity and insight, and the people of the TIC had longstanding relations with the banned ANC and had, stemming from the time of Gandhi, cultivated deep roots in the struggle. They were the 'Charterists', still firmly believing in the words, intentions and fundamental importance of the Freedom Charter for South African politics. As Cas told me, there was some measure of distrust of me in these circles. I had come, after all, from a Black Consciousness background, and that made some of them very uncomfortable. I thought them unnecessarily suspicious: my admiration for and commitment to the Charter was beyond doubt, I had thought. I did not blame them, however; they did not know me except from what they had read in the newspapers. How could they entrust a discussion on the government's proposals to someone whose politics they were not completely sure of? In fact, they had only the word of Cassiem Saloojee to go on. I was still to learn how deep suspicions can run in the movement, and how distrust can destroy ideas, relationships and people. But that suspicion was not exhibited publicly at all by anyone that day.

There are basically two versions doing the rounds as to how the idea for a UDF came to be mooted. It is important to remember that the ANC did not die when it was banned in 1960. I made the point before that the spirit of resistance was not broken. It must also be clear that this spirit did not aimlessly float around in some vacuum. It was rooted firmly in a long history of struggle, in the experiences, memories and political and spiritual values of people. So in a sense it could not have been otherwise: the UDF was part of the ongoing history of the struggle against colonialism and apartheid, a history in which the ANC stood central. The UDF, as child of that same struggle tradition, would find itself closely allied to the ANC, the more so because it was so deliberately built on the foundations laid down by the Freedom Charter. At the same time the ANC was not universally known or loved in all communities. It did not help that the ANC over the years had presented itself so expressly as an 'African' organisation, meaning 'black Africans' only. Historically though, the movement most readily associated with the freedom struggle had been the ANC.

Yet to say that the UDF was formed upon instructions of the ANC, as some people have persistently tried to argue, is simply not true. It is perhaps understandable that the ANC, in returning after exile, felt a deep need to re-establish its authority, and claiming the idea for the forming of the UDF was part of that need. This could also explain the myth that circulated for a while that shortly before the Soweto uprising Jacob Zuma supposedly slipped into the country clandestinely to 'organise' the youth. That they are still spreading the same untruth today regarding the UDF is a sign of a deeper malady, of a more profound political insecurity and immaturity than just some psychological post-exilic need. Of course the apartheid government saw the propaganda possibilities to justify its actions against the UDF by claiming that it was no more than the 'internal wing' of the ANC.

That there has always been some kind of continuous underground activity linked to the liberation movements is historical fact. But one cannot pretend that the 'underground' was a successful, effective movement that caused the apartheid government great harm. That is a natural problem with all clandestine political work all over the world where the leadership is elsewhere, in exile or in prison; logistics and communications difficult to say the least; and the government at all levels better equipped, better funded and specifically geared towards the curbing and elimination of that kind of activity. The sheer need for secrecy helped the apartheid forces more than we were ready to admit. That much was achieved by the underground nonetheless is a tribute to the single-minded dedication and unquestionable commitment of many ordinary people, and it should be acknowledged that that part of the political work was important, but not reflective of all the work done.

In these circles, I have been told, talk of a united front of some kind had been going on for some time. For many perfectly understandable reasons, however, not much had come of this talk. I heard of it the day I sat with Cas Saloojee at lunch talking about the meeting of that afternoon of 23 January 1983. Long after the launch of the UDF, I had heard that ANC president Oliver Tambo, in criticising the decision of the

Labour Party to join the Tri-Cameral Parliament, had urged the people 'to organize all democratic forces into one front for national liberation'. According to the *New History of South Africa,* journalist Howard Barrell, after interviewing Mac Maharaj and Joe Slovo in connection with these matters, commented that the formation of a front 'along similar lines' was prefigured in the strategy of the ANC. 'However, the idea of establishing a "united democratic front" originated in South Africa and the call was made without reference to the leadership in exile.' That is exactly how it happened.

Certainly I, and in the normal course of events, ordinary people on the ground in South Africa, would not have known about Tambo's call for some time. Personally, I had had no discussions with anyone at that time, certainly not the leadership in exile, about such plans. The Labour Party made its fatal decision on 4 January 1983 in Eshowe, the home of Buthelezi's Bantustan government. In an interview with the *Cape Times* on 7 January, I condemned the decision and talked of the need for such a united front to fight the decision and the Tri-Cameral Parliament. My mind was already made up by the time Oliver Tambo mentioned his idea in his 8 January ANC address: I was looking for the opportunity and the platform. During the luncheon discussion with Cas Saloojee, hearing his enthusiasm and his faith in my ability and readiness to speak on these burning issues, I was encouraged to share the idea with him. His response was immediate. With the accurate instincts of a true political animal, he sensed that the time was ripe. What I had spoken of in the *Cape Times,* but was not confident enough to speak of in the strange new political territory of Johannesburg, became a note in the margin – but it was the one sentence in the speech in which I called for the formation of the UDF. And here I must give Cas his due. History was knocking at the door, and I might not have answered had Cas not opened that door. I cannot help but gratefully think of the people I met at just the right time.

It was a speech in which the handwritten notes show how I had struggled to find the right words and phrases; how much I, after having typed it out on my old-fashioned typewriter on paper I still had left over from my visit to the US, thought of scrapping, adding and correcting; all perhaps signs of the nervousness the confident preacher but political novice felt at the prospect of speaking to such an august and venerable organisation of our country on such a historically important occasion. In the last paragraph of page 9 of that speech I began speaking of 'the politics of refusal' and the need for a 'united democratic front'. The first two paragraphs of page 10 explain it further and in the margin next to the second paragraph, I wrote the words 'Make the call clear!' That was also the first time I used the words 'all, here and now', words used by Martin Luther King Jr. to such great effect in another context, and which were to become the most remembered words of the address at the UDF launch. The call was almost an aside, but it was what the people had been waiting to hear, it seemed. In such ways history is made.

Built on the foundations of the Freedom Charter, the UDF was to be a decidedly non-racial movement. The significance of this was two-fold. First, there were those, the formidable Neville Alexander among them, who could not accept non-racialism. For them, this meant accepting all forms of 'bourgeois' values that had no place in the struggle. There was also the argument that however hard they tried, white people could never understand, could not free themselves from their white, middle-class way of life and their privileges, could talk the talk but could not walk the walk, and at the end of each day would leave us in our townships and return to the white, privileged, protected life of their suburbs. One could not make alliances with such people. Here were the echoes of the causes that had split the PAC from the ANC 20 years earlier.

The differences on these issues were so fierce that Bishop Desmond Tutu found it necessary to stay away from the launch and would not become a patron of the UDF. He found the politics too dangerously divisive. My response to these matters is found in the speeches included in this book.

The second issue, mentioned briefly above, was more personal. Some comrades looked at me askance because they wondered how I, having come politically of age in the Black Consciousness movement, could take up such a crucial role in a non-racial UDF. Perhaps it was hard for them to understand the impact of the Black Consciousness philosophy on my generation, especially on the young coloured people of our times. Black Consciousness was so much more than the slogans 'Black is beautiful!' and 'Black man, you are on your own!' imply. It was the rediscovery of our humanity, our pride, our ability to *be,* and in being, to discover our ability to resist the negation of our humaneness.

It was a political movement, yes, but it was a movement of profound and deep spirituality. It was a spirituality in which self-doubt and self-hatred deliberately created and nurtured by white racism had no place, in which the obsession with ethnicity had been replaced by the solidarity of the oppressed, and in which we learnt to understand non-racialism first as an essential part of our being and then as essential to our politics. It was an enormously liberating, powerful and empowering experience. Without that experience, I would never have been able to confront white racism, white superiority and my own black inferiority. I would never have understood the meaning of the concept of equality, would never have been able to understand the affirmation of my blackness as the constitution of my humanity and without that I, and a whole generation of my peers, would have been, to paraphrase Malcolm X, 'lost in the wilderness of white South Africa'. In short, for me, without Black Consciousness, there would have been no non-racialism. This was the treasure the ANC and all its leadership had so contemptuously cast aside, ignored and denied in their unseemly desire to reassert themselves as the only political movement that had made a difference in the lives of our people.

Between the sword and the soul

I was never part of any underground movement. Underground politics, as crucial and imposed upon us as they might have been, never held any attraction for me. This is not to say that the underground work had no value. Far from it. And one should not in any way downplay the unremittingly oppressive situations that had persisted through decades and necessitated underground political activities. Nor should one underestimate the extraordinary creativity and courage that went into the making of such politics.

But there were difficulties I found hard to overcome. Such as the fact that the real leaders were elsewhere while substitute leaders were inside but underground. These substitute leaders, young men and women who were not trusted with everything and therefore mostly unaware of what they were letting themselves in for, would, in their fiery enthusiasm and youthful naivety, have to face the fire. It always seemed clear to me that the government always knew exactly how to deal with strategies of underground violent struggle. Besides, I believed that the political scene had changed: those if us engaged in the struggle had a better chance than in the preceding decades. The international community was much more aware of, and sensitive to, the apartheid situation. Trade sanctions, the cultural and sports boycott and boycott of South African goods overseas had raised people's consciousness. The civil rights struggle in the United States had drawn attention to the efficacy and moral superiority of non-violence as a method of struggle, in ways that violent revolution never could.

Non-violent struggle had shown that in important ways it was much harder for an oppressive government to respond, and that the possibilities for violent repression with impunity were considerably less. The response could still be violent, and mostly was, but the government would not be able to get away with it without paying some price. Above-ground mobilisation brought the struggle into the open: from both sides. It drew people into open commitment and put them before open choices. It unmasked the intentions of government, exposed its weaknesses even as the regime showed its power and did not allow the world to remain mere onlookers, mere spectators to violence, as Bonhoeffer would have said. The more I think about it now, the more I understand that Tambo, being in the situation that prevailed, could never have meant to call for open, above-ground mobilisation of people. Not being there to take the lead and take the responsibility, he would never have made such a call. His was not that kind of leadership. He spoke the language he knew. For us inside the country, I was convinced things had to be different this time around.

But there was more. I was against the use of violence in principle. My radical Christianity and my understanding of the demands of the Gospel did not allow for violence as an option, even though I had an honest understanding of the reasons for the choice of violence in South Africa. I was, however, committed to a third way. My anger at the hypocrisy of Western governments and churches did not make me doubt my convictions in this matter. Besides, I had great difficulty in falling for the romantic notion of a 'democratic socialist revolution'. I remembered not only the Che Guevara who gave up his middle-class existence for a life dedicated to struggle. I also remembered the Che who with such ease became judge and executioner when he had tasted the intoxicating wine of power. The revelations about Stalin of which I learnt while in Europe (in that famous speech of Nikita Khrushchev, no less) still shocked me, but they did not totally surprise me. My Calvinist distrust of human nature to do good unless we are persuaded by the Spirit of God influenced my politics. My experiences with the Dutch Reformed Church family over the years taught me not to trust leaders blindly, and uncritically following the party line does not come easy to me. One should not attach more value to the voice of leaders than to the voice of the people. And even then one should be careful. From the Romans we have learnt that one should hear the voice of the gods in the voice of the people: *vox populi, vox Dei*. As Christians we should be even more precise: *vox victimarum, vox Dei*. We hear the voice of God most clearly in the voice of the victims. I will never forget the words of José Miguez Bonino of Argentina, theologian and friend with whom I met and talked to the women of the 'Disappeared' in that country. He wrote about our duty to 'stake one's life with and for the poor … those of unimpressive proportions, those whom the revolutionary movements tend to undervalue and even to annihilate …' It was from the revolutionaries that I learnt to look critically at all revolutions and their drivers.

There were strategic considerations as well. Why take on the apartheid regime on the very point where they were strongest and most powerful? Why attack them militarily and thereby give them the advantage of winning both the war and the political argument? In the eyes of a large portion of the world the South African government, albeit illegitimate, had at least the right and the duty to protect its citizens against violent attack. Although I thought I understood the philosophical distinction between oppressive and 'liberatory' violence, between violence and counter-violence, the practical realities made it difficult. I will never trivialise the sacrifices made by MK soldiers nor the circumstances that had driven them to those choices, but I could never believe that the ANC's military tactics could prevail against the overwhelming power of the South African Defence Force. We must be honest enough to admit that the struggle was not won by military victories and it is time to stop the illusion that it was. It was won by the commitment and the sacrifices, the extraordinary courage of our people inside the country. What gripped the imagination of the world and finally broke the back of apartheid oppression was the untamable spirit of our people, the wisdom of our elders, the strength of our mothers and fathers, the courage and determination of our youth, our unstoppable belief in our freedom and the inextinguishable fires of our faith.

I know, with my moral stand against the use of violence, I am far more child of the much-despised 'peace churches' of the Reformation than of the dominant Christian churches, Catholic and Protestant, with their 'just war' theology; far more inheritor of Gandhi and Martin Luther King Jr. than of Martin Luther and John Knox. The defencelessness of the prophet Jeremiah speaks more to my heart than the bloodthirstiness of the prophet Elijah; the quiet strength of Hannah more than the militancy of Deborah; the non-violent resistance of the early Christian church more than the muscled Christendom of ancient and modern Constantinianism; the powerlessness of the revolutionary Jesus far more than the throne-and-altar triumphalism of Western Christianity.

I do not believe that violence in the long run can offer lasting solutions. Violence destroys the chances for reconciliation in the destruction of the other. It casts the other in the mould of an unchangeable, incontrovertible enemy. It systematises as well as personalises enmity. After the violent blow is struck there are no more options left and the last word is already drowned in blood. Violence takes on a life of its own, feeds on ancient human emotions far stronger than we realise, releases a relentless, deadly dynamic we are not able, or prone, to stop. It sweeps reason and better judgement aside as in ritualistic helplessness not acknowledgeable to ourselves we respond to the call of blood to blood. Lifting the sword destroys the soul.

Non-violence appeals to our other, better selves, to the truth about ourselves and the other we know but too often deny: that in our creaturely, relational existence and our common humanity we are not meant to be reduced to mere instruments of destruction but are created to affirm, choose, and celebrate life rather than death. Non-violent resistance in a situation of conflict is the open gate to reconciliation and genuinely humane solutions. Non-violence affirms the humble acknowledgement of the possibility that we might be wrong, that openness to the other is the truly human way, that we can still, even at the very last moment, choose a different path. Non-violence opens the way to the ubuntification of the other, because it longs for the affirmation of our humanity in the humanity of the other. Violence, in its irreversibility, is a reach too far for mortals such as us. Non-violence acknowledges the existence of holy ground: such as taking the life of another. It is, quite simply, the way of Jesus of Nazareth. For this reason alone the UDF was a way I had to go.

I knew, however, that none of this could be taken for granted.

We were a people with a history, and it seemed almost as if all of our history agitated against this trend of thought. All the painful questions raised before returned with a vengeance. Would we, could we, reclaim the tradition of non-violence Nelson Mandela, with such righteous conviction, declared immoral in so many words?

Were our people ready to make that enormous mind-shift from underground resistance to open, above-ground resistance? Were we ready for the powerlessness of open-handed struggle, challenging the awesome power of the apartheid state? South Africa was as racist as the United States but the US at least had a Constitution and free media, and P.W. Botha was no John Kennedy. Were we ready to believe that there were real moral and political advantages to non-violent struggle, that it was strategically crucial for us to shift the terrain of battle, take the initiative away from the apartheid government, its police and its army, and to fight the struggle according to rules set by us?

Most important of all, could black people, after all this time, still *believe* in their own freedom, and that it would come in their lifetime? That they were responsible for their freedom, and that they could achieve it in this way? Was it possible to say farewell to the romanticism of the 'socialist democratic revolution', to the vision of MK troops marching into Pretoria, ANC flags waving, triumphantly emptying their AK47s into the air? Could we, and this was perhaps politically the most blasphemous question, understand that under the circumstances the ANC as organisation in exile and of exiles, could not effectively run a remote-controlled revolution, and that such thoughts would not be the epitome of disloyalty and betrayal? Could we make the distinction between genuine longing for freedom and the falsehoods of dead-end ideologies?

It was certain that things would happen that the ANC would not be able to control and would not be prepared for. Spontaneity was one of the strong points of the UDF and this would time and again catch the government, and by the same token the ANC, off-guard. That would cause all sorts of difficulties between me and some of the ANC leadership in exile as well as with their proxies at home.

When Cheryl Carolus and Trevor Manuel, working tirelessly and selflessly for what was to happen, came to brief me on the plans for the launch, I kept these thoughts to myself. I knew, though, that these arguments would be at the very core of our comings and goings in the years to come. Seven months later, on 20 August 1983, the UDF was launched in Rocklands, Mitchells Plain. Fifteen thousand people, young and old, black and white, Christians and Jews, Muslims and Hindus, people of all faiths. Representatives of almost 500 organisations were there, reflecting all the sectors of society I had so hopefully mentioned that day in Johannesburg. Graced by the presence of men and women of enormous stature, Francis Baard, Helen Joseph, Archie Gumede, Oscar Mpetha, who linked the present with the past, we were not just present at a historic event; we were a piece of history ourselves. It was an immense feat, under the circumstances, a triumph of organisational acumen. Through all the speeches, the songs, the poetry, the dancing and the joy, I sensed the awareness: the people were ready. South Africa's history was about to enter a completely new phase where we would again take politics to the streets.

What precisely lay ahead, we could not know, except that for all of us the struggle would now rest upon this new generation. I remain convinced and history has already borne this out: if it were not for the UDF, the struggle would not have accelerated the way it did, Mandela would not have been lifted up like he was, and the apartheid regime would not have been forced to begin talks and finally negotiations before the end of the decade. The ANC would have remained in exile much longer, the islanders would have stayed on Robben Island much longer, and we would not have seen that a non-racial, non-sexist, democratic South Africa was not merely an impossible dream, but could become a reality.

The speech I made that day reflected all the contestations we had to contend with, the hope, the ideals and the faith the people had brought with them to Mitchells Plain and had entrusted to me to articulate. The longing for justice, peace and reconciliation and the desire to fight for them, the commitment to a truly non-racial, democratic, non-sexist South Africa. The determination to see it through to the end. There was also amongst those gathered the sense of belonging and togetherness, which would remain a unique characteristic of the UDF through the years, and the shared sense of values that would inspire all of us.

That the ANC, so soon after its return, was so intent on getting rid of the UDF and all it stood for was a disaster in more than one way, for the organisation as well as for the people, and that I caved in to the pressure to participate in the UDF's 'funeral' will remain a personal shame. It makes no difference that its disbanding was a foregone conclusion more important to the exiles than I understood at the time, worked out in secret collusion with well-selected leaders from inside, or that Mandela himself urged me to comply. I should have been firmer, should have asked why the UDF, first claimed by the ANC as their 'internal vanguard', now suddenly became a threat to the ANC. I should have stayed at home that day and at least maintained some dignity. Instead, I became what, in the struggle against apartheid, I had never once been: a coward.

Nevertheless, that day in 1983, when the UDF was launched, remains in the hearts and minds of millions. And more importantly, all politics afterwards would be measured by what the UDF had achieved, for the country and within us.

5

Truth Crushed to Earth Shall Rise Again: A Crisis in Apartheid and the Politics of Refusal

The plan of P.W. Botha's government to introduce a new Constitution for South Africa in order to facilitate a new parliamentary dispensation was an important shift in the policies of apartheid. The new Constitution would create a 'House of Representatives' for coloured people and a 'House of Delegates' for Indian South Africans. There would also be a 'President's Council' where delegates from the three racially separated 'parliaments' would come together to deliberate and advise the President. Black Africans were supposed to find their political home in the Bantustans. These plans were the most important reason for the emergence of the black resistance politics in the 1980s. The rally called by the Transvaal Indian Congress (TIC) in Johannesburg for 23 January 1983 was the first public meeting where I addressed these issues. It was also the meeting where I first made the call for the establishment of the United Democratic Front (UDF).

The disintegration of a grandiloquent ideal

We are meeting at a time of crisis. Apartheid is in a crisis. This grandiloquent ideal, brought into the world and held before the eyes of white South Africa as an all-encompassing, soteriologically loaded

118

AB's prophetic view in retrospect was unwise.

policy of racial separation, which would solve all the problems of this country, is beginning to disintegrate. The pseudo-religious nature of the ideology of apartheid has been unmasked unmercifully. Churches in South Africa and elsewhere have branded apartheid a heresy and have stated quite unequivocally that any church that defends this policy cannot be regarded as an authentic member of the body of Christ.

Internally, the courageous resistance to apartheid and the determination of black South Africans to be free have made it clear to white South Africans in no uncertain terms that there can be no peaceful existence for them in this land unless it is peaceful coexistence with black South Africans. Little by little, the international community has come to understand the danger that the policy of apartheid poses to the stability of the region and to international peace. The total rejection by the black communities of the policies of the present government has put the lie to its claim that apartheid is the solution to our problems. The shame of racism, the brutal violence needed to sustain the system, the naked greed it tries to conceal, the shameless hypocrisy it generates, the sheer dishonesty in its assertions of the changes that are said to take place – all this now stands exposed for all who have eyes to see.

The politics of refusal

The South African government is tackling the present crisis by changes in the Constitution and the political system. The government and its supporters insist that apartheid has failed only partly – namely, in not providing political space for the so-called coloureds and Indians. Apartheid is succeeding, however, they assert, in that the homelands policy makes provision for the political and human needs of the almost 25 million black South Africans.

Blacks are not impressed. We have seen what has happened in the homelands. We know that the 'independence' of the four bush republics is a sham; that the homelands are no more than dumping grounds for the discarded people of this land; that they are places where our elderly die of misery and want, and our children are stalked day and night by hunger, sickness and the grim death that sits on the shoulder of hopelessness. These homelands are places where the signs and tokens of apartheid have been replaced by the relentless grip of black dictatorship. The government and its supporters know that these impoverished patches of land will never attain economic independence; that there will always be more black people in so-called white South Africa than in the homelands; that the very way in which the homelands were set up is the greatest stumbling block to democratic rule there; that this policy is beyond description in its immorality. But they are undeterred. For them, to quote a delegate of the white Dutch Reformed Church to the World Alliance of Reformed Churches meeting in Ottawa, Canada less than a year ago, 'the homelands policy is the ultimate solution to the problems of South Africa'.

At present, a vexing problem involved in apartheid policy has to do with persons classified as coloureds and Indians. A solution to *this* problem has produced the new constitutional proposals. The so-called coloureds and Indians may join with whites in a three-chamber parliament, divided on an ethnic basis, with whites in the majority. The whites will remain firmly in control. Greater economic benefits constitute the incentive for coloured and Indian cooperation in the new structure. Coloured and Indian officials will gain a degree of control over separate coloured and Indian affairs and will participate in joint consultation on common affairs.

Black people are being told that now that we have our 'political rights' in the homelands, it is 'unjust for coloureds and Indians not to have the same rights'. Suddenly the government's problems with the coloureds and Indians have become *our* problems! The crisis of apartheid has become *our* crisis!

We are being told that the decisions we make in 'our homelands' will determine not only our own immediate future, but also the future of our children. These decisions will determine the nature of the struggle for freedom and human dignity that will surely continue. Coloureds and Asians should likewise have a voice in determining *their* future. Has any national government ever been more conspicuously hypocritical? Suddenly there are no more 'lepers' in South Africa!

We must remind ourselves of some facts. Those who are talking this way are the ones who came to power in 1948 on a blatantly racist platform. They are the ones who took British segregationist policies and made them into a system that is terrifying in its totality and effectiveness. They are the ones who spent years trying to get the last few black people off the voter's role, and finally succeeded by packing the Senate and twisting justice in the courts. They are the ones who passed law after law to entrench racism: laws on racial classification, group areas, mixed marriages, separate education, the homeland policy. All these laws stripped Africans of South African citizenship. They are the ones who wanted the land, and took it; they saw our homes and claimed them. They built their palaces and their economic kingdom on the blood, sweat, and tears of our people. When we resisted, we were hounded, jailed, exiled, detained without trial, tortured and killed. Our peaceful demonstrations were turned into massacres: Sharpeville, Soweto, Cape Town. *All this they want us simply to forget!*

When white South Africans thought that they had broken our spirit, they gave us dummy institutions; they humiliated us with puppet leaders whom they themselves never would have accepted were they to have been in our place. This effort failed because of the refusal of the vast majority of the population to accept anything less than full democratic rights.

Now we are faced with this new situation. The steadfast determination of black people to fight for their human dignity, their successful recourse to the politics of refusal, the growing realisation in the world (in spite of the Reagan administration in the USA!) that apartheid is a cancer in the body politic of the world and the subsequent pressures on South Africa – through all this it has finally dawned on the government that something must be done.

The government says that the Westminster parliamentary system cannot work in South Africa. That is its basic point of departure. In our turn we ask: Why will it not work? There was nothing wrong with the Westminster system when it gave the Nationalists a winner-takes-all majority in the white parliament. There was nothing wrong with the Westminster system when it gave white South Africans the right to make laws for the whole of this nation, even though its officials were elected by a small white minority. There was nothing wrong with the Westminster system when it gave white South Africans an excuse to use the word 'democracy', although they knew they were oppressing the vast majority of this country's people and excluding us from meaningful political participation. Now that the pressures for change are becoming too hard to resist, now that real majority rule is staring them in the face, *now* they discover that the Westminster system will not work.

Perhaps white South Africans say the Westminster system will not work because the Nationalists themselves have set such a bad example within this system. They have used Westminster-style democracy as a cover for totalitarian rule. They use Parliament to enact laws that would have been labelled criminal if there had been an independent judiciary. They use the system to cover up shameful acts of dishonesty and corruption, as we saw in 'the information scandal'. Now they are afraid that black people will do the same to them if the system remains. Because, moreover, they are religious people, the white South Africans know that what the Bible says in this regard is true: 'You shall reap what you sow.'

The system they are now proposing harbours within its bosom the same danger. If one day blacks take over the government and a black electoral college elects a black executive president with such sweeping, almost dictatorial, powers and he sends the white Parliament home because it does not agree with him – what then? Shall we hear the same crocodile lament that we are hearing about Zimbabwe where the new government uses Mr Ian Smith's laws to keep him in check and now Mr Smith is angry?

There must be no doubt whatsoever in our minds. These proposals cannot be accepted and there can be no cooperation with the government on this basis. We must reject the government-proposed constitutional changes for clear reasons:

1) It is clear that these proposals are an entrenchment of apartheid and white domination.

2) The proposals accept as a basic premise that 'the homeland policy of the South African government is irreversible'.

3) The basic tenets of apartheid – the laws that are the lifeblood of the system – remain intact: racial classification, group areas, separate education, the so-called security laws, and the like.

4) Within the system as proposed there will not really be opportunity to change these laws: they fall under the jurisdiction of the white Parliament; and the new system is designed specifically to prevent coalitions with other groups,

walkouts, and boycotts.

5) Despite attempts to create the illusion of an 'independent' President's Council with an 'independent' contribution, it is quite clear that these proposals were devised to give shape to P.W. Botha's brand of Nationalist policy, geared to the needs of a streamlined apartheid. We had no part whatsoever in their making and in their interpretation. These proposals were designed to appease the Nationalist Party Congresses that debated and accepted them. Quite apart from the fact that we are sick and tired of being done for and spoken down to, there is no reason in the world why we should place our future in the hands of those who for so many decades now have shown with unabashed clarity that they do not have our interests at heart.

6) The proposals quite unashamedly accept ethnicity as the indispensable basis for doing politics in South Africa. All democratic-minded persons in South Africa have rejected this premise because they know that ethnicity does not solve differences; rather, it entrenches them. Ethnicity tends to emphasise group interests, keep alive tendencies toward tribalism, white and black, and foster narrow, ethnic nationalisms that can only aggravate an already volatile situation. Furthermore, ethnicity is inseparable from racism, however subtle it may be. The insidious nature of this evil is a warning that societies such as ours have enough problems without exacerbating their inherent racism by making ethnicity a basic, politically divisive factor.

7) These proposals exclude the majority of the South African nation, and, as such, they constitute a recipe for violent confrontation and disaster.

8) These proposals are not only politically untenable; they are also morally wrong and unacceptable. As a Christian I cannot and will not accept responsibility for the continuation of apartheid, a system that, in the words of Bishop Desmond Tutu, is the greatest evil since Nazism.

It is morally wrong to accept for myself rights and privileges when such rights and privileges are denied others who are fellow South Africans. We must say once more: justice denied one is justice denied all. With these proposals the injustice of apartheid will not be removed, and justice will continue to lie prostrate on the streets of our cities. Peace will find no refuge in this land until all of God's children in South Africa have the simple and indispensable dignity of full human rights. In 1977, when the government first made new constitutional proposals, the Labour Party rejected them for the following reasons: (1) they entrenched apartheid; (2) they were devised exclusively by the government – the South African people had no part in their formulation; (3) they would mean the inclusion of coloureds and Indians, and the exclusion of blacks; and (4) they entrenched white domination.

What is the difference between the proposals of 1977 and the new proposals of the President's Council? There are no essential differences. Yet the Labour Party and the South African Indian Council have accepted the new proposals. It is clear that once again the voice of Mammon has spoken louder than the voice of principle.

The new partners of the government are being validated constitutionally. These are the junior partners in apartheid. From now on they will share the responsibility for apartheid, for the creation of yet more homelands, for the resettlement of more black people, for the ongoing rape of our human dignity, for the death of those who resist this evil system. They will be co-responsible for the continuation – yes, the enhancement – of the civil war in which South Africa is already engaged. From now on, in terms of active planning and legislation, apartheid no longer has only a white face.

The inevitability of political tragedy

There is a great sadness in all of this and a persistent measure of inevitability. One ought not to play around with evil. Working within the system, for whatever reason, contaminates you. It wears down your defences, it makes easier the rationalisations needed for staying in the system. It makes you susceptible to the hidden and not so hidden persuasions that are at work within every system. It whets your appetite for power. The system even allows you some petty victories, so that you believe you can actually beat it. All the while it draws you closer, blunting your judgement, and finally exposes your powerlessness as you 'join the system to fight the system'. What you call 'compromise' for the sake of politics is in fact selling out your principles, your ideals, and the future of your children.

The situation calls for vigilance. We must not compromise the struggle we have been engaged in for well nigh a century. We dare not betray the ideals we have, the belief in a truly democratic South Africa. We must not betray the blood of our children. Today we are saying to South Africa: we will not do it! The dream of justice, of a free nation, of a humanised society, has not died. Those who have made these compromises never understood this dream, have never been part of this struggle.

Our response to the crisis facing us today is a dialectical one. It is the politics of refusal, which has within it both a yes and a no.

We must continue to struggle for the liberation, freedom, and human dignity of all our people in South Africa. While we say yes to *this* struggle, we say no to apartheid, racial segregation, and the economic exploitation of the oppressed masses in South Africa.

We must continue to show South Africa and the world that there are black people who refuse to be intimidated by the violence of apartheid or be tempted by the sugar-coated fruits of apartheid. While we say no, therefore, to hollow solutions built on personal gain and petty group self-interest, we say yes to integrity and commitment.

We must continue to work for a safe and secure future for our children, for a society where they will not be infected by the poison of racism. While we say yes, therefore, to a future built on genuine peace and justice, we say no to building that future on participation in greed, exploitation, and the narrow nationalisms that carry within themselves the seeds of destruction. We must refuse to let our children die in a war that is being waged for the protection of apartheid and the South African neocolonialist designs on Namibia and for frustrating the hopes of the Namibian people for freedom, democracy, and genuine independence.

This is the politics of refusal, and it is the only dignified response that black people can give in this situation. In order to succeed we need a united front. Most of the Christian churches, and all of the democratically minded organisations in our communities, have rejected unequivocally the proposals of the President's Council and the call to cooperate in their implementation. We all are committed to the struggle for a non-racist, open, democratic South Africa; a unitary state, one nation in which all citizens will have the rights accorded them by ordinance of almighty God. There is no reason why churches, civic associations, trade unions, student organisations and sports bodies should not unite on this issue, pool our resources, inform the people of the fraud that is about to be perpetrated in its name, and on the day of the election expose these plans for what they are.

Knowing truth from confusion

Those who have opted to join the government have agreed that it is necessary in order to 'help Mr P.W. Botha against Dr Treurnicht', or to help Mr Botha in his fight against the 'right wing' in his own party, because Mr Botha is 'on the right road'. This argument is as incongruous as it is incomprehensible. Apart from the fact that nobody, including the Nationalist Party leadership, is certain precisely where Mr Botha's road leads to, what business do blacks have trying to alleviate the problems caused by tensions within the National Party or within Afrikanerdom? To be sure, the turmoil within Afrikanerdom and the split in the Nationalist Party have been the most hopeful signs in white politics for many years. This is in fact exactly what we need. More turmoil means more creative tension, undermining the self-confidence and the arrogance that have become the hallmark of those in power for far too long. It means opening up possibilities for a re-alignment in white politics, for detribalisation, and for more effective opposition.

Why would any black person in their right mind wish to stop this process? It would be a blessing if this government were to fall! This would help to bring about the real, fundamental changes this government is so effectively obstructing. Moreover, do not the 'joiners' know that there is no fundamental difference between Mr Botha and Dr Treurnicht? The argument between these two gentlemen is not about the ideology of apartheid; it is not about whether apartheid ought to be removed or not. It is not about whether South Africa is to become an open, democratic society, or whether Africans should retain their citizenship in this country. They are not arguing about the necessity of white domination; they are not in disagreement on the issue of white control over the economy. The dispute is not about removing the racist laws from the statute books or about universal franchise. It is not about ways to redistribute the wealth of the country.

The real issue, the *only* issue, between Mr Botha and Dr Treurnicht is the most effective way in which white control of the economy and white political domination can survive in South Africa at this particular point in history at which pressure is being brought to bear on the government. In other words, the argument is about how to do the same thing in order to have all things remain the same.

Dr Treurnicht believes that white domination in politics as well as in the economy can be maintained by unchanged and unabashed racial separation, overt oppression, and a romantic call to the beleaguered Afrikaners to risk isolation as they cling tenaciously to their beliefs and depend only on their history, the conviction of their righteousness, their gun and their God.

Mr Botha, on the other hand, having a better understanding of the world today, believes there is an alternative solution to the present crisis in South Africa. His solution is to streamline apartheid (permits, mixed sports, etc.), to allow limited participation by coloureds and Asians in politics and the economy under strict white control (which he calls 'power-sharing'), and to generate the illusion of a challenge to the old, Afrikaner romanticism. By doing this, Mr Botha has succeeded in four ways. He has (1) created distance between himself and Dr Treurnicht, though it is mostly imaginary; (2) caused confusion in the ranks of English speakers who now feel that Mr Botha is indeed moving 'somewhere' and who cannot understand why their opposition party is so 'negative' ('After all, coloureds are playing for Western Province, and soon they will be in Parliament. What more do they want?'); (3)

lured some coloureds and Indians into this trap with the hope that more middle-class coloureds and Indians will join up; and (4) created the illusion of change so that conservative Western governments can support his government openly 'with good reason'.

What really matters, as I have shown, has not changed at all. The government has created a warm, cosy, middle ground where everyone who comes in may have their ethnic piece of the pie as long as no fundamental questions are asked. Many, including even some of the media, are joining this process, hoping somewhere there will be a reward for them, and that, miraculously, the agony caused by apartheid will end. Those who refuse to do so are branded leftists, radicals, and politically naive. But that does not matter; this situation is only temporary: *truth crushed to earth shall rise again, and no lie can live forever.*

I want to remind those Western governments that are now satisfied with this government that they should not be misled. The black people of this country *know* what they want, and it is not this. They know who their leaders are, and they are not sell-outs who need the Nationalist press to protect them against the wrath of their own people. We shall not be satisfied until we have our full human rights. Why can Britain go to war, in the words of Mrs Thatcher, 'so that the people of the Falklands may have the right to live freely under the government of their choice', but we are denied that right? Why can Americans have a system guaranteeing the equality of all under the law and justice for all, but we are denied it? The test of a good South African government will not be made in Washington, or in London, or Moscow; it will be made right here in this land. That test will be made by the suffering, struggling oppressed people whose determination to be free shall not be undermined by the violence of Pretoria or by the thinly veiled cynicism of Washington.

Allan Boesak

As we struggle, let us remember what Dr Martin Luther King Jr. taught us: that change does not roll in on the wheels of inevitability. It comes, rather, through the tireless efforts of men and women who are willing to be co-workers with God. Let us continue to believe that freedom will come; that justice will one day no longer stumble in the street; that violence will cease and peace will reign; that racism and apartheid will be merely a bad dream neither remembered nor mourned; that hatred will make place for love and true humanity. Let us believe the words of the prophet and work for the day when:

Babies will no longer die in infancy, and all people will live out their life span. People will build houses and they will live in them – they will not be used by someone else. They will plant vineyards and enjoy the wine – it will not be drunk by others. The work they do will be successful, and their children will not meet with disaster (Isa. 65: 20–23).

6

Between the Devil and the Deep Blue Sea: A Christian Response to the New Constitution

The apartheid government's constitutional plans made much of the 'Christian' character of the new Constitution, in the process laying claim to values Christians deem important and expecting support from the Christian communities on these grounds. The government's strategy also made clear just how crucial it was for them to convince Christians outside of the Afrikaner community. This address, given to Christian communities in Durban on 21 May 1983, is my response to this strategy.

Upholding Christian standards

The churches have to remain clear and unambiguous in our opposition to the new constitutional proposals for several reasons. The preamble to these new proposals states that the constitution seeks 'to uphold Christian standards' in South Africa. We are led to believe that that assertion is based on the fact that this country wants to be a Christian country, and that its government wants to be known as a Christian government. That also implies that the government knows and understands the commandments of the God of the Bible in terms of justice, peace, and human liberation, and that what the government does is to govern in such a way that these goals are realised and that the glory of God is served. There is of course the further implication that such a Christian government should have the full support of the Christian church.

But let us for the moment concentrate on what the government considers to be the Christian standards it is called to uphold through the implementation of the new proposals. Among these Christian standards, we are told, are:

- the integrity and freedom of the country;
- the maintenance of law and order;
- an independent judiciary;
- private enterprise;
- the duty to seek world peace.

Apart from the important question why the government should choose to ignore the pluriform nature of our South African society – after all, how should a faithful Muslim or a dedicated Hindu cooperate in upholding Christian standards? – there is another question. Should our Christian standards be forced down the throats of those who do not adhere to Christianity? Should we not rather live in such a way that others are attracted to the church and to the gospel, not because it will be politically advantageous, but because the witness, the lifestyle, the courage and faithfulness of Christians will be such that others will ask: 'Who is this Jesus whom you proclaim?'

But still another question remains, namely, what is Christian in what the government is trying to do? Something is not Christian simply because a government declares it so. Rather, it is Christian because it is in accord with the demands of the gospel of Jesus the Messiah. The Christian church in South Africa must not be intimidated or brainwashed by propaganda in our efforts to discern what is Christian or not. We are called, rather, to test the spirit, and to apply the criteria of the Kingdom of God – justice, love, peace, reconciliation – in this process of discernment. And these are the criteria we will apply in judging whether the constitutional proposals are in accord with the gospel or not.

The things that make for peace

Let us therefore look at these 'Christian aims' in the proposed constitution a little more closely. And in doing so we must look not only at the terminology used but also at the context within which it is used.

We must, as Christians, the constitution says, preserve the integrity and freedom of our country. But already here the questions abound. What is freedom? And who is free in South Africa? In other words, whose freedom must be defended? In what lies the integrity of our country? Does it not lie in the freedom of all its children, in the diligent pursuit of justice, in the recognition and faithful defence of the human dignity of all? Does it not lie in the fact that the practices and policies of the government are commensurate with the lofty ideals that it claims? Does a country have integrity when it destroys, systematically and by design, the human dignity of its citizens, when it makes as irrelevant and fickle a thing as racial identity the key to the understanding of human relationships, political participation and economic justice? Does it have integrity when in the name of Christianity it pursues policies which cause little children to die of hunger and malnutrition, which break up black family life and which spell out a continuous, hopeless death for millions of black people?

The vast majority of South Africa's people are *not* free – that is true. But neither are the whites, who think that their security and peace lie in the perpetuation of intimidation, dehumanisation, and violence. They will never be free as long as they have to kill our children in order to safeguard their over-privileged positions. They will never be free as long as they have to lie awake at night worrying whether a black government will one day do the same to them as they are doing to us, when white power will have come to its inevitable end.

One has to presume that the country's integrity and freedom have to be defended against 'the communists'. We have no reason to laud the communists, but we must not blame them for things they did not do. It was not the communists who took away our land, who created the homelands, who drafted the security legislation, who detained those who struggled for justice without trial, torturing them in the jails and banning them into virtual nonexistence. It is not the communists who created the Group Areas Act and thereby legally robbed millions of people of their homes. It is not the communists who killed Steve Biko and Saul Mkhize. So, while the communists have a lot to answer for, these things that have happened in this country they did not do. These are done by the South African government that claims to be Christian and that wants us to accept the new constitution because it claims to be a Christian constitution. No, whatever the communists have done, and God knows their misdeeds are many, they have not done them in the name of our Lord and Saviour Jesus Christ. Therefore God's judgement shall be harsher on this government because it, knowing the Name above all names, has deliberately and consistently profaned that Name. Therefore the churches, as deliberately and consistently, must remind the government: 'You shall not take the name of the Lord your God in vain!' And 'you shall reap what you sow!'

And what shall we say about law and order as a Christian aim? Does the government mean the racist laws that have become the hallmark of this country? The Group Areas Act, or the Pass Laws, the Mixed Marriages Act, or any of the other discriminatory laws which are designed to secure white people's whiteness and their privileged position? Does the Constitution speak about the so-called security laws, maybe? Is detention without trial, unexplained deaths in detention, and torture a Christian form of law and order? Is Christian law and order the killing of children on the streets who protest against apartheid and its evils? No, a thousand times no! The church cannot accept that. We must be clear in our witness that this kind of law and order is in fact a travesty of justice. The people are not there for the law, but the law, like the Sabbath, is there for the sake of people. Law and order are not the foundation of justice, but justice is the foundation of the law. Order is not the guardian of humaneness, but humaneness is the guarantee of order. Any order which is devoid of justice opens the door to tyranny and becomes the instigator of the chaos and disorder it pretends to prevent.

The constitution makes the glib identification of Christianity with capitalism. Is capitalism, with its overriding concern for profits and only profits, Christian? Is not God's economy an economy where people matter more than money and profits? Does not the Bible have explicit and disturbing things to say about wealth and about the rich? Contrary to the self-seeking, self-centred, selfish grab-ethic of capitalism, does not the gospel call us to share what we have, not to make us feel good, but in order to create equality among people (2 Cor. 8: 15)? Does not the biblical ethic demand love for our neighbour, so that we first seek the interest of the neighbour instead or our own (Phil. 2: 4)? In contrast to the capitalist theory that the rich must get richer so that the riches may 'trickle down' to the poor, stand the flaming words of the prophet Amos who did not believe that justice should 'trickle down' but rather that 'justice [should] roll down like waters, and righteousness like an ever-flowing stream'.

Finally, the Constitution talks about the duty of the government and the people of South Africa to seek world peace. This is a lofty ideal, and I wish that it were true. But to begin with, we will have to state that one cannot seek peace in the world when one is the destroyer of peace at home. It seems that it is forever necessary to repeat the well-known biblical truth: peace is not simply the absence of war; it is the active presence of justice. Peace is the shalom of God for the world and for the people of God's heart. It is the essence of the well-being of the community, and as such it encompasses *all* areas of life. Shalom is there also as a socio-political reality, as the gift of God which transcends any human ideas of success. It is a reality that goes beyond the purely personal and includes the totality of our human existence.

Moreover, in the Bible peace is always closely associated with *sedaqah* – justice – with which it shall join hands, according to Psalm 85: 10; and according to Isaiah 32: 17, peace is the child of justice. So in the Bible, peace has to do with human fulfillment, with liberation, with a meaningful life and well-being, and with the active presence of justice.

Again our question is: How can you create peace in the world when you create peace-lessness at home? The injustice of apartheid is an undeniable negation of the peace that the government is trying to seek. Apartheid, with its wanton violence, its destruction of human-beingness, its obscene overturning of human values, is the exact opposite of peace. South Africa's people are a threat to world peace, and certainly to the peace in this region, rather than a contribution to peace.

The essence of apartheid is the separation of people in society as well as in the church. The essence of the gospel is the truth that comes to us out of the mouth of Paul: 'Jesus Christ is our peace, he who has made the two one, and has broken down the wall of enmity that has separated them.'

In our situation the church must not succumb to the temptation of the false prophets who shout 'Peace! Peace!' where there is no peace. As long as the false god of racial superiority rules this nation; as long as the lives of black people count for nothing and our children have to grow up with hopelessness and despair; as long as justice continues to stumble openly on the streets of this tragic, beautiful land, as long as black and white people cannot learn to live together as brothers and sisters, there shall be no peace.

Over against the deliberate lie that apartheid can create peace must stand the sober warning of Jesus Christ, once spoken to Jerusalem and sadly true of South Africa: 'If you only knew the things that make for peace!'

Between the devil and the deep blue sea

I know about the many questions many of us must have. I know about the burning uncertainties, about the understandable desire to at least know where we are going. And we long for some certainty as we face the future. But you see, the way of liberation is never a way of certainties. There is not really a blueprint. It was not true when God liberated Israel from bondage in Egypt; it is not true today. In truth, the only certainty Israel had in those days was its experience in Egypt. This is vividly recounted in the 14th chapter of Exodus. There Israel is caught between the advancing armies of Egypt and the sea – between the devil and the deep blue sea.

The people of Israel become desperately afraid, and in their fear they

What is speech / light
... before a word is on our tongue ... you know it

long for the certainties of their life in Egypt. For there is a deadly kind of certainty in enslavement. We know the oppressor so well that we become used to a rhythm. In the process of liberation, however, there seems to be only risk and uncertainty. Besides, the power of the Pharaoh was much more concrete and tangible than the promises of God – which were all they had, really. A promise they had not heard (only Moses had heard it), a bush they had not seen as it burnt (only Moses had seen it), a land of promise which not even Moses had seen, a wilderness to go through that they did not know, and a leader whose stuttering explanations they did not trust. What was much more tangible were the fleshpots of Egypt (surely a wild exaggeration in that moment of dire distress), and the power of Egypt as represented in the king and his armies. So they shouted their anger at Moses and his God.

And poor Moses? He tries to comfort the people by promising them God's help: 'The Lord will fight for you, and you must be still.' But to Moses' surprise (and our own) Yahweh gets a little impatient with this comforting, pious theology. 'What is the meaning of all this clamour?' Yahweh asks. 'Tell the children of Israel to march.' To where? Into the sea of course, and beyond the sea into the wilderness. How? Simply with faith in the promises of this God who has taken hold of this people, who has tied their future to his own, and who shall liberate those to whom he has given his heart.

No, there is still no blueprint, there is still no military strategy, there is still no certainty – there is only the promise. *And it is the people of Israel who must take up the responsibility themselves and who must march.* In faith, in trust, and in the knowledge that the Lord is with them, determined to glorify God's name over against the might and pride of the Pharaoh.

I remind you of this story because it is so appropriate for us as we face the choices ahead of us. Behind us are the armies of the Pharaoh. In front of us lie the sea and the wilderness: that dark and uncertain future of which we know nothing. And the questions multiply. What if a black government is as bad as this white government? How do we know things will be different? If only we had some certainty.

But the choice is clear: we are called either to go with this God, on foot, into the sea and the wilderness, trusting only in his promises and willing to do what is right and just, or to climb onto the chariots of Pharaoh. And as with Israel, God will not make the decision for us, nor can we hope to hide behind the pious theological statements we make so often. The choice is ours, and we must not allow fear of the uncertain future to prevent us from doing what is right.

The future does not fall unexpectedly upon us, nor does it roll in on the wheels of inevitability, but it is shaped by the quality of our efforts in the present. So what South Africa will be, very much depends on the kind of foundations we are today laying for the future society.

But this is a false dilemma. The question is not so much what we should do *one day* if a black government should do something wrong. The question is, what are we doing *right now*, while this white government is doing what it is doing? While it is not wrong to have a legitimate concern for the future, it is wrong to use that as an excuse for not being concerned about the plight of those who are the victims of oppression and exploitation right now. And it is a tortuous logic to use fear of the results of oppression as a reason for the continuation of it.

But today we have to deal with another and even more dangerous false dilemma, and that is the argument that refusal to cooperate with the government in the new constitutional plan is participation in bloody revolution.

This is a clever political tactic, but it is as empty as it is misleading.

There is general consensus (even from coloured and Indian supporters of the plan) that the plans are an entrenchment of white political dominance and of apartheid. What does that mean? Apartheid is an exceptionally violent political system. There is, first, the *structural* violence embedded in the laws and the structures of our society. Every law that sanctions discrimination is an act of violence. When human rights are disregarded, when education is not equal, when there is economic exploitation, when a system by design causes deprivation, malnutrition, and hunger, when the law requires the breaking up of family life – this is violence. In fact, any act which erodes human dignity is an act of violence.

But second, there is also the violence needed to maintain the system, to safeguard the privileged position of the dominant group – the police and military violence without which apartheid will not survive for a single minute. We have seen it at Sharpeville, in Soweto, in Cape Town, and we are seeing it in the ongoing civil war on the borders of Namibia. , Sudan, congo

Saying yes to cooperation with the very government that maintains this violent system without first fundamentally changing it is taking responsibility for the continuation of the violence. The choice for violence, therefore, has not been made by those who resist the perpetuation of the system in the hope of working for a better society, but precisely by those who have abandoned the struggle for a better society by strengthening the present one.

So let us stand firm. Let us continue to speak out for what is right. Let us continue to seek ways toward genuine peace for the people of this country, and let us continue to seek ways to break the evil cycle of violence in which we find ourselves. Let us continue to resist apartheid, to say with Gandhi that non-cooperation with evil is as much a moral obligation as is cooperation with good. And let us continue to strive, to build, even now in the midst of the struggle, the foundation for genuine reconciliation between black and white in South Africa.

As you continue your work against so many odds, do not get weary. As you work in seemingly hopeless situations, as you see the light die in the eyes of those who have watched the pain too long, as you sometimes wonder whether anything at all will ever change the structures of power that so ruthlessly control our destiny in this land, do not lose faith.

Do not forget that every protest against injustice, every prayer for liberation, every act of compassion and love is an affirmation of freedom and a living sign of the Kingdom of God.

And if it sometimes seems futile and the dark clouds of despair threaten to blot out the sun and your hope, remember that we are guided, not by worldly strength and power, but by faith in God who through his Son loves us and through his Spirit nurtures us, and who has given us a vision that should not die: a vision of hope, truth, love, justice, and peace. God bless you!

7

All, Here and Now:
The Launch of the United Democratic Front

8 20 83

This is the keynote address at the historic launch of the United Democratic Front on 20 August 1983. It was the culmination of seven months of incredibly hard work by many dedicated activists. Amongst other things, this address sought to outline not only the principles on which the UDF was built but also the vision the UDF sought to hold before the people of South Africa.

The birth of a people's movement

We have arrived at a historic moment. We have brought together under the aegis of the United Democratic Front the broadest and most significant coalition of groups and organisations struggling against apartheid, racism, and injustice since the early 1950s. We have been able to create a unity among freedom-loving people this country has not seen for many years. I am particularly happy to note that this meeting is not merely a gathering of individuals. No, we represent organisations deeply rooted in the struggle for justice, deeply rooted in the hearts of our people. Indeed, I believe we are standing at the birth of what could become the greatest and most significant people's movement in more than a quarter of a century.

We are here to say that the government's constitutional proposals are inadequate and that they do not express the will of the vast majority of South Africa's people. But more than that, we are here to say that what we are working for is one, undivided South Africa that shall belong to all of its people, an open democracy from which no single South African shall be excluded, a society in which the human dignity of all its people shall be respected. We are here to say that there are rights that are neither conferred by nor derived from the state. You have to go back beyond the dim mist of eternity to understand their origin; they are God-given. And so we are here not to beg for those rights; we are here to claim them.

In a sense, the formation of the United Democratic Front both highlights and symbolises the crisis apartheid and its supporters have created for themselves. After a history of some 331 years of slavery, racial discrimination, dehumanisation and economic exploitation, what they expected were acceptance of the status quo, docility, and subservience. Instead, they are finding a people refusing to accept racial injustice and ready to face the challenge of the moment.

After more than three decades of apartheid, they expected humble submission to the harsh rule of totalitarianism and racial supremacy. Instead, they find a people ready at every level of society to fight this evil system.

After more than twenty years of apartheid education, they expected to see totally brainwashed, perfect little *hotnotjies* and *kaffertjies* who knew their place in the world. Instead, they find a politically conscious generation of young people determined to struggle for a better future.

After the draconian measures of the 1960s and the ever harsher oppression of the so-called security laws, they expected a people immobilised by the tranquillising drugs of apathy and fear. Instead, they find a rising tide of political and human consciousness that swept away complacency and shook South Africa to its very foundations.

After the tragic happenings of the 1970s – the banning of our organisations and so many of those who struggle for justice; the torture and death of so many in detention; the merciless killing of our children on the streets of the nation – they expected surrender. Instead, here we are at this historic occasion telling South Africa and the world: we are struggling for our human dignity and for the future of our children – we shall never give up!

In all of this, those in power in this country have made the fundamental mistake of all totalitarian regimes who do not depend on the loyalty of the people but on the power of the gun: they have not reckoned with the determination of a people to be free. Because they depend on propaganda, deceit and coercion, they have forgotten that no lie can live forever and that the fear of the gun is always overcome by the longing for freedom. They have forgotten that it is true you can kill the body, but you cannot kill the spirit and the determination of a people.

The positive side of evil

The most immediate reason for our coming together here today is the continuation of the government's apartheid policies as seen in the constitutional proposals. In recent weeks some people have asked me with greater urgency than before (and I am sure this question has been put to you also), 'Why do you not see the positive side of apartheid?'

Now, when you are white and your children's education is guaranteed and paid for by the state; when your job is secure and black people are prevented by law from being too much competition; when your home has never been taken away and your citizenship of the country of your birth is not in danger; when your children don't have to die of hunger and malnutrition, and when your over-privileged position is guaranteed by security laws and the best-equipped army on the continent, then I can understand why some people believe that apartheid has its positive side.

But for those of us who are black and who suffer under this system there is no positive side. How can we see something positive in a system which is built on oppression, injustice and exploitation? What is positive about a system which destroys, systematically and by design, the human dignity of people, which makes as irrelevant and unimportant a thing as skin colour the basis of society and the key to the understanding of human relationships, political participation and economic justice? How can apartheid be positive when in the name of Christianity it spawns policies which cause little children to die of hunger and malnutrition, which break up black family life, and which spell out a continuous, hopeless death for millions of black people?

How can apartheid be positive when it keeps part of South Africa's children manacled in the chains of slavery and the other part in the chains of fear? The time has come for white people to realise that their destiny is inextricably bound with our destiny and that they shall never be free until we are free. I am so happy that so many of our white brothers and sisters are saying this by their presence here today.

But we must also ask the question, what is positive about the government's constitutional proposals? In order that there should be no misunderstanding, let me as clearly and briefly as possible repeat the reasons why we reject these proposals.

Racism, so embedded in South African society, is once again written into the Constitution. All over the world, people are beginning to recognise that racism is politically untenable, sociologically unsound and morally unacceptable. But in this country, the doctrine of racial supremacy, although condemned by most churches in South Africa as heresy and idolatry, is once again enshrined in the Constitution as the basis upon which to build the further development of our society and the nurturing of human relationships.

All the basic laws, those laws that are the very pillars of apartheid, indeed, those laws without which the system cannot survive – mixed marriages, group areas, racial classification, separate and unequal education, to name but a few – remain untouched and unchanged.

The homeland policy, which is surely the most immoral and objectionable aspect of the apartheid policies of the government, forms the basis for the wilful exclusion of 80 per cent of our nation from the new political deal. Indeed, in the words of the proposals made by the President's Council, the homelands policy is to be regarded as 'irreversible'. So our African brothers and sisters will be driven even further into the wilderness of homeland politics; millions will have to find their political rights in the sham independence of those bush republics; millions more will continue to lose their South African citizenship; and millions more will be forcibly removed from their homes into resettlement camps.

Clearly the oppression will continue, the brutal breakup of black family life will not end. The apartheid line is not at all abolished; it is simply shifted so as to include those so-called coloureds and Indians who are willing to cooperate with the government.

Not only is the present system of apartheid given more elasticity, making fundamental change even harder than before, but in the new proposals the dream of democracy is still further eroded.

So, while the proposals may mean something for those middle-class blacks who think that the improvement of their own economic position is the highest good, it will not bring any significant changes to the lives of those who have no rights at all, who must languish in the poverty and utter destitution of the homelands, and who are forbidden by law to live together as families in what is called 'white South Africa'.

It cannot be repeated enough that all South Africans who love this country and who care for its future, black and white, Jew and Gentile, Christian and Muslim, have no option but to reject these proposals.

Apartheid is a cancer in the body politic of the world, a scourge on our society, and an everlasting shame to the church of Jesus Christ in the world and in this country. It exists only because of economic greed, cultural chauvinism and political oppression, maintained by both systemic and physical violence and a false sense of racial superiority. And therefore we must resist it. We must resist it because it is fundamental opposition to the noble principles of our Judeo-Christian heritage, and of the Muslim faith. We must resist it because it is a fundamental denial of all that is worthwhile and human in our society. It is in opposition to the will of God for this country. We must resist it because in its claim to be Christian, apartheid is a blasphemy, idolatry, and a heresy.

To be sure, the new proposals will make apartheid less blatant in some ways. It will be modernised and streamlined, and in its new multicoloured cloak it will be less conspicuous and less offensive to some. Nonetheless, it will still be there. And we must remember, apartheid is a thoroughly evil system. As such it cannot be modified, modernised, or streamlined; it has to be irrevocably eradicated. And we must continue to struggle until that glorious day shall dawn when apartheid shall exist no more.

And so, to those who ask *why* we are not satisfied and *when* we shall be satisfied we must say in clear, patient terms: we shall not be satisfied as long as injustice reigns supreme on the throne of our land. We shall not be satisfied as long as those who rule us are not inspired by justice but dictated to by fear, greed and racialism. We shall not be satisfied until South Africa is once again one, undivided country, a land where there shall be meaningful participation in a democratic process of government for all our people.

We shall not be satisfied until the wealth and riches of this country are shared by all. We shall not be satisfied until justice rolls down like waters and righteousness like a mighty stream.

The challenge of non-racialism

We must turn to one other important question, namely the question of whites and blacks working together. This has been mentioned as a reason why the United Democratic Front has been so severely attacked by some and why they have refused to give their cooperation.

They are saying to us that white people cannot play a meaningful role in the struggle for justice in this country because they are always, by definition, the oppressor. Because the oppression of our people wears a white face, because the laws are made by a white government, because we are suffering so much under a system created and maintained by white people, they say there can be no cooperation between white and black until all of this is changed.

I would like to say to those who think this way that I understand the way they feel. We have seen with our own eyes the brutalisation of our people at the hands of whites. We have seen police brutality. We have experienced the viciousness and the violence of apartheid. We have been trampled on for so long; we have been dehumanised for so long. But it is not true that apartheid has the support of all white people. There are those who have struggled with us, who have gone to jail, who have been tortured and banned. There are those who have died in the struggle for justice. And we must not allow our anger for apartheid to become the basis for a blind hatred for *all* white people. Let us not build our struggle upon hatred, bitterness and a desire for revenge. Let us even now seek to lay the foundation for reconciliation between white and black in this country by working together, praying together, struggling together for justice.

No, the nature and the quality of our struggle for liberation cannot be determined by the colour of one's skin, but rather by the quality of one's commitment to justice, peace, and human liberation. And in the final analysis, judgement will be given, not in terms of whiteness or blackness, whatever the ideological content of those words may be today, but in terms of the persistent faithfulness we are called to in this struggle.

Besides, the very fact that we are talking about the constitutional proposals already reveals the paradox in this argument. The government has been pushing ahead with these proposals precisely because they have been supported and accepted by some people from the black community who think that the short-term economic gains and the semblance of political power are more important than the total liberation of all South Africa's people. So our struggle is not only against the white government and their plans, but also against those in the black community who through their collaboration seek to give credibility to these plans.

But there is something else that we must say. South Africa belongs to all its people. That is a basic truth we must cling to tenaciously for now and for the future. This country is our country, and its future is not safe in the hands of people who – white or black – despise democracy and trample on the rights of the people. Its future is not safe in the hands of people – white or black – who depend upon economic exploitation and human degradation to build their empires. Its future is not safe in the hands of people – white or black – who need the flimsy and deceitful cloak of ethnic superiority to cover the nakedness of their racism. Its future is not safe in the hands of people – white or black – who seek to secure their unjustly required privileged positions by violent repression of the weak, the exploited, and the needy. Its future is not safe in the hands of people – white or black – who put their faith simply in the madness of growing militarism. So for the sake of our country and our children, whether you be white or black, resist those people, whether *they* be white or black.

So let us not be fearful of those who sit in the seats of power, their lips dripping with the words of interposition and nullification. Let us not be intimidated by those who so arrogantly, so frighteningly, echo their master's voice.

We are doing what we are doing not because we are white or black; we are doing what we are doing *because it is right*. And we shall continue to do so until justice and peace embrace and South Africa becomes the nation it is meant to be.

Three little words

In the meantime, let me remind you of three little words, words that express so eloquently our seriousness in this struggle. You don't have to have a vast vocabulary to understand them. You don't need a philosophical bent to grasp them – they are just three little words. The first word is the word 'all'. We want *all* of our rights. Not just some rights, not just a few token handouts the government sees fit to give – we want all our rights. And we want *all* of South Africa's people to have their rights. Not just a selected few, not just coloureds or Indians after they have been made honorary whites. We want the rights of all South Africa, including those whose citizenship has already been stripped away by this government.

The second word is the word 'here'. We want all of our rights *here*, in a united, undivided South Africa. We do not want them in an impoverished homeland, we don't want them in our separate little group areas. We want them here in this land which one day we shall once again call our own.

The third word is the word 'now'. We want all of our rights, we want them here, and we want them now. We have been waiting so long; we have been struggling so long. We have pleaded, cried, petitioned too long now. We have been jailed, exiled, killed for too long. Now is the time! And as we struggle, let us remember that change does not roll in on the wheels of inevitability. It comes through the tireless efforts and hard work of those who are coworkers with God, who are willing to take the risk of fighting for freedom, democracy, and human dignity.

As we struggle on, let us continue to sing that wonderful hymn of freedom: Nkosi Sikilel' iAfrika. I know: today we are singing that hymn with tears in our eyes. We are singing it while we are bowed down by the weight of oppression and battered by the winds of injustice. We are singing it while our old people languish in the resettlement camps and our children are dying of hunger in the homelands. We are singing it now while we suffer under the brutality of apartheid and while the blood of our children is calling to God from the streets of our nation.

But we must work for the day when we shall sing it when we are free. We shall sing it when our children shall no longer be judged by the colour of their skin but by the humaneness of their character.

We shall sing it on that day when even here in this country, in Johannesburg and Cape Town, in Port Elizabeth and Durban, the sanctity of marriage and family life shall be respected, and no law shall require of man to put asunder what God has joined together.

We shall sing it on that day when in this rich land no child shall die of hunger and no infant shall die untimely, and our elderly shall close their eyes in peace, and the wrinkled stomachs of our children shall be filled with food just as their lives shall be filled with meaning.

We shall sing it when here in South Africa white and black will have learnt to love one another and work together in building a truly good and beautiful land.

With this faith, we shall yet be able to give justice and peace their rightful place on the throne of our land; with this faith, we shall yet be able to see beyond the darkness of our present into the bright and glittering daylight of our future; with this faith we shall be able to speed up the day when all of South Africa's children will embrace each other and sing with new meaning:

> Nkosi sikilel' iAfrika
>
> God bless Africa. Guide her rulers. Bless her children. Give her peace!

PART THREE

Raising a Sign of Hope

8

Courage is Contagious:
The Consequences of Struggle

'Beyond our wildest dreams'

The growth of the UDF was undoubtedly phenomenal. Starting with over 500 organisations, it grew to almost 1 000 within the next few years. This was not as implausible as it may sound. Every town, every township with any kind of organisation at all who wanted to join, did so. The only real criterion was genuine commitment to the struggle. Besides, many such organisations already existed; most of which were ideologically aligned to the ANC. It is certain that some of them were secretly funded by the ANC, though many were not.

The enthusiasm on the ground was amazing and infectious. Youth, student, civic, trade union, professional, political and women's organisations proliferated. Each knew it could make a contribution to the struggle unique to its own situation. Students would talk to students, workers to workers, health and education professionals to their peers. Pressure would build up to the level of national leadership in those organisations which had such national structures, and mostly this leadership would respond. New Christian youth groups were formed, existing ones were transformed. For instance, the Student Christian Movement and the predominantly Afrikaans-speaking Association for Christian Students, radicalised and politically conscious now, came to bear no resemblance at all to their conservative white counterparts, and the national leadership supported them in their choices. These organisations had a strong presence in and enormous influence on high schools and college campuses right across the country. Every Christian student camp became a workshop for Christian participation in the struggle. The UDF was everywhere.

The UDF was truly a peoples' movement. Not only the cities but also the rural areas became, as the establishment media would define them, 'hotbeds of radicalism'. The message of the UDF spread like wildfire. The 'coloured' communities, unlike other political organisations who drew their support mostly from the English-speaking elites in Cape Town and the peninsula, launched an onslaught on the rural areas. Often it would be the politicised students from UWC and the teachers' colleges who would return home and light the fires of political consciousness and participation.

To hear the youth, and eventually the older generation of the conservative *platteland*, till now so quiet, so submissive, speak the language of liberation, sing the songs, chant the slogans, in Afrikaans, evoked emotions which even today I find hard to describe. The language of the oppressor had been stolen from us and possessed by those who denied its very origin and roots, distorted by those who in their clumsy attempts to make it white and aristocratic and European succeeded only in making Afrikaans an orphan. That language, uprooted from the soil of the soul from which it had grown, its sounds robbed of all melody by the harsh words of subjection and *baasskap,* that language had been redeemed in our eyes. It had come home to the dusty streets of Oudtshoorn and Steytlerville, of Graaff-Reinet and Calvinia, of Lamberts Bay, Elandsfontein, Springbok and Upington. It was in the Afrikaans *platteland*, where the rhythms of the *rieldans* had for years shyly slumbered just under the skin and where toes were not too dainty to kick the dust and hips not too girdled up to swing, that they responded and did the UDF's Afrikaans trademark chant with such brave and joyful abandon, the lilt and intonation so different from the Afrikaans of the Cape Flats:

> Die mammas, die pappas,
> Die oumas, die oupas,
> Die boeties, die sussies,
> Die hondjies, die katjies,
> Is saam in die struggle!
> Amandla, Awethu!

I would come on to the stage and before saying anything else would begin the rhythmic chant. The first pair of words (*Die mammas*) would be mine, the crowd would take up the second pair. The hall would vibrate, the roof would come down. Outside, the coloured policemen, batons and guns in hand, faces grim under the watchful eye of their white bosses, would feel the yearning in their hearts but would not dare move. Inside, swaying bodies and stamping feet would echo ancient Khoisan rituals and awaken rhythms we had all but forgotten. The sheer joyfulness of it would obliterate our fear but stoke other fears outside. I would add any category at random: nurses, lawyers, doctors, teachers, (*die nursies, die prokkies, die dokkies, die onnies*); the crowd would follow. That night after the meeting or the next day they would smell the tear gas, run before the dogs or feel the rubber bullets, after

I had gone, taking the media with me. Then they would feel the fear, and the pain. But for the moment our hearts were singing. It was like church. It was awesome.

Translations of such songs and slogans never really work, but here goes. As one reads it, one should get into the sway of things, or one misses the point.

> The mothers, the fathers,
> The grandmas, the grandpas,
> The little brothers; the little sisters,
> The puppies, the kittens,
> Are all in the struggle!
> Power to the people!

As I said, it never works, but hopefully you get the idea.

So when the historians write that 'the UDF immediately (and completely) transformed the nature of black opposition politics', they are of course right. But they really don't know the half of it. Unless they were there. Crowds of thousands marching down the street through rural towns like Cradock, Oudtshoorn and Graaff-Reinet (once for over 20 km in heat of over 40 degrees) were a sight these places had never seen – ever. And this was just the Western Cape, where, together with the old Transvaal and Natal, the UDF was initially strongest. It would be the same all over the country, and the Eastern Cape's place in history is secured. I will never be able to recall precisely the number of times I spoke, the number of marches I led.

Even though the UDF's first objective was to target the phony elections for the tri-cameral parliament and the new Constitution, and the real battle for that issue lay mostly in the Cape and Natal, the

UDF also gave the struggle a national character. In addition, it gave the struggle a decidedly non-racial and non-violent character. It forced the government to abandon their idea of a referendum. They held elections instead. This suited us perfectly. The anti-election campaign was on. The polls for the tri-cameral parliament and the black local authorities were dismal. The boycott was a resounding success. Then came the consumer boycotts, the stay-aways, the strikes, the closing of the schools as protest against coloured and Bantu education. The agenda was a national one, exactly as we had spelt out on 20 August – the creation of a non-racial, non-sexist, democratic South Africa – and that goal necessitated the destruction of apartheid.

I have always been a bit surprised at two issues regarding the UDF which some keep on raising. The UDF, they argue, claimed to be a non-racial organisation and yet in opposing apartheid, a race-based policy, their actions invariably took on a racial character. The logic escapes me totally. Why should the UDF's non-racial character be questioned because it was fighting a racist system? Why should the character of the UDF be determined by the kind of system it fought? Such arguments remind me of how completely, even if unknowingly, the subjection to apartheid's racist mindset dominated some people's thinking. The UDF refused to be defined by apartheid – not in its politics, its attitudes or its actions. Would the same people argue that because Marxists were fighting capitalists the Marxists couldn't help but be capitalists themselves? Taking on the apartheid regime and its myth of racial superiority did not make one's opposition to racism 'racial'. It meant dealing with a political, economic and social reality in order to debunk the myths and untruths, establish new ways of thinking and, create new realities.

It makes more sense to argue, as for example Neville Alexander did, that the UDF 'subjected itself to race' in accepting racially based organisations, such as the Indian Congresses of Natal and Transvaal (the TIC and the NIC), and organisations based in the separate and racially divided townships. The UDF argued then, and I still think it is a good argument, that one should take into account the historical contexts in which those organisations were formed. They served a very specific purpose then, and their goal was to keep the tradition of struggle alive in those communities, while building firmly on the principles laid down in the Freedom Charter. The TIC and NIC had that special link with Gandhi which had vested them with great authority in the Indian communities. What purpose, political or otherwise, would have been served if the UDF had high-mindedly refused to recognise the existence of these organisations, or demanded them to disband in order to be re-established as non-racial organisations? It was wise under the circumstances not to try to uproot those organisations but rather, as in the case of the TIC and NIC, to strengthen their mobilising capacity in the Indian communities for the sake of the broader struggle. It was also simply good political strategy. Every community has its own needs and dynamics, its own ways of doing things, and subsequently needs a unique approach. Honouring that is honest as well as politically sound. I would never be so arrogant as to think that as a Christian I am equipped to deal with the Hindu community as well as a Hindu person, even if I shared their political views. There are always dynamics involved that are greater than just ideology and politics, and one should be respectful of those. Non-racialism does not mean the obliteration of all cultural or religious identities, of language, of community styles; it means honouring and treasuring the wealth of diversity within one, unified non-racial reality. To dismiss this in the name of some purist pretext is, in my view, too ideological to stand the test of reality.

The second argument concerns the widespread protests. Many protest actions, the argument goes, have been attributed to the UDF when in fact they were driven by UDF *affiliates*. Again, the argument mystifies me. From the very beginning the UDF knew (and the ANC feared) that much action in the course of struggle was perforce going to be spontaneous; that is, not planned from above and handed down with precise instructions and therefore not subject to 'control'. While there was always going to be great danger in such spontaneous action, and that danger had to be recognised, it was also the UDF's hallmark of authenticity. And it was unavoidable in a truly people-driven movement. People would react and respond to situations in their own environment as they saw the need. They, better than anybody from outside, could gauge the political temperature, know what was possible and what the consequences would be for them. In that sense there always was an autonomy that naturally belonged to communities and their organisations. It would have been wrong, and foolish, for the UDF leadership to tamper with that. So of course first responsibility for action was always with local leadership. But while some of those base organisations might have existed before the formation of the UDF, they were hardly organised enough, or strong enough on their own, to embark on actions that would have meaningful political impact. The UDF coordinated them, brought them under one, strong, national umbrella and gave them a platform and political stature they did not have before. Whereas earlier they might have engaged in some action as say, the local branch of the Congress of South African Students (COSAS), now they could act under the banner of the UDF.

One must also not underestimate the power of the UDF to inspire. I witnessed what just one visit could do to poor, neglected but determined communities. It was something the apartheid regime, despite its propaganda and security forces, its remunerative power and military might, did not and could not budget for.

Last but not least, these small organisations now had access to funding they might not have had before. I am sure underground ANC organisations, as argued previously, whether MK affiliated or not, had easier access to funding mainly because the ANC approved of them. Hundreds of others did not enjoy such approval and remained under-funded and therefore mostly impotent to launch meaningful political action. Or they were simply not known. The Foundation for Peace and Justice (FPJ), which I headed during those years, made such funding possible on a large scale. Hundreds of marches, funerals and rallies were funded through the FPJ. In that sense, the UDF did not have to 'claim credit' for the myriad actions of protest across the country: they were in essence UDF activities, precisely because these organisations or groups or unions *were* UDF affiliates.

Within a year, the UDF had become a formidable organisation with support at levels and among people that no organisation, including the ANC, had ever experienced before. By 1985, the newly formed Congress of South African Trade Unions (Cosatu) had joined the UDF. In this manner, the National Union of Mineworkers (NUM), under the brilliant leadership of Cyril Ramaphosa, became part of the UDF. Now we had the powerful backing of the unions and a different kind of leadership strengthened the UDF. We were seeing things, as one UDF leader told a Dutch journalist, 'beyond our wildest dreams.' There was talk of a 'Mass Democratic Movement' rather than the UDF, but the name never quite stuck. Certainly not with ordinary people. Today, when people recall the struggle years during the eighties, they still speak only of the UDF.

The UDF was not only internally the apartheid government's most impeccable foe; it simultaneously exposed the make-believe resistance of groups like Chief Buthelezi's Inkatha Freedom Party, the fraudulent nature of P.W. Botha's so-called reforms and the pathetic political posturing of apartheid-created ethnic politics, all of which tried to convince our people and the world that 'working within the system to fight the system' was the only way. Internationally, the UDF had become a household name. Of all the international gatherings, rallies and marches I attended and addressed, sometimes with international celebrities and film stars, nothing spelt out this fact clearer than what happened one day after I had just got off a train at Penn Street Station in New York, city of cherished anonymity. A young African American man walked by, stopped, and with unabashed directness pointed at me and shouted: 'Hey! UDF!' I smiled: we had truly become an international force.

The consequences of struggle

But the clouds were gathering and the rumbling of thunder could already be heard. By 1984 South Africa experienced a veritable uprising. Rebellion against the imposed black authorities had broken out in the Transvaal townships. Spreading rapidly across the country, it would not stop until the middle of 1986. Strategically better organised and better reported by the media than before, the rebellion made headlines across the world. For one brief, shining moment, the South African media had no reason to take a back seat to their international colleagues. The *Rand Daily Mail* and the indomitable Allister Sparks, Tony Heard of the *Cape Times* and his unforgettable interviews with Oliver Tambo, 'Let Tambo be Heard!'– and the incomparable cartoonist Tony Grogan. On the Afrikaans media side in early 1989 there was Elna Botha and her audacious series for Afrikaans radio on the unavoidability of negotiations with the ANC. Her bosses at the SABC refused to put it on air and she, with the whole Monitor team, resigned en masse. The courageous journalists of the community and alternative media: Rashid Seria, Zubeida Jaffer, Moegsien Williams, Ryland Fisher of *Grassroots* fame, Max du Preez and Jacques Pauw of *Vrye Weekblad*. The few who worked for the international media: Jimi Matthews, Sahm Venter, Craig Matthews and Rashid Lombard. I wish I could mention them all. They exposed the dark deeds of the regime, gave voice to the silenced, carrying our message beyond the townships and the borders of self-besieged South Africa.

The stay-aways, consumer boycotts and strikes intensified. Church leaders across the country played a tremendously important role. Even though hardly mentioned now, the role of those clergy, sometimes backed by their denominational structures but mostly not, acted out of deep-seated evangelical conviction. There were the well-known names: Desmond Tutu, Smangaliso Mkhatshwa, Frank Chikane, me, but many were totally unknown, local pastors who knew the demands of the Gospel and understood their responsibilities toward their communities. There were the Catholic nuns, Sister Bernard Ncube first among them. They were everywhere. Without them, the struggle would not have been won, and without them the violence that did ensue would have been so much worse.

The reaction to the rebellion was inevitable and not unexpected, but its ferocity was nonetheless fearsome. The security forces were let loose. Police attacked peaceful marches, rallies were broken up, church services banned and worshippers attacked with tear gas, shot at with rubber bullets and hunted down by dogs. Thousands across the country were detained without trial. There were daily battles in the streets. We tried desperately to keep the protests and demonstrations peaceful. Mostly we succeeded, but many times, and it would become a pattern as time went on and the regime got more desperate, police and soldiers would deliberately provoke the marchers. One tactic that always worked: students would begin to march, or be on their way to a march by bus. They would be stopped, police would wade in with the dreaded shambok and begin by beating the girls. Always the girls, and always they hit them across the breast. The boys would go crazy.

The atrocities were piling up. Affidavits poured in and we exposed as much of this as we could. After the first state of emergency was declared in 1985, things inevitably got worse. The security forces were given a blank cheque, the restrictions on the media were very effective indeed, and we had to smuggle information out of the country. Children as young as six years old, like little Thabo Sibeko of Sebokeng, were deliberately shot and killed. Bernard Fortuin of Elsies River was only ten when he was shot by police. While he lay bleeding to death, his mother tried to push through the crowd, explaining that it was her son lying on the ground. 'Let the bastard die!' shouted the policeman, pushing her away. The cold legacy of Jimmy Kruger lived on.

Things got worse. Human Rights activists, lawyers and Black Sash workers like Di Bishop in Cape Town and Molly Blackburn in Port Elizabeth brought affidavits, witnesses and reports. In 1985, in Cradock, two young soldiers breaking into a home ostensibly looking for 'terrorists' beat and raped an elderly grandmother. On a regular basis, tear gas would be fired into homes, schools or churches. As people came running out they would be indiscriminately beaten up, detained, fired at. At a prayer service for the release of Mandela at my own church in Bellville in 1985, police did the same thing, and then threw rocks in the church yard and in the road as 'evidence' that the worshippers had been the first to use violence.

It went on and on. In March 1985 in Uitenhage in the Eastern Cape, police fired into a peaceful funeral procession killing at least 27. Reports here, as almost always, differ. Newspapers at the time reported 22 killed; so does at least one history book. At the time, the community spoke of over 40 dead, and of the police refusing to release the bodies. On the day of the funeral in Langa township, Archbishop Tutu and I preached. I counted the coffins lined up on the field: 27. Many of the coffins were small. A few weeks later there was yet another funeral. Molly Blackburn took me through a heavily-cordoned township to see a mother whose ten-year-old boy had been killed. As we talked she kept folding and unfolding a T-shirt in her hands. It had been white once, with a picture of a little bear on the front. Now it was torn and blood-stained. He had worn it the day he was shot. The anger I felt and expressed at the funeral in Uitenhage remained. It burnt and burnt. I did not fight it. It kept me keenly aware of the justified emotions sweeping our communities, and consciousness of its explosive power forced me to temper my public utterances.

Cape Town, late October 1985. A government truck was driving down a main road in Athlone, a coloured township. It was loaded with crates, but very few noticed that for such an ostensibly heavy load, the truck looked remarkably high on its axles. Athlone had been turned into what the activists called 'a site of struggle'. There had been rioting, tyre burning in the streets and stone throwing at police vehicles. The Palestinian boys we see on television today, in their frustrated and hopeless anger throwing stones at Israeli tanks, and soldiers firing live ammunition in retaliation: that was us. On that day, some young people were standing on the corner engaged in idle talk. Suddenly the crates burst open, policemen with guns rose up and fired live ammunition at the youths. Three were killed. It became known as the Trojan Horse killings. The community seethed in anger, the Cape was in uproar. The killings were caught on film and the world was enraged. Yet another service. Yet another funeral.

The assassinations of the Cradock leaders Matthew Goniwe, Fort Calata, Thomas 'Sparrow' Mkontho and Sicelo Mhlawuli raised the levels of arrogance and brutality of the regime, but they also raised the stakes, even as they raised the level of our anger. My funeral address battled with both my own anger, that of the community and the need to speak in such a way that my anger did not incite recklessness. It was never easy, but that day the balance was even harder to find. The theme of my address was the result of much prayerful wrestling, and it was both genuine and necessary.

These funerals were not just occasions to mourn the dead and comfort the families. They were politically charged, emotional gatherings at which we sought to inspire people not to allow the oppressive forces to win: our struggle had to continue. They were rituals of struggle. I understood, and I participated, but I always left such funerals with a strange sadness. Not just for the dead and the family, but for something else too. The struggle was an overwhelming thing. What counted, always, was the common struggle against apartheid. Few would dare to raise questions of oppression internal to the struggle, or what would be considered 'private' pain. Few would dare to raise questions about the insensitivity of the liberation movement to groups or persons who felt themselves locked out, sat upon or disregarded, even as they marched and sang and suffered with the rest of us. They were expected to subject their own, real pain to the greater suffering of the masses. Their own suffering did not count, or if it did, was not allowed any public space, lest they should 'think more of themselves than the struggle or claim more attention for their pain ...' Gays knew it, women, knew it, dissidents knew it; those whose human rights were trampled underfoot in the camps in the bush knew it too. And so did those who had lost a dear one, a father, an only son or daughter. We needed to remain focused. We needed to remain together. And our togetherness could not abide attention to the terrible loneliness of the individual caused by us. The cause was always greater. ✓ ?

At those funerals the cry was 'Don't mourn, mobilise!' Mourning itself became a sign of weakness: an admission that the regime had won. Those in power should not be allowed to see it, lest they should rejoice in it. The grief of loved ones had to be a deeply private, deeply buried grief, so that the rhythm of the struggle would not be disturbed. I have often prayed for forgiveness for having been part of that. Even so, it was always awe-inspiring: the way the people came back, time after time, wave after wave, facing the dangers, the dogs, the tear gas, the guns. Out of detention and solitary confinement they came, the scars of torture on their bodies, their sleepless nights filled with dreams of terror one could only guess at, organising, mobilising, working for liberation. Many would be arrested, others wounded, some killed. Others would take their place. It is true: courage is contagious. But no less awe-inspiring was the fact that those who kept on coming back too were those carrying the invisible burden of unrelieved grief, unattended pain, unspoken sorrow. And they too joined us – again and again. Maybe the church will one day think of that, call them together, ask for forgiveness and pray for healing.

But there was something else that happened at Cradock and the funeral of the Cradock Four on 20 July 1985. And that, perhaps more than my words that day, symbolised and captured powerfully what I wanted to say. Beyers Naudé went with me. As we entered the township and were met by the leadership, we could hear the singing at the stadium. We could the see dust rising as the comrades danced and toyi-toyied. The anger was palpable, a living, breathing thing. As I entered, a cheer went up and I was lifted shoulder high and carried into the stadium. But here's the thing: next to me was this white man, not known to many. But they lifted him up as well, showed him to the crowd and proclaimed him loved and accepted. In the midst of all that pain and anger. They may have been blinded by tears, but not by hatred. It was almost as if they knew what I was going to say. In lifting Beyers on their shoulders, they lifted up their hope that white South Africa might yet listen and understand the things that make for peace. They held shoulder-high their determination that evil shall be overcome by good. They held him up for all the world to see that they understood the difference between him and the security policemen who murdered their leaders, the politicians who gave them their orders and the whites who simply did not care. I drew such strength from amazing moments like these.

That same year, on a visit to Australia, I spoke in interviews of the atrocities committed by the security forces. Louis le Grange, minister of police, was livid, and made a number of very threatening speeches. Upon my return the UDF organised a special rally for me to respond to the threats of the minister. Almost the whole first half of that speech was devoted to reference to affidavits from all over the country. I read out first a definition of 'atrocity' as found in the dictionary, then read from the affidavits: event after event, fact after fact, killing after killing, with dates, names of the victims and registration numbers of police vehicles. I challenged the minister to a public debate on television where we could discuss the actions of his security forces. Le Grange did not respond. In the rest of the speech I attempted to explain the policy of non-violence to which the UDF had tried to adhere. I spoke of the violent response of the state to our peaceful protests and I tried to urge our people not to give up that principled stand. But it was becoming more difficult by the day.

The government, as in 1960, had again crossed that fatal line. But the people too had taken a step towards the abyss. During that first wave of the uprising, the people forsook non-violence and attacked the homes of local black councillors, the most visible and personalised presence of apartheid in the townships, the symbol of collaboration with the system. They were the personification of our willingness, despite everything we knew and believed in, to become an instrument of evil, the personification of our acceptance of the disrespect and indignity heaped upon us by apartheid. The crowds burnt down municipal buildings, shops and liquor outlets. The homes of black policemen were firebombed to drive them out of the townships, and suspected informers were killed. The suspicion of guilt was enough.

For the first time, too, the world heard of a thing called the 'necklace', a tyre placed around the neck of a person, doused with fuel and set alight. Crowds stood around as the person burnt, jeering and shouting and singing freedom songs. It would happen more than once. It was, I was told, an execution, not murder. He was an *impimpi,* a police informer, the most despicable being in any struggle. There was even a 'hearing' in a 'peoples' court', modelled on the kangaroo courts of the young revolutionary Cuban republic, with Ché Guevara as presiding judge, jury and executioner. It was justified. 'Those who live by the sword shall die by the sword,' Cheryl Carolus responded to my agonised questions. This was a reference to the Gospel of Matthew 26: 52, perhaps intended to help me understand better and to take some comfort from that biblical truth. Rather, it reminded me of Matthew 4. In Matthew 26 Jesus does not condone or justify violence, he condemns it, exposing the downward spiral of inevitability violence creates in its origins and in its consequences. It is not a justification, it is a warning.

I wept when I heard of it. Violence initiated and carried out by us, in its irreversible finality and soul-destroying guilt, had settled itself upon us. Our own brutalisation had begun. I was almost witness to it once. In Lawaaikamp, an informal settlement near picturesque George in the southern Cape, I was to preach at the funeral of three young people killed by the police. A priest speaking before me mentioned that the community knew the identity of the informer who had sold out the three youths. I was taken by utter surprise at the speed of events. A man stood up, clearly panicky, shouting loudly that he knew they were talking about him, but that he was innocent. They had the wrong man. Immediately others jumped up and ran toward him, grabbed him and pulled him outside. I realised what was happening and driven by fear, panic and some instinct, I suppose, jumped over the pew and ran outside, pushing into the crowd. They had already hit him badly and he was bleeding, his eye swollen. Someone was already pouring something that smelt like petrol over him. I battled my way toward him, all the while shouting and pleading with them not to do this. With the man clinging to my back I urged the crowd to let him go, not to do this gravely wrong thing. By God's grace, and the level-headedness of UDF marshals, they listened. I got to a car and drove him away. The photographer for the Detroit *Free Press,* David Turnley, got it all on film. David Turnley, thoroughly professional, kept his camera clicking all the while, even as he was searching for his car keys, found them, and threw them to me. Funny how one notices such little irrelevant details at such moments.

It was the swiftness with which it happened that stunned me. Archbishop Tutu had the same experience when he saved the life of a man condemned to a similar death by a crowd in Johannesburg. The shock and disorientation came later. I trembled like a leaf as I slowly realised what had almost happened. I still preached that day – an emotional sermon about the noble character of the struggle and about the temptations of struggle, about our ideals and our vision and how to keep them pure. I spoke about the responsibility to create a just society even as we struggled for that just society. What kind of country do we really want? I asked. What kind of people do we want to be? I spoke about the love of Christ, about forgiveness and about reconciliation. I spoke about non-violence as the more difficult, but the more noble, way. I pleaded for a peaceful revolution as I never had before.

In the recent past I met some of those who were part of the congregation that day at Lawaaikamp. As I write, just weeks ago at the unveiling of Madiba's statue at Drakenstein Prison, three men who, as fiery youngsters, were members of Peter Mokaba's 'young lions', came to speak to Elna and me. They recalled those long-ago events as they introduced themselves, and thanked me for helping to restrain them on that fateful day. 'We know we were wrong, Rev,' they said. 'It would have been a terrible thing.' 'We would all have been guilty of that terrible thing,' I told them. I told them also of my meeting mid-2005 with the man they almost killed. I was speaking in George at a community workshop and during the lunch break I was approached by a man. 'I do not suppose you still remember me,' he began. I shook my head. 'I am the man from Lawaaikamp, the one who almost got killed.' As I stepped forward to embrace him, I saw someone behind him. 'This is my daughter,' he said, introducing me to a beautiful young woman, now a student at the University of Cape Town. 'When I heard you would be in George today, I wanted her to meet the man who saved her father's life.' She came forward to greet me. I looked at her. Gorgeous, bright, full of life. She was just a few months old when he was attacked, and had he been killed she would have had to grow up without a father. What would her life have been then? Now here they both were. Am I a sentimental crybaby? I probably am, but I couldn't help it. How does one explain life, and the ways of God with one's life?

Not all were this fortunate. Desmond Tutu and I could not be everywhere, and even if we could, we would not have been able to intervene every time, and, I am sure, people would not always have wanted to listen to us. The anger was a blazing fire. The provocation was too much to withstand, and the urge for revenge just too much part of human nature. Besides, the violence paid rich rewards. The necklacing of informants caused the police's sources of information to dry up, the black town councils collapsed, and black policemen moved out of the townships. The townships were made ungovernable. The people smelt victory. The blood of the martyrs was being avenged.

From then on, and right through the eighties, the issue of violence remained a painfully divisive one. The tensions surrounding it grew. It was incredibly hard to continue to make the argument, but Desmond Tutu and I persevered. Not everyone in the church agreed with us. Frank Chikane spoke about the violence as necessary self-defence. The Just War theory justified the theology of the Just Revolution. Some questioned my credentials as a liberation theologian, out of sync with many of my colleagues in the rest of the third world. One journalist from the US, no doubt with the civil rights struggle and Martin Luther King Jr. vs. Malcolm X in mind, raised the question whether the non-violent argument (and, by implication, I) had lost our relevance. I took comfort from the fact that my arguments and pleas were not made from the safety of an armchair: I made them from the frontlines of the battles, and they could not be so easily dismissed. In the end, and given the circumstances, the violence could have been much more horrific, white South Africa could have burnt and burnt, and those 'rivers of blood' the revolutionaries spoke of and all the pundits expected could have flowed. But it did not happen. Amazingly, the non-violent core of the struggle held, the frenzy of violence passed and by 1988 the final defiance campaign had started. But it had cost blood, sweat and tears. And prayer. The influence of the church and of Christian leaders was immense and decisive.

Through it all, I had lost the desire to judge, but I knew nonetheless that our submission to the temptation of violence had been a wrong turn. The so-called mainline churches and their leadership had been caught out by their own shameful history and did not have an idea of how hollow, false and hypocritical their indignant arguments against violence sounded. The South African government felt and responded more confidently now: this was something they could handle. Even though very few white people died during this period, and fears of whites about white suburbs being overrun and burnt down by mobs of angry blacks were never realised, violent resistance did give the regime reason to act with extraordinary brutality, not just in retaliation but in pre-emptive measures. Troops in the townships were an almost permanent presence.

The politics of divide-and-rule took on a new, deadly and sinister character. As the apartheid government set out to win hearts and minds in the black areas (a political programme of appeasement, promises and bribery called WHAM), it simultaneously set up bands of armed vigilantes in the townships. It was well advised by the Reaganites: the pattern was the same as we had seen in El Salvador, Paraguay, Nicaragua. In Cape Town these vigilantes became known as the *witdoeke*. In KwaZulu-Natal that role was played by Inkatha and the violence there reached horrific proportions. The media spoke of 'black-on-black violence' as if this was an internal, tribal war white people could only shake their heads at in exasperation. Political assassinations followed: the Pebco Three, the Gugulethu Seven, the Cradock Four, to name a few. For a while the war was everywhere. In that short, miserable period, instead of fighting the apartheid regime, we were mostly fighting each other. Historians sometimes refer to the period during the second state of emergency as a period of 'fragmentation' and 'demoralisation' for the UDF. In my view, this had everything to do with the violence and its eroding influence on what Luthuli called 'the moral character of the resistance'. It had to do with something else as well.

'No middle road'

In his book *Pale Native* Max du Preez also discusses the violence of this period. The 'only logical conclusion' he can come to is that the anger and frustrations of the youth were such that these could not be controlled or stopped by those from outside the immediate circles of these communities and organisations. And that the violence provided the youth with attention that they had never had. Of course, too, there was the fact that the real enemy, the white government, was unreachable and hence untouchable. They vented their anger on the proxies in the townships. Coupled with the deliberate provocation from security forces this became an extremely dangerous mix. I think that is also true. But I propose we consider some other contributing factors as well.

The frustration the ANC in exile must have felt at not being able to control and direct events in South Africa after 1976 has, I think, been long underestimated. The spontaneity I have spoken of before, the unpredictability of events, the very style of the UDF, made that impossible. But it left the ANC with a serious dilemma.

First of all, it flew in the face of the dogma of 'democratic centralism', a vital communist dogma, which most of us at home did not know, or we did not understand how central it was to ANC thinking. Lenin, like Marx, believed in the participation of the masses in the struggle for the 'democratic revolution'. However, Lenin argued that given its lack of cohesiveness and limited focus, the working class required a (communist) vanguard leadership to control the spontaneous and 'decentralised' actions of the masses. Advice may be given from below, but decisions are taken at the top. In the unified, hierarchical structure, decisions, and therefore guidance from the top down, were regarded as the most efficacious. That principle is called 'democratic centralism'. For a political programme to be successful, the leadership must be the vanguard. In this thinking the task of political transformation could not be left to ordinary people, but required a select group of the political elite to plan and execute the process. Along this line of Leninist philosophy, a select group of intellectuals had the task of thinking and acting on behalf of the masses, in the process directing, and thus controlling the actions of the masses. Studies show how, despite many practical adaptations in other matters such as the switch from Marxist economic policies to neo-liberal capitalism, the ANC as an organisation consistently held on to this principle during its period in exile as well as after its return to South Africa in the 1990s. There are numerous examples of how this principle has impacted on political attitudes and decisions as well as on the country as a whole, to the decided detriment of the democratic ideal. It is argued that democratic centralism is the ideal philosophy for underground political work or for an organisation in exile; however, communism held onto the principle whether it was in power or not. The ANC would fall into the same trap. It is clear that precious little space is left for independent thinking or the proclaimed 'wisdom of the people', let alone space for a theologian whose operating motto for theology as well as politics is a 'hermeneutics of suspicion'. It is this principle that allows the ANC to say, as they did in 1969, that 'the primacy of the political leadership is unchallenged and supreme, and all revolutionary formations and levels, whether armed or not, are subordinate to this leadership ...' Hence, too, the ease with which Nelson Mandela, in 1997, quite harshly and uncompromisingly described the hesitant and cautious criticism levelled at the ANC by churches and some organs of civil society, as posing an 'illegitimate challenge' to the leading political role of the ANC. Mandela would have none of this 'watch dog' politics. As it happens, Mandela made his remarks in response to criticism pertaining to the disbanding of the UDF. In a bitter twist of irony, it is the persistence of this principle that raised the ire of communist Jeremy Cronin, prompting him to coin the now-famous phrase, the 'Zanufication of the ANC' under Thabo Mbeki. In referring to Mbeki's leadership style, Cronin did not hesitate to speak of Stalinism.

Second, it undermined the ANC's claim to be the only voice of the oppressed people of South Africa, their only legitimate representative in the eyes of the world. Now there was another voice, other internal actors not necessarily connected or subjected to ANC underground structures. The ANC often heard of events after the fact: they read about them in the media the same as other people abroad.

Third, not being able to control and direct events undermined quite seriously the authority with which the ANC could speak of those events and, by implication, the struggle. They could *claim* that the UDF was only following instructions, but that claim, they knew, was not always sustainable, and in important ways sometimes contradicted.

Fourth, if the ANC were the only legitimate voice of the people of South Africa, their choice for violent revolution and the violent overthrow of the apartheid regime had to be seen as the legitimate choice of the people as well. But now the people were making a choice for non-violent resistance, and while it was firmly within the tradition of the ANC, it was not current policy and had not been since 1960.

Fifth, that very same fact created an uncomfortable credibility gap in the language the ANC spoke and the language that emanated from inside. This was not just 'mixed signals' or semantics. It was fundamental. It caused more than just embarrassment when, for instance, Desmond Tutu or I shared an international platform with ANC representatives in exile, on which occasions our arguments often found greater response. It raised, finally, without our having deliberately sought it, the question of authenticity, which brings with it the question of authority. I do not believe that either Desmond Tutu or I wanted to provoke a fight with the ANC leadership in exile or that we revelled in the tensions that sometimes arose. But tension is almost inescapable in such circumstances. We spoke not just with the authenticity of people having come to New York, London, Geneva straight from South Africa, still smelling of tear gas, the dust of the townships still clinging to our feet as it were; we spoke with the authority of the church. We were firmly convinced that our mandate did not derive from political organisations, however powerful these were, but from God. Our arguments were nevertheless political arguments, our analysis political and socio-economic analysis – just as theirs were. But the source of our thinking was fundamentally different. I had read Marx and Lenin, I admired the erudite Gramsci, but my deepest source of inspiration for my politics was the God of the Exodus, the prophets of social justice, the song writers of the Hebrew Bible, and Jesus of Nazareth.

Some say that the ANC, in adhering to the armed struggle, sought to please its sponsors in the Soviet Union and Cuba more out of need than conviction. Under the prevailing circumstances, it had to do so. It was, they argue, more a tactical than a principled stance. I am sure that for some in the ANC that was true. Thabo Mbeki could not have been the only one who knew the military struggle was futile when he told the *New York Times* on 20 June 1980 that the ANC could not possibly win a 'bush war', especially when there was no bush. 'Look at the map,' Mbeki said. There is no bush: 'The masses must serve as our bush …' But there were others, and they remained influential, who did not think it was just talk to 'please Moscow'. They *believed*. Now, there were leaders of the struggle inside who passionately believed that non-violence was the only way. The revolutionary reference now was not Stalin, or Castro, or Ho Chi Minh, but Jesus of Nazareth. The masses were following them, and the results were there for all to see.

It must have been earth-shaking for those to whom, and on whose behalf Joe Slovo spoke, in 1985, at the Kabwe Conference of the ANC. While the non-violent revolution was in full force in South Africa, Joe Slovo reminded the ANC, the world and those of us inside that the ANC had made up its mind. The only way to victory was the successful revolutionary overthrow of the apartheid regime. 'No Middle Road', he called his address. And while Thabo Mbeki saw the fall of the Berlin Wall coming earlier than most of his comrades, and understood earlier than most also the political consequences of that momentous event, for the die-hards it was a shock from which they never really recovered. Up until the 1990s the language of the ANC, and the litmus test for true commitment and genuine comradeship, was the violent revolutionary struggle: the 'socialist, democratic revolution'. My own insistence that our struggle inside was a true non-violent revolution, that it was as much about values and ideals as about politics and economics (I sometimes said 'the only revolution that mattered'), must have sounded like heresy. So till late in the game the ANC's way of thinking, the climate it created, the very air it breathed, was 'the revolution' with its attendant vision of bombs and AK 47s, its songs of victory drummed into the youth through the *toyi-toyi,* its dreams of 'taking' Pretoria and enjoying the fruits of the 'democratic socialist revolution'.

But the strangeness does not end there. In July 1989, at least a full year after secret talks had been initiated with the apartheid regime spearheaded by Neil Barnard, head of South Africa's National Intelligence Service and, arguably, according to journalist Terry Bell, 'the most powerful individual in South Africa by the late eighties', Mbeki chaired the SACP's 7th congress in Havana, Cuba. As a member of the SACP politburo, Mbeki had helped to write the insurrectionary 'Path to Power' programme that spelt out the belief in the violent overthrow of the apartheid regime. This he clarified and defended and steered to acceptance within the congress while he was finalising the details of a negotiated settlement with apartheid South Africa. Some might regard this as deft political footwork, but it spells out an ambiguous, even contradictory, stance in the ANC that bordered on political schizophrenia. It also shows a carelessness, stunning in its casualness, toward the sacrificial struggles of the people inside the country who were not good enough to be let in on the secrets even though they were good enough to spill their blood as they responded to the ongoing calls for a people's revolution according to the injunctions of the 'Path to Power'.

So while the people marched and demonstrated, broke laws and clashed with security forces, went to prison and the torture chamber, battled with banning orders and internal displacement, there was an incremental militarisation of the struggle and as a result a militarisation

They who have no life give no liberty
(. Jefferso)

of the UDF. Stone Sizane, UDF leader in the Eastern Cape, was probably the first to openly extol the virtues of armed struggle and the role of MK at the funeral of the Cradock Four. The white media were hung up on the presence of the SACP flag that day, which was not so strange when one considered that Matthew Goniwe, for example, was a committed member of the SACP. But the picture of me speaking before the backdrop of that flag got more space than what we said, once again depriving the reading public and white people in particular of vital information they should have had. It provided the government with propaganda fodder for years: they now had their 'proof' of what I truly was. But the thing that disturbed me that day was not the SACP flag; it was Stone's speech. Our language was changing.

When I visited Los Angeles as a guest on a popular radio talk show, the host confronted me with the unforgettable words of Winnie Mandela: 'With our boxes of matches and our tyres we shall liberate this country.' These words caught me completely off-guard. My first, instinctive reaction was to try to explain them. I had great admiration for Winnie Mandela. Things were never that simple, I tried to say, there was a historic and political context, the violence of the comrades was provoked, counter violence. I could not sustain the argument. The logic of my own passionate stance on non-violence placed too much weight in the scale. The more I tried to explain the more it sounded like justification. I had to condemn it. Much later I saw the video clip. Winnie Mandela was wearing her MK uniform. I understood: she was speaking expressly as an MK commander. The body language, the uniform, the words, they were all conveying the same message. We were, she was saying, engaged in a war. In the townships self-defence units were getting underway. Formed on instructions of the ANC, they were meant to protect the people against the violence of the state. In the event, they inadvertently became valuable tools in the hands of state propagandists: they were linked to most of the violent attacks against individuals in the townships. Despite our fine words about a 'disciplined revolution', we, like the government, did not know where to draw the line. Not because we did not want to, but because we could not, even if we did. Violence never allows one to draw the line, and we had forgotten that.

Meanwhile the underground was busy. Early in 1980, the ANC initiated in exile an operation called Operation Vula, an underground intelligence network, to prepare the country internally for the violent overthrow of the apartheid regime and the take-over of the new revolutionary government. The leading figure in this operation was the brilliant and articulate Mac Maharaj. Seemingly nothing of what was happening under the leadership of the UDF had given the ANC pause. Nor had the prospect of a negotiated settlement deterred them. While the ANC, through Nelson Mandela, Thabo Mbeki and Cyril Ramaphosa were engaging the South African government in vital preliminary talks and real progress was being made, the operation went on. A large and influential section of the ANC still had no faith in non-violence or negotiations. As Simphiwe Nyanda wrote in *The African Communist* early in 1990, 'passivity' does not contribute to governmental takeover. And even if there were to be negotiations, he wanted to be clear that negotiations can only be conducted 'from a position of strength'. That strength, in his view, came from the power created by the 'militant actions and other revolutionary activities of the oppressed masses'. Passivity was not just the negotiations; it was also the non-violent struggle. They were both the symbol of untrustworthiness as far as the people's struggle was concerned. Unlike the masses who believed in their imminent freedom, the ANC did not.

Van Zyl Slabbert's observation in this regard is both true and instructive: 'What one must keep in mind,' he says, 'is that those who planned Operation Vula were not a bunch of ANC romantics or a few hot heads.' The planners included Joe Slovo, Jacob Zuma, Ronnie Kassrils, Mac Maharaj and Oliver Tambo. One could hardly get more senior than this. I read this and I wondered about the pressure put on Tambo in this matter. So the talk went on: the masses were to be mobilised for a 'popular uprising', but this was not the uprising we'd envisaged: it was 'a people's war' led by MK, if not with tanks, helicopters and fighter jets, then with bombs, AK 47s, Molotov cocktails and pangas. The argument that such internal violence could only be bad for the international image of the ANC, especially since they claimed the UDF as their own, was true, but it merely underscored my point. Violence develops a deadly logic of its own. It cannot allow for a moment of critical hesitation, for the pause of self-critical reflection.

At the funeral of the UDF in 1991, Mac Maharaj was also a featured speaker. He strode to the podium and began with the words that would become his theme throughout the speech. 'I am a soldier!' And indeed, it was as a soldier that he spoke, extolling the virtues of the armed struggle and the underground movement. The UDF we knew and had embraced was clothed in a distant strangeness few of us recognised. The masses who had swept into the streets in protest, filled the jails with freedom songs and toppled the apartheid idols from their thrones were turned into lonely children, orphans standing on the corner as the tanks rolled by. It was as if the years of struggle we knew had been simply and effortlessly wiped away. It had all come from outside. I understand better now that Maharaj had a job to do that day, and I have no idea how much of it he believed himself, but the incongruity of it all mystifies even history.

In my view, the climate of violence created, the language, the deliberate fashioning of a revolutionary dream of violence, even though it was a deception, the normalisation of violence through the romantic portrayals of war, sacrifice and death, played a vital role in the militarisation of the UDF. It was also, I think, a desperate measure to gain control over an internal movement that had committed itself to the same struggle, the same ideals, the same goals, but had elected to walk a different path.

It is also true that the different messages coming from the ANC were signs of confusion and indecisiveness, of people at different levels of understanding. I am not questioning their commitment: I believe they all truly had that, but the understanding of the situation and the end goal, and especially how to get there – these had become diffuse and vague. Besides, the end was drawing near, some knew. The lines inside the movement were being drawn differently. We would discover that in other ways as well.

'The Righteousness of our strength'

There came a point in the testimony of Steve Biko in the SASO/BCM trial in May 1976 when he felt compelled to explain why the Black Consciousness Movement had elected to make non-violence its firm policy. He spoke of the desire to make South Africa an open, non-racial democracy, a home for all its people, but a home in Africa for Africans, not just a European province on the African continent. He spoke of black peoples' struggle for justice and freedom and of his belief that they would succeed: 'We certainly don't envisage failure.'

He explained that he understood why the ANC and PAC had chosen for violence, but said 'we don't believe it is the only alternative'. He expressed his belief that white people would eventually listen, that they would not 'be deaf all the time'. He exhibited that pre-1976 innocence we had before the killing of the children. The regime, he said, had not yet been 'Hitlerised'. Even if it took time, if there were bannings and imprisonment and suffering ahead, eventually South Africa would have no alternative; there would be freedom because, he said, 'We believe ultimately in the righteousness of our strength ...' It is vital that we understand these words. In saying this, Biko spoke not of the power of the gun, for he did not believe in violence, but of the power of belief. He spoke not of the weakness of others that is there to be exploited, but of the strength of the oppressed that is there to inspire and to share. In saying this, Biko affected a fundamental and crucial reversal: it is not those with the power of government, socio-economic status and position, or military strength who are strong, but those who are powerless and exploited, oppressed and victimised. They are strong because their strength is righteous, rooted not in the desire for power but in the longing for freedom and justice; not just for themselves but for all. He spoke not of 'the strength of our righteousness' for that would have been too arrogant, too self-righteous and hypocritical, but of the 'righteousness of our strength'. He knew that black people were not strong because they were powerful, but because they were right. They were right to believe in themselves, in their own freedom, in the justness of their cause, and in their freedom lay also the freedom of their oppressor. He knew that they had to show that the way they had chosen was indeed the right way, the righteous way. In following that way lay our strength. In the words of Benjamin Dube's marvellous Gospel song: 'Humble yourself by the side of the Lord, and he will lift you up.'

That is how we felt in the 1980s. We had to show that the way we had chosen and believed in, the way of non-violent resistance, was the righteous way. We had to do that not only in response to the new signs of willingness of support shown by the international community, but also in the face of the violent challenges at home. Apart from the demonstrations, marches and protests all over the country, we had found that sanctions were a powerful instrument of non-violent action.

By 1984 we knew that the existing trade and economic sanctions, though they undoubtedly enlarged the vulnerability of apartheid, were not going to be enough to force the South African government to change. I had already met Terry Crawford-Browne, at that stage an international banker with Nedbank and a man with amazing courage and commitment. Crawford-Browne talks in great detail about this in his book *Eye on the Money,* so here I will just touch on the highlights. In long conversations we had, Crawford-Browne convinced me that the most effective sanctions would be financial. On this, Desmond Tutu, Beyers Naudé and I agreed, and we worked together with Terry. We already knew that the only way to awaken the deeply-buried conscience of the white community, and especially the business community, was to hit their pockets. Consumer boycotts right through the country did that admirably.

We had different strategies. Government thought it had scored a massive win by organising so-called rebel rugby and cricket tours. First National Bank had been seduced by the government to sponsor the 1989 rebel World Rugby Tour. The tour was of great political importance for the government and for white rugby fans. I had read in some novel how a disgruntled community had created chaos in a bank. I ran the idea past Terry Crawford-Browne when we discussed civil disobedience in the area he understood so well. He came up with a simple but brilliant plan, '15 easy ways to disrupt a bank'. Ngconde Balfour, an Anglican social worker at the time, took the organisation of the action in hand.

A 20-minute blockade of the bank on a Saturday morning followed. Peaceful and effective. The tour was cancelled the following Monday and for the subsequent planned rebel cricket tour no sponsors could be found. It was absolutely delightful.

As the situation deteriorated, the international community got more and more jittery, especially the banks which had lent all those billions to the apartheid government. As Crawford-Browne observes, the government failed to see that domestic political repression might have undesired international economic repercussions. In the worsening situation, the government prevailed on a Dr Fritz Leutwiler, a Swiss banker, to help. After months of rioting and the failure of P.W. Botha's 'rubicon' speech, I encouraged Crawford-Browne to draft a statement on behalf of South African church leaders to deliver to Leutwiler in London and to bankers in New York. The letter was signed on our behalf by Archbishop Desmond Tutu and Beyers Naudé, in his capacity as general secretary of the South African Council of Churches. The pressure was building up.

The violence at home called for heightened non-violent activism. The campaign for sanctions and disinvestment reached new heights. In the US, we finally got Congress to agree on a comprehensive sanctions bill, which got vetoed by Ronald Reagan, but then the veto was overturned by the Senate. It was a bi-partisan action, and I remember working for almost a full year with the Congressional Black Caucus, Andrew Young and politicians such as Senators Edward Kennedy, Joseph Biden, and Frank Church, and on the Republican side with Senator Nancy Kassenbaum and some of her colleagues who turned against Reagan on the apartheid issue. David Dinkins, an African American, was elected mayor of New York City. The new mayor urged New York to withdraw its banking business from any bank that did business with South Africa.

All across the US, states, cities and universities engaged in some form of sanctions against South Africa.

We had to now concentrate on the banks and their loans to South Africa. We had worked hard on a proper plan and in concert with Desmond Tutu, Beyers Naudé and Frank Chikane, I went around the world propagating this plan, including visiting president George Bush in Washington. Meanwhile I had been detained, placed in solitary confinement, released and put under house arrest and charged with sedition. My passport had been withdrawn and eventually returned as a result of the intervention of a Dr Danie Prins, who worked in P.W. Botha's office.

I had come to know Sir Shridath Ramphal, or Sonny, as his friends call him, Secretary General of the Commonwealth. When the Commonwealth Eminent Persons Group was sent to South Africa in 1986, Sonny asked me to serve as their informal adviser. The night before P.W. Botha bombed Botswana to show the Commonwealth just what he thought of them and their efforts, some of them listened to me preach in Port Elizabeth on a sermon from the Gospel of Luke: 'I saw Satan fall like lightning from heaven.' They found the sermon moving, entertaining, strong, courageous under the circumstances – or so they told me afterwards. The crowd in the church knew it to be prophetic. In 1989 the Commonwealth Heads of State would meet in Kuala Lumpur. The sanctions issue was to be the most hotly debated matter on the agenda.

F.W. De Klerk had just been elected president of South Africa to preside over what Frederick van Zyl Slabbert called 'the last white Parliament'. During that week at least 23 people had been shot and killed in Mitchells Plain in the Western Cape alone. At a media conference in Cape Town's Anglican Cathedral, held together with Archbishop Tutu,

I spoke of Mr De Klerk sitting on a throne 'swimming in blood'. At a meeting between De Klerk, Desmond Tutu, Frank Chikane and I in October of that year, he was not very pleased with me at all. But he also knew I was on my way to Kuala Lumpur, where much was to be at stake.

At the Commonwealth meeting, Britain's Margaret Thatcher, true to form, took up the cudgels for De Klerk and white South Africa. She argued strongly that De Klerk 'should be given a chance'. Terry Crawford-Browne, on a visit to London, remarked how surprised he was to find how 'out of touch' the ANC was with events in South Africa. Not only were most of them under the impression that they would never see South Africa again, the confusion Van Zyl Slabbert spoke of was evident. I experienced that myself.

In Kuala Lumpur just about all the other Commonwealth countries were for continued pressure on South Africa. Thabo Mbeki was there, representing the ANC. We had met before of course, but had not had long conversations. On the day before the great debate, Sonny called me. 'We might have a problem,' he began. It seemed that contrary to all expectations, Thabo Mbeki and I differed on the question of sanctions. He wanted existing sanctions to continue, but would have none of our idea of banking and targeted financial sanctions. We talked, of course, and I argued hard, but Mbeki was adamant: his view was official ANC policy. He expected of me to fall in line. I could not agree, could not understand how he could take such a stand and could not understand why he could not see how crucial it was for the pressure to remain, especially at that moment. Abdul Minty who was also present, tried in vain. In the end, we agreed to disagree, but it left the Commonwealth in a bit of a quandary. Two opposing viewpoints from South Africa? Sonny Ramphal made a decision. There would be a committee of seven member countries. We would each have an opportunity to put forward our case and the proposal of the person who convinced the committee would go on the floor the next day.

We met the committee and argued our case. Of the seven countries, only India accepted Mbeki's argument. So that evening, while Thabo Mbeki was attending a dinner arranged by Kenneth Kaunda and Robert Mugabe, I was on the top floor of the hotel, briefing Bob Hawke, prime minister of Australia, who would put the case for sanctions to the meeting the next day. Thatcher fought hard: sanctions would only hurt black people by weakening the economy at a time when the opposite was necessary; they would be a betrayal of De Klerk, a 'brave man' who had wanted change; Mandela was a 'communist and a terrorist'; sanctions would not work because the banks were not 'ready'. She concluded by announcing that South Africa's foreign debt had been rescheduled for another three years.

But it did not matter. The killings in South Africa that accompanied De Klerk's election were taken hard by the delegates. On 3 October, Herman Cohen, the US government's secretary for Africa, gave an ultimatum to South Africa, saying that the Bush administration would tighten banking and other financial sanctions in 1990. The Commonwealth voted for banking sanctions. In the US, the Financial Sanctions for Democracy Bill gained renewed support from the public and in Congress. A new round of congressional hearings was going to be scheduled for early 1990. One of the bill's most important provisions, writes Terry Crawford-Browne, was to prohibit American banks from holding deposits from South African banks or conducting correspondent services with them. The Commonwealth was not going to lag behind George Bush. I was elated: this was a victory of major proportions. At home, these events inspired a final surge of actions. As

Biko said, we were sure of the righteousness of our strength.

For me, personally, though, a new, difficult drama unfolded. At Schiphol airport in Amsterdam, on my way back to South Africa, a friend awaited me with the news that I was 'in trouble at home'. He held up a copy of the *Star* newspaper. It was on the front page: an attack on me by the venerable, just-out-of-prison Walter Sisulu because of my 'stand on sanctions' at Kuala Lumpur. I was hurt, mystified and angry. Frank Chikane met me at Johannesburg airport and took me to see 'Uncle Walter'. Apparently Thabo Mbeki had 'reported' home and told them about our difference of opinion. But in his version, I was the one who pleaded for the 'soft option', wanting to spare De Klerk and asking for no more sanctions. He made me sound like Thatcher. I had dared to fly in the face of official ANC policy and I was going to be punished. I was shocked, and deeply disappointed. Walter Sisulu did not know me that well, but I felt he could at least have asked about my views, which had been known for years. But I suppose he thought he should believe Mbeki. I had to convince him by telling him the truth – both about Kuala Lumpur and myself.

We spent a long time talking that evening, and I explained exactly what had happened. As we were talking his telephone rang. It was Nelson Mandela, calling from Drakenstein prison. It was the first time I had heard Mandela's voice. It was an unexpected surprise. Walter held out the telephone. 'Talk to Madiba,' he said. I told my story again, holding nothing back. The upshot of it all was a press conference Walter and I held together the next day, during which the record was put straight.

This incident gave me an idea of what went on inside the ANC, but it was only much later that two things were confirmed. First, that there had already been exploratory talks, not just between Nelson Mandela and the government, but since at least 1987 between emissaries of the government and the ANC. Thabo Mbeki was central in those talks. At that point very few of us inside knew anything about this. I could only draw my own conclusions as to what kind of promises had been made in those talks towards the end of 1989, why, and to whom.

Second, at that point there had been apparent disagreement in the ANC on the issue of sanctions. There was the camp who favoured tougher sanctions and more pressure on the government, and there were those, under the leadership of Thabo Mbeki, who felt otherwise. This was the group involved in the secret talks. What scared me was the length to which a leader of the ANC would go to cover himself, to protect his ego and to serve an agenda that might have been important for the country, but that he had not seen fit to share with one who was a leader of the internal resistance. It was the first time I saw that now-famous closed and immobile face. It was also frightening how he refused to listen or reconsider his viewpoint, even if an argument made eminent sense. He would rather disparage my name and twist the truth about our respective positions on such a vital matter as sanctions, on such a crucial platform as the Commonwealth Heads of State and Government.

I discovered something else. I was now afraid of Thabo Mbeki and that ANC he represented. I had, I feared, made an enemy. In early December 1989, a journalist friend who was working for the foreign media and had close ties with the ANC in exile called me. She had just returned from attending some meeting of the ANC leadership. She was distressed. 'They are going to shaft you!' she said. A week later, another supportive journalist told me what she was told by 'someone in the know': 'You are backing the wrong horse. Boesak's time is over.' When on 2 February 1990 a rally was held to make our presence felt as President De Klerk made his watershed speech in Parliament announcing the unbanning of the liberation movements, the release of prisoners and the return of the exiles, I stood at the back of the crowd listening to the speeches. It was the first time in more than a decade that I was not asked to speak at a major rally. I knew then that my friends were right. I was being shown my proper place. Not just on that day, but in the struggle, and in history. De Klerk was announcing the fruits of our struggle, and I was not going to be allowed to taste any of it.

That I nonetheless became ANC Western Cape leader was due to mostly two things, I think. One was Nelson Mandela's insistence, and the other was popular demand. The story of the internal dynamics within the Western Cape ANC prior to, during and after the elections of 1994 is a different and as yet untold one. But as I mention elsewhere, by October 1994 I found the situation such that I had asked the President to consider me for a position outside the ANC, preferably abroad, working on issues that I felt I could make a contribution to, such as human rights. Geneva, headquarters of the United Nations' human rights agency, is what I had in mind. But I would never get there.

When Biko spoke about the 'righteousness of our strength' this is what he meant: the call to rise above adversity, not to nurture the anger and the pain, to forget about the humiliation and to continue to struggle for what is right and just. Where does one find this strength? Jeremiah said it differently: 'You have only run with foot soldiers and they have wearied you. How will you run against horses?' In situations such as these, as in others far more testing that I would yet come to know, I would discover the amazing difference faith makes in one's life.

9

Standing in Threatened Space: If this is Treason, I Am Guilty

This speech, held on February 27, 1985, addresses the detainment of a number of UDF activists with the charge of 'treason'.

A fraud that continues

We have entered a decisive phase in our struggle. Those of us who have warned that the South African government cannot be trusted, that the reforms that they are talking about are cosmetic, that apartheid and racism still reign supreme, and that the South African government still has only one goal, namely absolute power for itself and for the white minority and continued control over the majority of our people in this country, were right. Subsequent events since we have begun to make this clear have shown that this government indeed cannot be trusted. While the South African government talked of reforms and while they were engaged in a massive effort to mislead the international community, they instituted a racist constitution. While they were talking about reform they continued the homeland policy. While they were talking about reform they continued the denationalisation of South Africa's people, robbing our black people of their birthright and of their right to stay in this land. While they were talking about reform they continued their forced removals, their policies of subtle genocide by forcing our people from the lands where they had lived for so many years into those concentration camps the South African government calls 'relocation areas'.

While they were talking about reform and while they were signing peace treaties with countries like Mozambique, they detained us, they shot at our people, they tear-gassed us when we peacefully, so powerfully demonstrated our rejection of their policies and of their constitution. While they were talking about peace with other nations they sent their police and their troops into our townships, they broke up our funeral services with violence, they threatened our unarmed people, and they murdered our children on the streets of the townships. While they were talking about reform and while they were lying to the world saying that apartheid is dead, the unrest all over the country proved that the struggle for justice and our struggle for genuine liberation shall continue. The boycott not only proved the discontent of our people but also our determination. And these are the things that the South African government cannot even begin to understand or begin to stop. While they spouted their propaganda across the world we proved to the world and to the government that neither smear campaigns nor dogs nor guns nor tear gas can undermine the determination of our people to be free.

So now the South African government is in trouble. They don't know what to do. There is no direction, there is no sense of where they are going. If you go and ask people who sit in the parliament what it is that they want before the end of this year, no one will be able to tell you. Because they don't know what they want. There is such a state of confusion that one is justified in saying that not since Sharpeville in 1960 was the South African government so vulnerable to pressure, so confused, as now. There is no control over the economy – and you know the reason the rand is so low is that it has become so expensive to live abroad these days.

The problem that we have to face is how we, in this situation, keep the initiative that we have gained. The fact is that international pressure is growing; in the United States, in spite of constructive engagement – maybe also *because* of constructive engagement – there is an unprecedented movement of protest against the South African government and its policies and against constructive engagement. Never before have people in the US been so engaged in solidarity with the people of South Africa. And this will happen again and again and again. They are engaged in the struggle not simply because they feel like it, but because you, the people of South Africa, are engaged in the struggle, and you have made them see that it is worthwhile for them to throw their weight behind us. And that is important.

A struggle that cannot be stopped

All over Europe the movement against apartheid is growing. I spoke not so long ago to a new organisation called Western European Parliamentarians for Action against apartheid, and they have pledged themselves to try to put pressure on their own government and through them to put as much pressure as possible on the South African government so that fundamental change can take place. These people are doing that because in South Africa there are people who believe in the struggle, who fight for what they believe in, who believe in justice, who believe in liberation, and who believe that they ought to be participating in that struggle. As long as you are involved, the people of the world will more and more become involved. To the chagrin of the South African government, President Kaunda goes around the world and asks for pressure on the South African government and calls for disinvestment. The Danish government this morning announced that it will no longer allow its companies to bring new investment to South Africa. You see, the campaign is working.

In response to this unprecedented international pressure the South African government is trying to show that it is really changing, so they say that Nelson Mandela can come out of jail and that Walter Sisulu can be released from prison. But while they say to Walter Sisulu, 'Please come out of jail' and to Nelson Mandela, 'Please come out of jail,' they take Sisulu's wife and put her in prison. And they take fifteen other people and put *them* in prison. What is the matter with this government? You know, our problem in this country is really that we sit with a government that can only think so far. There must really be people in that government who cannot think very well. One wonders where they went to school. If we knew, we could go talk to those schools and say, 'If you turn out any further governments for this country, please advise us.'

I noticed something when the government made Nelson Mandela the offer of release. A magazine in this country wrote that Mandela should accept that offer because in doing so he would not endear himself to the people who now want to claim him – like the United Democratic Front. He would instead establish his credibility with all the peace-loving, thinking people in South Africa, namely 'them'. I read that article and I thought, what a cheek! Who are they to now claim Mandela for themselves? They are the ones who created policies which made it impossible for black people to live in this country like decent human beings. They are the ones who, when we started to resist these policies, made laws that made it impossible for us even to resist them by peaceful means. Then they banned Mandela's organisation, they drove him to violence, they locked him up for 22 years, they banned and banished his wife, they locked up in Robben Island and the prisons of this country the people who worked with him, they called him a terrorist, they called him a communist – and now, when they are in difficulty, they want to offer him a conditional release and say that *we* must not claim him because he must establish his credibility with *them*. Mandela does not need to establish his credibility with those people. Mandela does not need to establish his credibility with anyone but the people who are still in the struggle for justice and liberation in this country, and that's you. And he doesn't need to establish his credibility with you.

But of course, since the South African government is facing all these problems, someone has to get the blame. This time it is the turn of the United Democratic Front. Mr Le Grange made a speech last night. As usual, it was a speech brimming with threats, intimidation and promises of more intimidation. And he singled out, again, the United Democratic Front as an organisation that is 'creating a climate of revolution in South Africa'. I want to say to Minister Le Grange: 'Mr Le Grange, I am actually getting a little sick and tired of all these threats. The people of South Africa are getting a little tired of these threats. We are engaged in a struggle for liberation, not because we want to die, but because we want our people to be free. We are engaged in a struggle for liberation, not because we wish to die, but because you oppress us, and as long as you continue to oppress us we will have to resist you. We are people, and we are people who belong in this land. The climate of revolution, Mr Minister, is not created by those who struggle for justice and peace, but by those who make policies that despise and undermine the human dignity of people. The climate of revolution is created by those who make policies that exploit our people, who take away the necessities of the many to give luxuries to the few. The climate of revolution is created by those who make policies that create hunger and starvation in the homelands while the tables of the rich in white South Africa are sagging with food that will be thrown into the dustbin. The climate of revolution is not created by the United Democratic Front, but by people like you, Mr Le Grange, who refuse to listen to the voice of reason, who refuse to listen to our people when they say we want our rights, and we want them here, and we want them now, because they are our rights. The climate of revolution is not created by the United Democratic Front, but by people like you, Mr Le Grange, who detain without trial; by those who allow our people to be tortured in their jails; by those who allow the wanton killing of our people on the streets of our nation.' These are the things that are creating a climate of revolution in our nation, and Mr Le Grange must not blame the United Democratic Front – he must put the blame where it belongs, right in front of the door of the South African government, of which he is a part.

If this is treason ...

Now the government has charged some of our brothers and sisters with treason. As I have said over and over again tonight, this is a serious charge. Treason is described as organising, or taking part in, or instigating, armed revolt in order to overthrow the government. Actually, they are being charged under a section of the Internal Security Act in which any act of 'subversion' – which can include speaking out against the South African government or calling for pressure on the South African government – is also treason. It is wide, it is irresponsible, but it is a law that is on the statute books of this country. So these comrades will be charged with treason.

I want to say that I consider this a scandalous, dastardly, and cowardly act. I have worked for a long time with the people who are being charged. I have not heard them call for violence. Not once. From its inception, the United Democratic Front has been an organisation committed to non-violence. Under the most difficult circumstances, we did not ask people to take up arms. We said to our people, 'Let us find ways and means, with all of the odds against us, even at this late hour, to try peacefully to express our legitimate political aspirations in this country.'

We know that we have had a long battle behind us. We know that every single effort toward peaceful change in this country has been met by the government with violence and ended with a massacre. We know how our people marched peacefully on 21 March, now 25 years ago, in Sharpeville. One day soon we shall be commemorating that tragic event, when their peaceful demonstration ended in bloodshed, most of them shot in the back. We know that in 1976 our children took to the streets with nothing in their hands except placards which said to the South African police, 'We do not want to fight. Please release our comrades and our friends.' Those children were shot down by the police by the hundreds. And we know that in 1980 in Cape Town our children took up the challenge and marched peacefully for a better future for themselves, expressing only that they do not want to grow up in a country where racism is rife, and where oppression is the order of the day, and where exploitation is around every corner, and where our people are being pushed into little holes in the homelands where they will die of hunger and despair. The answer the South African government gave once again was guns, and dogs and tear gas – and our children died. And you will remember that when little Bernard Fortuin, ten years old, was shot on the streets of Elsies River, lying there bleeding to death, his mother wanted to talk to him. But they refused, and they shoved her away with their gun butts, and when she said to the policeman, 'Please! He is my son,' he said the words that reverberated around the world, to the shame of South Africa: 'Let the bastard die!' You know that.

And then we formed the United Democratic Front and we said to our people, 'Let us not despair; let us not say that the only answer to the South African government's violence is violence; let us not seek to repay them with the same things that they are doing to us; let us not seek to be overcome with evil, but indeed to find a way to overcome evil with good by peacefully demonstrating what it is that we want.' We made this organisation into a force that even the whole world will now have to reckon with. We never picked up a single stone, but they came again with their dogs and their guns and their bazookas, and they killed our people even on the night of the election. We in the United Democratic Front said, 'Let us try to find ways of telling our young people to commit themselves once again, even now, to a strategy of non-violence.' And we did, and the world respects the United Democratic Front for it. It was the South African government who turned around and detained our people. It was the South African government who turned around and sent their police to our demonstrations on the night of the election, and it was they who started again to shoot at our people. What is it that we have done? We in the United Democratic Front have created a unity that this country has not seen for almost three decades. We brought back the spirit of the struggle that we knew in the 1950s. We were the people who were able to bring people together even in this racist land – where hatred is the order of the day because hatred is the theme of the South African government – to make it possible for black and white to work together in the face of strong criticism from others. We have been able to say to the people: 'Do not look at the matter simply by the colour of a person's skin, but try to judge that person in terms of that person's commitment to the struggle for justice and liberation.' And we have succeeded in doing that.

In one single year, in a short 12-month period, we have brought together a mass movement now representing millions of people in this land. We have challenged the South African government's constitution and, what is more, we have won. We have made people aware of their rights in South Africa. We thereby exposed the violent, oppressive nature of this government. We have given the people of this country back their self-respect, we have given them a faith in the justice of our struggle, we have given them a belief that we shall overcome. This is the United Democratic Front. We stand for things that the South African government cannot understand. We stand for democracy. They don't know the meaning of the word. We stand for non-racialism. They cannot stand it when people of different races can live and work together. We stand for an open democratic society. They cannot stand it, because then they know that their violence will have come to an end.

But there is something more. We must ask the question, 'Is what we have done treason?' I, brothers and sisters, have called for the foundation and the formation of the United Democratic Front. I have spoken more than anybody else over the last year. I have said publicly that apartheid is evil, that it is a blasphemy, and a heresy. I have said that the South African government is unjust, undemocratic and unrepresentative; it does not have the love or the support of the people, it has no right to exist, it is illegitimate, it should not exist. I have said openly that the South African government is a violent government. I have called for Christians and people of other faiths to pray for the downfall of the South African government, to pray that God should give us another government, that God should remove them. I have from the very beginning resisted this government on the basis of my Christian commitment and of my Christian faith. And I shall continue to do so as long as God gives me breath in my body. If this is treason, then I am guilty of treason, and I would say to the South African government tonight, if I am guilty of treason, then charge me with treason and put me in jail.

I say this, brothers and sisters, not out of a sense of bravado. I have no desire to be a martyr – God knows my life for the last month or two has been hell enough. I say this not out of defiance, because I know that the minister to whom I am speaking now is a very powerful man, a man without conscience who can do whatever he likes and get away with it. But I say this because in a perverted, unjust and cruel society such as ours, where those who fight for freedom, peace and human dignity are banned, detained and charged with treason while criminals sit in Parliament and receive accolades from those who share in their power and privilege, this is the only decent thing to do. And if I have committed treason by resisting the South African government – which is exactly what our brothers and sisters who are now in jail have done – the South African government must now put me in jail and charge me with treason.

But you must know that we are indeed at the beginning of a decisive phase of our struggle in the history of our land. This is the beginning of the end of apartheid. Their [the apartheid government's] days are numbered. And what you must do, Mr Le Grange, you must do quickly, for your day of judgement is near. You must remember that the struggle does not depend on one or two or three or four people, and that the strength of the United Democratic Front has always been that we do not simply depend on those people that we have put in positions of leadership. The strength of the United Democratic Front has always been the people, has always been your commitment, has always been your participation in the struggle. So in the end it is not a question of whether the UDF will survive the onslaught because a few of the leaders are in jail facing trial, but in the end it is a question of whether you in your own commitment will remain faithful. I say to you my people tonight, do not begin to fear the future, do not begin to give up faith in our struggle and in the justice of our cause. Do not be overcome by the evil that this government represents, but overcome evil with good.

So in the midst of trial and tribulation I exhort you to remain a faithful people. In the midst of hopelessness and despair that sometimes overcome us because we think that the powers standing against us are so invincible, remain a hopeful people. In the midst of fear and uncertainties that come up in our own hearts because we do not know what tomorrow will bring, and we do not exactly know what will happen to us inside those jails or whether we will even come out alive, be a strong people. In the midst of unfaithfulness by so many who turn around and for a mess of pottage sell the birthright of our people just to sit in a bogus parliament and be given power and be given honour by people who do not even know the meaning of these words, be a committed people. And in the midst of violence of this South African government which shall continue and which shall increase because they have created the monster that in the end is destined to devour even themselves, in the midst of the destruction that may come, remain a peace-loving people. In the midst of the madness of racism and hatred that still reign in this country, be a compassionate people. And in the end, if we remain faithful, if we take the risks that are necessary, and if we remain committed to what we believe in, we will be also a victorious people. God bless you!

10

Raise a Sign of Hope: Address at the 'Cradock Four' Funeral

This is the address at the funeral of the 'Cradock Four' on July 20, 1985. Their deaths were followed by a wave of violence and other actions across the country.

The spiritual children of Adolf Hitler

My brothers and sisters, I am grateful that I can be with you today. I have come to Cradock often in the past years. The first time was when Matthew Goniwe and Fort Calata were detained, and the people of Cradock asked me to come and visit with them, to come and see for myself what was happening in Lingilihle.

Since then I have learnt to admire those men who have been such wonderful leaders in this community, and it has been a singular honour for me to work with them over the last year. I will not forget the last time I spoke in this very town of Cradock, some five or six weeks ago. The people who came to listen were willing to wait from eight o'clock in the evening until I arrived at almost eleven o'clock that night. They did not move, which was a sign of the spirit that lived in Cradock. And that in turn was a tribute to the leadership of the brothers whom we mourn today, and whom we will bury. When I think of their lives, when I think of what they have become – symbol of our struggle, of our hope, of our determination, of our genius that we have in the black community in South Africa – and I think that we must bury them today, I must say so that all the world and this country can hear: if we have to bury men like Matthew Goniwe, Fort Calata, Thomas ['Sparrow'] Mkhonto, and Sicelo Mhlawuli, then I say this country is digging its own grave. South Africa is setting fire to its own future.

As I stand here today I am overcome by a terrible sadness and anger, and I know that this sadness hangs all over our land. Because yet again, as so many times this year, we must mourn; yet again we must bury our people. Yet again we must come and lay to rest some of the finest sons and daughters of our country. Yet again this government has shown that it will be utterly ruthless in its determination to hold on to power and to keep apartheid alive. Yet again we must say that something terrible is happening to this country. Look at where we are! Look at where we are! Apartheid with its racism and its exploitation is not only alive but is being defended with uncommon harshness. The church is being persecuted for its obedience to God and for its decision to stand alongside the poor, the weak and the oppressed of our country.

There is unrest all over South Africa, for the cause of all the unrest and the violence has not yet been removed. The police and the army have laid siege to our townships. As our brother has said, indeed 'our townships are infested with them'. The police and the army are conducting a reign of terror against our people. Our people disappear; we do not know what happens to them. Over the past few months more than ten thousand people have been detained and kept in jail. Thousands have been wounded, hundreds have been killed. Over the past few months there has been the emergence of death squads. I am not so sure that they are simply death squads put there by the so-called right-wing, for they have received too much protection over the last year. Our children die, like little Johannes Pochter the other day in Steytlerville, only 12 years old, beaten to death by the police. Our children die like they have been dying for so many years now in those concentration camps in the resettlement areas where there is no food and where there will be no nourishment from the moment they are born until the very week that they die, which will not be long after that.

This says to me that we must face up to the fact, my brothers and sisters, that in this government we are facing truly the spiritual children of Adolf Hitler. This is where we are. And today we are burying our brothers who have not died by accident, nor is their death a mystery to us.

Our people who live here in the townships have testified, and they know what the truth is about these people and about the deaths of our brothers. Therefore we do not believe those newspaper reports which talk about the 'mystery' of the death of the four that we will bury today. The UDF has raised certain issues and has asked certain fundamental questions about the deaths of Matthew Goniwe, Fort Calata, Sicelo Mhlawuli and Sparrow Mkhonto. We have said publicly that only a very few people have known about the meeting that they were attending in Port Elizabeth and that there was no public announcement as to when they would leave that night or whether they would come back to Cradock that evening. Only the people in the office knew that they were going to go back to Cradock that night, and the only other people who could have known were people who would listen in to that conversation with their sophisticated instruments. We know who they are.

We have been told that Matthew had said that evening that he would not stop the car unless he was stopped by uniformed police. We know that there was a roadblock that night. The question that must therefore be answered is: Who killed them? They were not struck down by lightning, the car did not mysteriously go up in flames. Our brothers were killed by the people who stopped them at that road block. Our people believe that the police dit it – and I believe it too! It is time that we must say to this government: 'Stop protecting these murderers who kill our people!' Who has been responsible for the systematic death of a number of our civic leaders over the past year? For they die mysteriously, they disappear mysteriously, they are being assassinated one after the other. Who is responsible for that?

And I want to say to the South African government: Do *not* protect those people! Why have you created a climate in which the police can kill? Why have you created a climate in which death squads roam around and can do whatever they like as if the lives of our people do not matter? Why have you created a climate in which people know they can kill our leaders and they will not be brought to justice? Why have you created a climate in which the police can kill 43 of our people without any provocation; you set up a commission of inquiry, and still the police will be held blameless? I must say to the South African government: We have said to you before and we are saying to you again, 'There is a God in heaven who knows about justice, and you shall reap what you sow!'

And yet, my brothers and sisters, while this is happening, it seems that most of our white brothers and sisters in this country cannot be bothered. They are more concerned about the cancellation of a rugby tour than they are about the lives of our people! I have seen more concern in our newspapers for the All Blacks who are not coming to South Africa than for our people who have died. In most of white South Africa, they are calling for stronger action by the government.

Most refuse to hear the truth, most refuse to listen to the voice of the oppressed and of our people who suffer. They would rather listen to the propaganda on South African television than they would to the voice of Mrs Goniwe, who will tell them about her husband and what he did and the work he had done for the sake not only of our people but for all of South Africa. While we are suffering, and while we are crying out, white South Africa mostly wants to make heroes out of those black people who are willing to sell their souls for money and the little bit of political power that P.W. Botha will give them.

Not only your hearts

I must say to our white brothers and sisters, I am so grateful that some of you are here today to show your solidarity. I hope that you will go away from this funeral today with more than mere sympathy in your hearts, because we do not need that. We need your total commitment to the struggle; we need your joining in the struggle; we need your voices to be heard. We need not only your hearts; we need your bodies in the struggle. And so we hope that you will go and use the power that you have, so you can go and tell the government tomorrow that they must stop killing our people. I hope that you will use the opportunities you have to do just that and thereby forge links of brotherhood and sisterhood that cannot be broken even by the evil of racism or by the propaganda of the South African government.

I would plead with white South Africa, please do not be deceived by what you hear and see and by those who so cunningly can twist the truth even by quoting the Bible. The State President spoke a week ago to hundreds of young white people. He said to them that it is his duty to stop terrorism just as Jesus drove out the money changers from the temple. I would like to ask the State President whether he knows what he is doing when he tries to read a theology of violence into the life of the Man whom the Bible calls the Prince of Peace. I would like to know why those church leaders who are so quick to condemn us when we ask to pray for the removal of unjust rule and who say that we want violence don't rise up and tell the State President: 'You cannot use the name of Jesus to justify your violence.' Why are they silent? It is their duty to preach to those who have the power to change this country tomorrow if they want to.

I would like to say another thing. The State President must think about whether he is right in simply assuming that the terrorists he is talking about are those brothers who have to fight from across the border. The experience of black people in this country is different. We do not think that the terrorists are those who are the freedom fighters of this land. The ANC, Mr Botha, did not shoot our people when they were defenceless at Sharpeville 25 years ago. The ANC, Mr Botha, did not kill our children in 1976 when they were walking peacefully on the streets of Soweto. The ANC, Mr Botha, did not kill our children during the school boycotts in 1980 in Cape Town. It was not the ANC who killed little Thabo Sibeko, who was six years old, last year on the East Rand. It was not the ANC who killed 43 people at Langa township on 21 March at the massacre of Uitenhage. It was not the ANC who killed our four brothers whom we are burying today. *Your* government did it – so *they* are the terrorists! It is a most dangerous thing when people in power begin to believe their own propaganda!

And I urge those white people who are serious about the future of South Africa to look a little further than your newspapers, to listen a little deeper than to the voices of the commentators on South African television, and to come and talk to our people in the townships. There you will hear the truth. There you will see the truth. There you will see what it means to live under apartheid.

Raising a sign of hope

I know that today's funeral will not be the last one. I know that our mourning will not end today. I know that tomorrow and tomorrow and tomorrow there will be more tears that will flow. There are difficult days ahead. The violence of the South African government knows no end. More of our brothers and sisters will be detained. There will be more whose names will be added to some hit list and more will be killed by those faceless murderers who hide behind balaclavas and their guns and behind the protection they receive.

But this is the price that we have to pay for our freedom. We are here today, but we will do more than just mourn. We have heard it over and over again. We will not simply mourn; we will wake up from mourning and we will dedicate ourselves anew to the struggle for justice and liberation and freedom and peace.

If I die tomorrow, do not come to my funeral and sing freedom songs if you are not willing to participate today in the struggle for liberation and justice. If I die tomorrow, do not avenge my death with more senseless violence and hatred, but raise up a sign of hope that this country will become what it must become and that we will make our contribution to that future. If I die tomorrow do not give up and do not despair, for I know that our victory is near, that apartheid and injustice will never endure and that our people shall be free. If I die tomorrow, raise up a sign of victory and hope; for the future of this country is not written in the guns, the violence and the armies of the South African government, but it is written in the hearts of our people, in our determination to be free and in our willingness to give our lives for this struggle we believe in.

I know that as we have to go from funeral to funeral many of us will become tired. Many of us will become tired of protest, tired of knocking at the door, tired of seeing our brothers and sisters dying. But as long as our people, black and white, are shackled in the chains of oppression and racism, there will be a fight to fight, and we must not give up. As long as our children die needlessly and untimely there will be a fight to fight – do not give up. And as long as injustice still reigns supreme in this land there will be a fight to fight – do not give up. As long as little children are born just to die, too soon, there will be a fight to fight – do not give up. For this country is yours, this land is yours, the future is yours – do not give it up!

So while we mourn, let us commit ourselves again to the struggle for justice and freedom and liberation. There are things that we can do. We can begin to ask ourselves what those of us who come from Natal, the Western Cape and from Transvaal should ask: Why it is that the people in the Eastern Cape can have a successful consumer boycott, but we do not do anything about that in the Cape or Natal or Transvaal? One of the things that should come out of this funeral is for the people of this country to go back home and organise those boycotts, and we will lay low those who think they are the powerful. We will keep away from them our buying power. We should begin to do that. We must do it in Cape Town, we must do it in Johannesburg, and we must do it in Durban.

And to our people in the townships who have shops, I say you are part of this struggle too. When we say that we shall boycott the white shops we want your full cooperation. We want you to make it possible for our people to do that. You do not raise your prices, you lower them. You lower them because it is the cause of the struggle. And if you do that you shall be known as people who fight with us and who struggle with us for justice.

I must say that if the only thing we do when we go back home is to raise a sign of hope for our people, so that we can see and the world can see that in spite of what is happening to us we are not a defeated people, we will have achieved a noble purpose.

So raise a sign of hope and continue the fight for justice and for peace. Raise a sign of hope and struggle for a truly non-racial democracy in South Africa. Raise a sign of hope and continue to believe that in South Africa the day shall dawn when the people shall govern. Raise a sign of hope and do not give in to hatred and violence, but seek peace and genuine reconciliation. Raise a sign of hope and be a brave and courageous people. Raise a sign of hope and be a committed people. Raise a sign of hope and the God of peace and justice shall be with you – and we shall have our freedom! We shall have our freedom! We shall have our freedom! God bless you all!

PART FOUR

Coming Home?

11

The Morning After: Exiles, Inziles and the Loss of Treasure

Fools rush in ...

A song from the sixties, 'Fools Rush In (Where Angels Fear to Tread)', based on the well-known saying by Alexander Pope, plays through my mind as I write. My favourite version of this song is by Lou Rawls, the singer with the deep, resonant, drawling voice. He is what we used to call a 'crooner'. It is a lovely, catchy tune, with an infectious, swinging rhythm. The saying 'fools rush in' refers to saying or doing things that a wiser person would prudently avoid. The 'wiser' person knows to tread carefully lest she or he should bring harm to her or his career, slip a rung or two down the ladder or suffer similar repercussions. But the saying is also about belief, conviction and integrity. Bible readers will know what I mean. St Paul talks about the challenge to be 'fools for Christ', and the wisdom of God that is foolishness to the world.

In politics the saying means that the party line is paramount. In the liberation movement, though, the term 'party line' is not used – that term is for liberals and conservatives. Rather, the term 'the collective' is used. But 'collective', I have found, does not mean 'the people'. I thought it did, until I learnt about democratic centralism, the vanguard, the lumpen proletariat and their designated role in the 'national democratic revolution'. What did I know of the seriousness with which the ANC took the political theory of Rosa Luxemburg, which holds that once the collective leadership has taken a decision there can be no dissent – public or private? Everyone in the collective, as well as those on whose behalf the wisdom of the collective has spoken, must abide by those decisions. Those who insist on thinking further or differently become 'counter-revolutionaries'. The terminology differs, but the fact remains that all political formations, whether liberal, conservative, right-wing or revolutionary, have strong expectations of adherence to the party line.

I am not sure that I am offering my unawareness of these political traditions as an excuse. Of course one reads, but reading and experiencing are vastly different. My political tradition was the Black Consciousness Movement – whose philosophy was meant for ordinary people – and the UDF, a truly people's movement. There was an openness in the UDF that today I sorely miss.

Another thing that made an uncritical political mindset hard for me to sustain were my theological convictions, which are firmly rooted in radical Calvinism and liberation theology. I am an inheritor of the Calvin who warns that 'kings are much pleased with their own greatness and wish their own pleasure to be treated as an oracle'. So we have to be vigilant since 'their obstinacy utterly perverts justice'. I am a spiritual child of the Abraham Kuyper who was clear that 'as a man I stand, free and bold, over against the most powerful of my fellow men ... in the sphere of the state I do not yield or bow to anyone who is a man, as I am ...' Liberation theology taught me more than I can say, for instance that it is possible, after liberation, to create a worse tyranny than the one before. And we had known this long before Robert Mugabe the liberator became the undoing of Zimbabwe and the executioner of his people.

From all available evidence it is clear that this critical independent thinking is not an attitude to be recommended; not in politics, anyway. But independent thinking, critical distance and self-critical engagement are precious things, too precious to easily give up. From Biko we have learnt that the greatest ally of the oppressor is the mind of the oppressed. Conversely, we have discovered that the greatest ally of the freedom struggle and of the democratic ideal is the liberated mind of the oppressed. It seems inevitable that when one enters party politics it is expected that one should give up independent thinking. This was, I would later often reflect, the deepest concern of Desmond Tutu as we talked in those years and he raised his unhappiness that I would leave the church for politics. I had thought then, and argued, that critical thinking was characteristic of theology.

Calvinism, with its theology of the Lordship of Jesus Christ over every single inch of life, its conviction that Christian witness ought to enter the real world and challenge it, shape it, subvert it, revolutionise it until it conformed to the norms of the Kingdom of God – justice, equity, peace, humaneness – had produced radical politics and politicians and the world's first cogent revolutionary theory. It had produced John Calvin and Abraham Kuyper who were both theologians and politicians who made a tremendous difference in their societies in their time. Besides, in our times we have had Albert Luthuli and that long line of Christian leaders before him who gave such extraordinary leadership to the ANC. I also thought that the UDF had proven that one does not have to give up the ability to think critically. I was confident; too confident, I think now, too sure of myself and my abilities, arrogant enough to think that it was possible to do in the ANC what could be done within the UDF.

I was wrong and I would pay for that hard-headedness. Desmond Tutu was right. A born politician would probably do well to toe the party line, but for an accidental politician like me this particular form of political correctness would be much harder, and a lot less safe. But others insist that entering politics was the right decision for me at the time, taking into account the needs of our people and the situation in which we found ourselves. It remains a vexing question for me, though, and developing circumstances are not making it any easier.

But there was something else. The differences between the Black Church and the UDF in our country and the political party the ANC had become were huge, and the differences between the ANC of Luthuli and the ANC after exile were even greater. We discovered that almost immediately, but found it too hard to admit even though it was seen in all sorts of ways, in little as well as greater things. This discovery was a truly traumatic thing for all of us who had gone into the struggle to fight for those ideals and dreams and values we had built our life around. I know of struggle activists, veterans of pain and sacrifice, who have not in the years since 1994 been able to come to grips with, and overcome, this reality. It is only now, years later, that they dare to speak of these things, that they are ready to say that the ANC that came back from exile is not the ANC they had held up to the people throughout all the years of struggle. The ANC had come home, but this home would be changed in ways we could not have imagined.

Where angels fear to tread

In the discussions and the debates throughout the first three years of the nineties around all those exciting issues so fundamental to South Africa's future I sat on the National Executive Committee (NEC), listened and participated. But from the start I found it a strange and uncertain space.

At first I thought it was because we were, all of us in the NEC, more or less strangers to this new situation, even though many of the exiles seemed confident enough. Later we would find that that confidence was mostly bluff. We in fact knew far more about the situation at home than did the exiles, more about what it took to get where we were, and far more about the people represented by those who sat on the other side of the negotiating table. But we knew very little about power and its political permutations. We were overawed, not so much by the exiles as by the romantic aura they had brought with them. It must be said, though, that for some of them I will always have the greatest respect. They did take charge, the exiles, and firmly, but equally true is that we surrendered. We had simply, without questioning, laid the staff of authority in their hands.

The issues on the table were not the problem. It was the approach, the underlying, foundational arguments, the style that was so very different, almost disorientating, for me at least. The values we had held so dear and on which we had built our struggle, the ideals in which we believed, the dreams which shaped our actions, the faith that gave content to our hopes and sacrifices – all these were as nothing here. There was no understanding, no connection. Like Noah's turtledove sent out after the flood, these hopes and dreams hovered uncertainly in the air without finding 'a resting place for its feet'. The ANC had the words and the slogans, but there was no *belief*. There was a fascination with realpolitik and underneath the friendliness there was, in some of them, a hardness to which I found difficult to relate. They had been away too long. All of a sudden, dreams, hopes, ideals and values such as faith, which had made up the spirituality of the struggle, attained a dream-like quality, almost as if they had never really existed. The exiles had brought home the world they knew and were comfortable with, and this was home to them. But it was not home to us. Hesitant at first to be honest about the imposition of an exile culture, we are now ready, it seems, to call the attitude of the exiles what is was: sheer arrogance.

In October 1994 I was asked to speak at a conference where representatives of churches were gathering to discuss the role of the church in the new democratic situation, especially with regard to the Reconstruction and Development Programme (RDP). It was by all counts an important conference. It took place before the ANC discovered (or was told) that the RDP did not reflect the new ideological commitment to neo-liberal capitalism, and before President Nelson Mandela's cabinet canned the whole idea and scrapped the RDP ministry. I was then appointed minister for economic affairs in the Western Cape legislature, but within this position I continued to speak also as a Christian activist, as a pastor to my colleagues. I tried to speak as I always did, openly and honestly. In 2001, after a widely publicised sermon preached before 3 000 worshippers at a service of thanksgiving on the night of my release from prison, a respected scholar of the left and SACP stalwart Anthony Holliday, writing in the *Mail & Guardian,* angrily called me 'the demagogue of the poor' who ought to be disciplined by the ANC. I thought that was quite a compliment, when the self-styled champions of the poor felt so threatened by a sermon that they would react in such panic. In 1994, the reaction of the ANC to my public utterances was not as public, but strong enough to prompt me to ask the president that I be redeployed as a diplomat at the United Nations. This, however, was not to be.

I have not reproduced that speech in its entirety, but the reader can gain some idea of the issues I regarded as important at that time from the following extract.

The UDF 'Don't Vote' campaign against the tri-cameral parliament, 1983. The success of this campaign proved to be a turning point for the UDF and the country.

At one of the very many funerals for victims of political oppression in the 1980s.

With UDF supporters after a church service, 1980s.

With Senator Ted Kennedy during his visit to South Africa in 1985. It resulted in a decisive breakthrough in the sanctions campaign.

Saving the life of an accused 'informer' at Lawaaikamp, George, moments away from him being 'necklaced' by the angry crowd.

At a protest march in Cape Town with Beyers Naudé, early 1980s. One of the many called for and led by the churches.

With Winnie Mandela at D.F. Malan airport, Cape Town in 1985. She was on her way to visit Nelson Mandela at Pollsmoor Prison to discuss our planned march for his release.

It is fitting that we should talk about this centrepiece of government policy at this conference. It is also fitting because the RDP came into being after a long process of consultation, not only within the political structures of the ANC, but also with all sorts of players outside the ANC – the churches, organisations of civil society, academics and business communities. And we have gone through at least six or seven drafts before it was adopted as ANC policy in the end. So in a real sense the RDP reflects not so much ANC thinking as the thinking of all those who cared enough to engage the ANC in conversation to make their contributions. The end product thus reflects the contributions of a broad range of participants who we hope will continue to be participants as this programme is translated into action.

What you will be doing here today, therefore, is not just examining the RDP. You will also be asking the question what exactly it is that we, separately and together, must do. What exactly is the role of business, educational institutions, non-governmental organisations and the churches with regard to the RDP? I said that it is about time [we discuss these roles], since the church has always been at the centre of humanising activity in South Africa. The nation is in need, not merely of philosophical reflection as to where we are going, not only of political clarity in terms of our future. I believe firmly that South Africa as a nation is in need of spiritual direction. The same kind of spiritual and theological direction that has inspired the church over the many decades past in the struggle against apartheid, racism and the dehumanisation of our people is the kind of theological clarity we need now, as we talk about rebuilding the nation.

The bringing together of our people, reaffirming and redefining the goals we have set for ourselves, giving meaningful content to the vision that we have [is now of paramount importance]. Let me be clear: politicians and politics alone cannot shape a vision for the people of South Africa. We need the creative input of the church, very clearly based on our understanding of the Gospel and its demands for the times in which we live. And I would further suggest that the church do that without any apology, without unnecessary false modesty – even though we know that we have not always been as modest as we claim to be – but rather with the humility that befits people who call themselves servants of the Living One. There is a huge difference between politically correct modesty and the genuine humility the Gospel is so insistent upon. That is the kind of contribution we hope and expect the church to make.

During the struggle we knew that the incarnation of Jesus Christ was not just some ethereal, doctrinal truth we believed in our hearts. It was the identification of God with us, the affirmation and redemption of our humaneness, the encapsulation of the humanisation of the world. We knew and confessed it then; we must know and confess it now. So when you talk about the RDP, I would suggest very strongly that you once again look seriously at this tradition the church has left for us.

May I also suggest that the RDP is not only about material things. You have seen the lists: so many houses in so many years; so many homes to be given electricity in so many years; so many schools and so many clinics to be built in such and such a time; raising the levels of literacy and skills before such and such a year. You have seen all that, and all those things are important. But they are in a real sense only the one side of the coin of the RDP. The other side says that the RDP has to do with the reconstruction of minds, the changing of hearts and attitudes. In short, it has to do with conversion, with an RDP of the soul, so to speak. This is crucial. For without this reconstruction of the soul and the mind we will not find the peace we are looking for in our process of reconciliation and a lot else besides. If, therefore, we have a problem with the call to conversion in the 1990s, we will have a problem with the RDP. If conversion for you means that we must once again retreat into the old, one-sided spirituality – although that is too good a word for that kind of religiosity of the past – then you will have a problem with the RDP.

Let me repeat: at this time of our history the church continues to need theological reflection that will enable us to do the necessary political, economic and developmental work that will help us to do the right thing in terms of our contribution. I have been pained by the absence of a clear, prophetic word and action from the church in this process of transition, after the decades of struggle, culminating in the leadership the church has been able to give in the 1980s.

I do not think that the voice of the church is clear enough and loud enough to make the contribution we need to make South Africa understand what the transition from apartheid to democracy really means. We knew well enough what we wanted to do in the struggle against apartheid. I am suggesting that since that struggle has taken on a new dimension we have failed to understand both the nature of the struggle now and the dimensions it has taken on. And therefore we will not be able to give the kind of direction people have been waiting for. There is a vacuum there.

My fear is that the vacuum will be filled by those with a theological and political agenda that is in principle fundamentally different from what the nation really is in need of now. This is a statement of intended provocation, because I firmly believe we need to think about this more clearly than we apparently do. Perhaps some other time, Chairperson, you might want me to come back and talk about this, as a brother rather than as provincial minister.

I think the church was so relieved at the political settlement we have reached that the urge to continue to be prophetic disappeared completely. And I speak as someone with political responsibility and a deep desire for the kind of spiritual nourishment and guidance I hope some in the church will try to give. Without that spiritual guidance, without that spiritual nourishment, all politics, all economic reconstruction, all developmental work in South Africa will only be piecemeal. Little bit by little bit, maybe, but it will not reach nor fulfill the goals we have set for ourselves as a nation.

Where Wise Men Never Go ...

We have to deal with major issues confronting the people of South Africa and therefore confronting the church. These are issues that have an impact most directly on our ability as a nation to unite, to change what needs to be changed, to transform ourselves from what we were and in many ways still are, into what we ought to become and what God has in mind for us to be.

Firstly, a major challenge that lies ahead, not in terms of years but right in front of us, is how to deal with the legacy of apartheid. There are some of us who think that since we now have Nelson Mandela as president, to use the word 'apartheid' is a sin. Think about it: it is *apartheid* that was declared a sin by the churches; now it is talking about it and its ongoing devastation that is the sin. That we cannot talk about the past because that would be against reconciliation is a point I will come to later. That we cannot face the issues that still lurk in the background and that constantly poison whatever we try to do because raising these issues will upset some people. The legacy of apartheid is there for all to see and will remain with us for a long time. Just the physical evidence of our past in the remnants of the group areas will remain for decades, and that is only the surface of it.

Secondly, there is the lingering racism in South Africa. It is a reality in every community. Let me also say that in the Western Cape the elections we have just had were not just about change or transformation or the RDP. They were as much about racism as about anything else. Racist fears, racial prejudices. We need to deal with that as a reality. It is not true to say that racism is a thing of the past. If President Reagan succeeded in the 1980s to give racism in the United States a new cloak of respectability, how long do we think it is going to take us to properly cure all our people from that particular evil?

Thirdly, there is the matter of amnesty, and yes, this too is a matter of politics. It has to do with the army, the police, and the members of liberation movement armies. It is concerned with murder, the corruption of cover-ups, with torture, but also with justice. It concerns the feelings of revenge that ordinary Christians feel although we might not admit to those feelings. It has to do with restitution, not so much in the sense of restoring material goods, but rather in the sense of the restoration of our human dignity. How do we keep these things apart in our minds and in our worship and our theological reflection? If we preach what we profess to believe, 'Judgement is mine, says the Lord', what does that mean practically, and how ready are we for it? How many preachers, I wonder, have over the last six months preached on that text, and how many mentioned the question of amnesty? But it is a reality for our parishioners, especially for those who have undergone unforgettable, unforgiveable experiences.

Another thorny issue facing us is reconciliation. Through the years we have insisted that reconciliation is necessary, that it cannot be cheap, that Jesus Christ paid with his life on the cross in order to reconcile the world with God. How then can we expect to get away with less than that? In our time reconciliation has become a cheap, easy buzz word. Reconciliation has been hijacked from the life and language of the church by the politicians, the journalists and the analysts who, with all respect, know not always what they are talking about. Why has that happened? It has happened because we, the church, refused to understand and witness to the biblical injunction, which demands that reconciliation is not possible without confrontation – confronting what we are, what we have been, what we have done. We never wanted to understand, nor insist that reconciliation is not possible while one tries to cover up the sins of the past, compounded by the sins of the present, by painting over the cracks. These cracks have to be exposed in order for true reconciliation to take place. We did not want to recognise that reconciliation is not possible without restitution and so we conveniently skipped over the story of Zacchaeus in Luke Chapter 9. We did not want to be reminded of what Zacchaeus and the Gospel understood reconciliation to be: 'that everything I have stolen from anyone I will give back, fourfold'.

I think that we will discover that there shall be a price to pay for watering down the evangelical injunction in a political situation like ours. And the church must not allow the politicians, whomever they may be, to dictate to the church the meaning of reconciliation. We need, furthermore, to speak of the Truth Commission. Apart from the few brave voices here and there, I did not hear the church pronouncing on this at all. And I can foresee that by the time we do hear such a voice it will be, like in the political world, not a voice of prophetic clarity, but of clever compromise. I am afraid that is not enough.

The Truth Commission is not about nailing people to the wall, although in my less sober moments I sometimes think that might not be such a bad idea. The Truth Commission is about healing the wounds by uncovering the truth. Let us be clear: there *are* wounds, there *are* victims in South Africa. We cannot act or pray or worship as if there were no victims, as if there were no system or people who inflicted these wounds. We have got to face the issue. What does it mean for all of us, and what does the Bible have to say about it? Oh no, we don't hear an Evangelical word, we rather hear from eminent theologians that tired old slogan from 19th-century European liberalism: the Bible is such an open, inconclusive book, so difficult to interpret that it can be misinterpreted by anyone. Therefore it is best to leave it alone. For our situation it has nothing to say. We need to speak of ethnic mobilisation. There is a danger here. It may still be rumbling under the surface, but in this country I believe we are facing a new ethnic mobilisation. This will have serious implications for the church and for theology. We have fought to overcome it, and mostly we did. But all of a sudden ethnic passions have become the basis for political bargaining. Ethnic interests are used as the foundation for seeking some kind of nation that in effect would forever remain balkanised. I plead for vigilance.

Furthermore there is the issue of Armscor. What does it mean that South Africa has a leader in the person of president Nelson Mandela, respected by all the world for his moral integrity, his ability to forgive, his ability to lead his nation along the path of reconciliation, and yet this man's country sells arms to countries like Rwanda, where there is a devastating civil war, to Saddam Hussein's Iraq, to Angola and Yemen? These are so-called trouble spots that threaten a whole continent, are costing the lives of millions, and South African arms are being sold there. All our government has to say is that we must not make an issue out of this: South Africans arms constitute 'hardly' 2% of all arms sales in the world. We must not make an issue of this, they say, because the very nations that tend to lecture us, like America and Britain, are those members of the United Nation's Security Council who are amongst the largest arms dealers in the world. Oh, we must not make an issue out of this, they say, because nobody in the world has hands clean enough to climb on their moral high horses and give South Africa lectures as to what to do with our guns. We must not make an issue out of this because making guns provide jobs.

I despise this line of argumentation, and I think the church should speak out. This is an issue on which the church should challenge our government. You should speak to me as representative of this government: 'What are you doing, Allan Boesak, sitting there and not saying to whoever should hear that the arms trade is wrong?' But we all wait for the 'opportune moment'.

It seems clear that there are serious moral and theological issues involved here. What have we fought, bled and died for? What are we, and what kind of nation do we want to be? Are we saying that we want to be as bad as America as an arms manufacturing, arms selling nation? Can we be a nation of reconciliation as well as a merchant of death? These are questions that politicians, maybe because of their own political and personal situations, cannot even mention. But the duty of the church is to say what politicians are afraid to say. It is to see what politicians will not, and cannot afford to see, to bring to the fore what politicians regard as too sensitive, perhaps in terms of their own constituencies, to put on the agenda. That is our responsibility. For what is at stake here is not only shelter for our people, but pitching the tent of God in our midst. What is at stake here is not only pure drinking water, but in a very real sense the water of life. What is at stake here is not simply the prosperity of our people, but the essential character of our nation.

We will never again in history have an opportunity like this. If

we do not use it now, we will not see it again. It seems to me
that what comes into play here is that well-'known sentence
from the old marriage vows we use in church: 'Speak now or
forever hold your peace.'

The church is called upon to be a partner of government in this
effort. But it will be a unique kind of partnership. Although
the animosity of the past between church and state is gone, the
critical distance remains. But clearly, ladies and gentlemen, the
government cannot walk this road alone. It is a long, winding
road. It is a difficult, uphill path. When it rains it will be a
slippery path. But it is a necessary path.

But wise men never fall in love …

It would have been wiser, I suppose, if not easier, to choose some other
path. But I had fallen in love with my country and its people, with
justice and the politics of justice. The song with which this chapter
begins is talking about romantic love, of course, and almost always
our tendency is to put all love in the category of sentimentality and
romance. Yet talk of love in connection with politics and justice is seen
as wild, unattainable fantasy, unable to stand the test of realpolitik.
Love is the stuff of the wild-eyed populists or the romantic preachers,
not of politics in the real world. Mixing love and politics is not just
a matter of confusing the issues; it is, argues academic Jakes Gerwel,
a matter of 'pathologising the nation'. Thabo Mbeki also had a few
scathing words to say about love and politics.

And in a sense I guess the arguments are true. Unguarded talk of love
in a political context fuels fears of emotional manipulation. It replaces
reason and logic, suspends clear-headed thinking. Or so we think. It
demands that we live as if we were not in the real world. At some deep

level, we suspect that it wants to rob us of our hard-earned adulthood, our political and personal maturity, and bring us back to the pliable impressionability of childhood. But we have come of age; *Mündigkeit*, the Germans call it. We have seen too much, experienced too much, heard too much, been lied to too often. The 20th century has been a steep and tragic learning curve, and it has left us cynical of life, distrustful of each other, wary of the world of ideas and the power its exudes, suspicious of God inasmuch as we think God still matters. We now want to deal with reality on our own terms, and in our terms, 'love' was life's first victim. It is also our greatest weakness, leaving us open and vulnerable to all sorts of manipulation and exploitation. We hate to be treated like children who cannot see the woods for the butterflies.

But the love I am speaking of is not romantic or sentimental. It is the love that in fact removes childish notions. Believing in the infallibility of the leadership or the party, in the unchallengeability and unchangeability of the world in which we live, clinging to the myths created by the powerful and thereby sanctifying your own powerlessness – that is childish. Thinking that Machiavellian machinations can replace integrity because they understand better the politics of power, and that mediocrity is achievement because it never takes risks – these are the childish things love compels us to set aside. But love that rejoices in justice, that fosters humility, that seeks peace, that is willing to make room for others – that is putting away childish notions. It is a love that makes choices: for the truth and rejoicing in it, rather than to profit from evil; to expose the foolishness of realpolitik by choosing for justice, peace and genuine reconciliation; to seek, precisely in politics, to do what is right instead of just what is popular. To seek the strength of the nation not in the flawed and delusional 'security' of arms and the boastfulness of the language of violence, but in securing the rights of the poor, protecting the weak and the needy, creating a safe place for the vulnerable, the marginalised and the excluded.

The love we have for the country of our birth, for its people to whom we are bound with ties stronger than blood, is the kind of love that empowers us to distinguish between truth and myth. It is the kind of love that helps us to understand that 'law and order' is not the enforced state of confusion when the law and the threat of violence are used to keep the poor impoverished and subjugated, which is then called (in that often lethal but always abusive combination) 'law and order'. Order prevails when justice is done and there is no confusion about right or wrong in society.

Years ago, I was convinced by my teacher Paul Lehmann, matchless theologian and personal friend of Dietrich Bonhoeffer, that freedom is the presupposition and the condition of order; order is not the presupposition and condition of freedom. Justice is the foundation and criterion of law; law is not the foundation and the criterion of justice. These are, he says, the 'proper priorities of politics'. When one truly loves one's country and its people, these issues become clear, and one will insist upon the 'proper priorities of politics'. Is this 'pathologising' the nation? Far from it, I should think.

In 2004 Madiba, in giving the annual Steve Biko lecture, finally gave Steve Biko his due, something the ANC had withheld for too long. I quote him at length, as the point he is making is crucial.

> We South Africans have succeeded quite admirably in putting in place policies, structures, processes and implementation procedures for the transformation and development of our country. We are widely recognised and praised for having one of the most progressive constitutions in the world. The solidity

of our democratic order, with all of its democracy-supporting structures and institutions, is beyond doubt. Our economic framework is sound and we are steadily making progress in bringing basic services to more and more of our people. It is at the level of what we once referred to as the RDP of the soul that we as a nation and people might have crucially fallen behind since our attainment of democracy. The values of human solidarity that once drove our quest for a humane society seem to have been replaced, or are being threatened, by a crass materialism and pursuit of social goals of instant gratification. One of the challenges of our time, without being pietistic or moralistic, is to re-instill into the consciousness of our people that sense of human solidarity, of being in the world for one another and because of and through others. It is, as Biko did at that particular moment in history, to excite the consciousness of people with the humane possibilities of change ... To bestow on South Africa the greatest possible gift – a more human face.

This is the notion of love of which I am speaking. Nelson Mandela is right, of course, and it is better that as a nation we face that truth and deal with it. The situation Mandela describes is largely due to three things. First, we are faced with the paradox of a government that has the most admirable ideals, but in whose actions often compassion and caring are seen as weaknesses, as a subtle undermining of their resolve to engage the world of realpolitik. Second, as a nation we have not been able to sufficiently resist the temptations, or embrace the responsibilities that come with power, rights and freedom, hence our difficulties with corruption, greed, instant gratification and our carelessness towards our responsibilities in regard to public service, commitment to transformation and a genuine, gentle patriotism. Third, our selectivity in dealing with our past has prevented us from an honest assessment of the way that our past intrudes upon our present and future. That explains our inability to understand the root causes of our frightening levels of violence, for example, and our pretended satisfaction with our shallow reconciliation. Like Samson who awoke unaware that he had lost his hair and his strength, we have, from all sides, become beguiled, and hence misled, by the entitlements of our romanticised past and our imagined, but unimaginative future.

All this brings not only new forms of injustice, or the worsening of old ones, but also an unravelling of the relations of caring and responsibility. This unravelling takes on different forms. It manifests itself in our media, which far too often regards itself as wholly inured to the healthy corrective of honest self-criticism, proving true George Seldes's dictum: 'The only holy cow the media do not touch are the media themselves.' This attitude is evident in the two Cabinet ministers who, as a joke, went to stand on a Cape Town street corner, checking the time to see whether it is true that in South Africa a woman is raped every 20 seconds. Or in their colleague seven years later who poured scorn on the agony of victims of violent crime by telling concerned and worried South Africans to either shut up or leave the country.

Jacklyn Cock describes this unravelling of societal relations: in reports of the nurse whose patient dies while she chats to the driver in the front of the ambulance, the builder who erects sub-standard RDP houses, irregularities in tendering processes, corruption in the arms industry, the police officer who takes bribes, the currency speculator whose concern for profit obliterates any concern for the well-being of fellow citizens, the public servant falsifying pension claims, the teacher who abuses or neglects his pupils, as well as owners and drivers of minibus taxis who are indifferent to the safety of their passengers.

To this we could add a Governor of the Reserve Bank who preaches sobriety in spending and the tightening of belts to the rest of us, hikes interest rates that strangle the poor and already struggling middle class, and castigates unions who ask for salary increases in keeping with inflation, while he himself accepts a whopping 28% raise in an already stupendous salary. This is nothing short of scandalous. This is what the Bible calls lack of love for one's neighbour. No, the pathologising is not done by those who insist on justice and equity, but by those who believe that while the rich in their yachts and schooners are riding the waves, the rest of us in our leaky little rowing boats battling against the currents do not matter, and in the end our society and our planet can sustain such contradictions.

Meanwhile, students of societal dynamics tell us, the ramifications of unravelling relations continue to spin out. Apart from the privatisation of state assets and functions, South Africa also knows a phenomenon called the privatisation of social relations. People retreat from public engagement in pursuit of individualised goals. The social bonds of caring and solidarity that marked the struggle, exactly as Mandela pointed out, are fast disappearing. Strong, cohesive group identities have been replaced by a defensive and aggressive individualism, a fierce competitiveness, an atomisation of our collective life.

As a society, we have to a large extent lost the meaning of togetherness; we have thrown away the solidarity of human-beingness. We have not lost the art of sloganeering, though, and somehow that just makes it worse. We speak glibly of ubuntu, but we live lives of self-centred individualism. We call upon the 'spirit of the ancestors', but we exude the spirit of post-modernist cynicism. Our political discourse is mostly empty bombast, our public discussion is pathetic rudeness and the verbosity of violence parades as 'robustness'. A civil society that has lost its civility has lost the meaning of its existence. And civility without care and compassionate justice is not possible.

We have begun to think that we now have to seek private solutions to socially produced problems. People believe they cannot trust the state to provide all that is needed in the most pertinent issues that touch their lives: unemployment, illness, security and safety, health care and proper education. Hence the protracted battles about gun ownership, safe neighbourhoods, crime statistics and the consequences of a growing and absolutely shocking xenophobia. We need to change this. We need to rediscover our sense of community, our sense of values and a common destiny. And we need to reclaim the public square that we have abandoned to make it happen.

In her book of essays *Between Past and Future,* Hannah Arendt describes the perplexing crises societies face as a result of loss of meaning of the traditional key words of politics: justice, reason, responsibility, virtue, glory. Taking as her point of departure the French Resistance against Hitler, she describes how the brave men and women, when the war was over and a new situation virtually erupted upon them, became almost disoriented. They became, she says, 'separated from the world of reality'. She does not mean the world of realpolitik, she means the reality of real values or, put differently, the things that really matter. Not understanding what justice, virtue, glory or responsibility meant in the new situation, she argues, they 'could only return to the old empty strife of conflicting ideologies which after the defeat of the common enemy once more occupied the political arena to split the former comrades-in-arms into innumerable cliques which were not even factions and to engage them in the endless polemics and intrigues of a paper war … They had lost their treasure'.

These brave fighters for justice during the war were neither the first nor the last to lose their treasure, Arendt continues. 'The history of revolutions – from the summer of 1776 in Philadelphia and the summer of 1789 in Paris to the autumn of 1956 in Budapest – which politically spells out the innermost story of the modern age, could be told in parable form as the tale of an age-old treasure which, under the most varied circumstances, appears abruptly, unexpectedly, and disappears again, under different mysterious conditions, as though it were a *fata morgana*.'

Once again Hannah Arendt has it spot on. If she had lived, she would have added South Africa to her list of countries that have undergone revolution. That might indeed be at the heart of the crisis that has burst so unexpectedly upon us even as I write. We are seeing it all: the confusion after the common enemy has been vanquished, the cliques and paper wars, the loss of meaning of that which gave our struggle infinite value but now which seems a dream that never existed – justice, virtue, responsibility, glory. In our revolution we have, like all other revolutions, lost our treasure.

Let this fool rush in

Those who scoff at South Africa's miracle are wrong, I wrote in *The Tenderness of Conscience*. What happened in 1994 *is* a miracle, because it went beyond our abilities to project or control, and against great odds. But it was not beyond our imagination. That we did not wade through rivers of blood, as so many had expected and even more had feared, because they knew there were those who had actually wanted it, was more than we could have planned. But it was not a miracle that fell out of thin air, as if God as *Deus ex machina* lifted a finger from outside our history to create something out of nothing. The miracle, in a very real sense, was the fruit of struggle, of faith sometimes wavering, always under attack but never diminished, of a believing people who with sacrificial love, an amazing endurance and a God-given gift for forgiveness refused to give up hope. They recognised within themselves the hope that God had planted in them, and with that hope cried their cries for freedom and justice. And it was, as Calvin said, 'as if the Lord heard himself, when God hears the cries of the oppressed'.

Those who claim that nothing good has happened, that in the days of apartheid we actually were 'better off', are wrong too. Desperately so. They are caught in the foreign language of yesterday, and can find no words to describe the tomorrow we are striving to build. In continuing to struggle for meaningful change and ongoing transformation, for genuine reconciliation and the building of one nation, we must not merely be satisfied with reaching our goals. We must grasp our destiny. In doing this we must not make the imperfect our yardstick as if this is the best we have to offer, nor must we make the mediocre our consolation. We must not measure our progress by the comfort of the rich, but by the contentment of the poor. Judgement on how we walk must not be taken from the privileged, but from the powerless, the ones of unimpressive proportions, those the Bible calls 'the least of these'. The authority with which we rule must not be derived from the approval of the mighty and the boastful, but from the voiceless who have invested their hope in the reality of justice.

Our strength should not be found in weapons made by human hands in order to destroy and maim and kill. It should be found in the power that only the love for justice can bring. The health of our nation can never be found in the determinations of the Washington Consensus, but in the security of all our people, the safety of women and children, the integrity of our laws, the inclusivity of our democratic life. Our true confidence should not be found in the indexes that measure our compliance with rules not our own and not geared towards or guided by justice. It should be found in the faith of our people who continue to dream the dreams their parents and elders, their siblings and their children died for. Here is something to think about. Mapungubwe, the ancient kingdom in the Limpopo Province, is one of South Africa's most precious archeological and historical treasures. This kingdom, 'The Hill of the Jackal' in Sesotho, and which reached the height of its power in the 13th century, was first settled in the 8th or 9th century AD, archeologists tell us. The place has a fascinating and proud history. This is where gold was melted 600 years before that particular technology was mastered in Johannesburg and where those stunning golden images, now on display at the University of Pretoria and in the Gold of Africa Museum in Cape Town, were fashioned with African hands. It was also probably the first place in South Africa where cotton was grown and weaved into material.

The point I want to make is not about the amazing achievements of these South Africans or the level of civilisation they had reached, even though these achievements are impressive enough and South Africans should be justly proud. There is, I think, a valuable lesson to be learnt here. At the epitome of Mapungubwe's power the population was around 3 000–5 000, living in an area of more than 30 000 km². This was a powerful people. Over time a curious arrangement developed. The people were directed to live in the valley and on the plains surrounding the hill. The king and his chosen elite lived on the hill itself, the rest of the royal family and whoever the king favoured lived on the terraces of the hill.

This arrangement was deliberate. The king and his privileged few were isolated from the people but protected by the people who perforce formed the first line of defence in case of an invasion. By physically isolating themselves from the ordinary people, the king and his trusted circle heightened their status and their power. This was a new development for the culture and the people, the scholars say, and brought with it a new symbolism: the ritualisation of leadership. It created distance and aloofness and put communality and solidarity under immense pressure. I am sure that for some it was the 'natural' outflow of the immense civilisational achievements, the just rewards for their leadership, this re-arrangement of ancient societal relationships, and for them it placed the proper emphasis on their perceptions of status and relations of power. But it was a temptation that should have been resisted. The kingdom did not last.

History is full of lessons like this. In the last few years, the combined results of exile, democratic centralism, the vestiges of Stalinism, the effects of centralised power and the deadly casualness which has marked leadership's attitude towards the poor and voiceless masses have brought South Africa closer to this ritualised leadership than we realised. The Union Buildings, and with it Luthuli House, and by extension Parliament, symbols of our ritualised power, were in danger of becoming another Mapungubwe, another Hill of the Jackal, removed, distanced and insulated from the people with their cries for justice and their search for hope. In South African society, as a result, the temptation to create a ruling elite that cocoons itself inside the 'hallowed halls of power', behind gated communities and the closed doors of privileged schools and the disinfected luxury of private hospitals has become very real indeed. Emerging from our pain-filled and fractured past, we are seeking to build a nation with shared values, common dreams and mutual aspirations. Every 'Hill of the Jackal' in South Africa must be laid low.

The Venda people still have a saying that refers to this time in our history: 'To climb the mountain [where the king lives] one must walk in a zig-zag pattern.' This means that one cannot approach the leadership and speak directly; one must have an intermediary, since the leadership is too exalted. But 'exalted' in this context is close to 'unapproachable' or, worse, 'feared'. And this fear has very little to do with love, respect and trust. Is this what ANC members mean when they speak of the 'closing down of democratic space'?

Our people today must not find it necessary to seek the intervention of intermediaries or climb a winding uphill path in order to speak to their leadership, to make their voices heard, to let their hopes be honoured. They deserve better. For through it all – the centuries of struggle, the many battles for survival, the endless stream of disappointments, disillusionments and dislocations, the bitter failures, the amazing victories and the stunning achievements – the South African people have never given up the hope that beyond the darkness the dawn awaits, that we are capable of more than we allow ourselves to believe, that nothing we do for good shall ever be in vain.

Jonathan Sacks, rabbi and philosopher, has called hope a human virtue with religious underpinnings. At its ultimate, he writes, 'Hope is the belief not that God has written the script of history, that God will intervene to save us from the error of our ways or protect us from the worst consequences of evil, but simply that God is mindful of our aspirations, with us in our fumbling efforts, that God has given us the means to save us from ourselves; that we are not wrong to dream, wish and work for a better world.'

12

Prayer, Prophecy and Political Piety: An Open Letter to Minister Kader Asmal

Goodwood Prison
Private Bag X04
Edgemead
23 March 2001

Prof Kader Asmal
Minister of Education
Parliament Buildings
Cape Town

My dear Kader

It was with great sadness that I read of your attack on the Christian prayer gathering held on Wednesday 21 March. I must confess to some, though not total, surprise. I have sometimes wondered how long it will take for our government to launch such an open attack on Christians for being Christians. The ANC, it is known, has a culture of tolerance, not only for the wide divergence of viewpoints and beliefs in society as a whole, but also for within the movement itself. You yourself are a cultured man with a high level of understanding for the views of others; an erudite man, for whom I have much respect. What is it, then, that made you lash out so harshly against Christians gathering to pray in public for issues that must, surely, trouble the government as deeply as they do us?

I was not present at Newlands on Wednesday (what would I have given to be there!) because I am, as you know, still incarcerated, my hopes of an early release having been dashed again and again. But we prayed here too, the prisoners at Goodwood Prison, for peace and genuine reconciliation, for true justice and an end to violence, mayhem and crime, for good government and for the fulfillment of the dreams of the poor, for the kind of transformation of our society and our country that is more than mere change. So in spirit we were at Newlands and we felt ourselves one with those persons, lifted up together by the songs of praise and worship while we lay in our cells, and joined together before the throne of God. I praise God that such an event was possible and actually happening, where Christians from all persuasions, black and white, Protestants and Catholics, 'mainline', Pentecostal and Charismatic, could be united by the call for prayer and the firm belief that God answers prayer. So when your attack came, you were also attacking me, as well as all those Christians who are members of the ANC, and I feel obliged to respond.

I tried to seek some understanding of what it is that so vexed you and caused such an ugly, ill-advised outburst of intolerance. I know that some are already saying that it was pure frustration that the ANC rally itself could draw no more than about 300 persons, and that on such an important day on our political calendar, in contrast with the Christian prayer service which attracted over 45 000. Surely it cannot be that. If there is unhappiness about the numbers the ANC is able to draw at public meetings on such auspicious occasions as Human Rights Day, then surely the ANC must search for the answers within itself. And we must take note of the fact that a Christian gathering *is* able to draw the masses in such huge numbers. Something very special is happening in our country, and politics in general, and the government in particular would be wise to learn from it.

One should hardly have to mention that Christians, like any other group, have the right, constitutionally, to gather and give public expression to their beliefs. No apologies, no excuses, no explanations. More important, over and above the constitution, we believe that Christians have a calling, a *duty* to pray. I will not bother you with references to biblical texts, but I can assure you, they are all there. Trust me. We are called to pray for all persons in authority, for the government, for the church, for all people in need. We pray that the world in which we live may be changed, that *people* may be changed because we hold the conviction that all real and lasting change somehow comes from within. And prayer is not doctrinal formulations or the mumbling of magical formulas. Neither is it an escape from our earthly responsibilities. Rather it is a call to take up those responsibilities, not on our own, but in total dependence on the grace of God and in the power of the Holy Spirit of God.

Yes, for this very reason our prayers are sometimes political. They must be, because all the world is the Lord's, and there is no area of life, not a single inch, that is not subject to the Lordship of Jesus Christ. So politics and politicians cannot consider themselves outside the demands of the gospel or outside the circle of prayer. We pray for politics, not because we feel so much at home there, in that world of intrigue and compromise, of betrayal and power, of immense temptation and awesome responsibility, but because even there we must assume our positions as believers. Even there we must dare to name God, to confess God from within the womb of politics, and so challenge every idolatry that seeks to displace God in the lives of God's people. And so we came together to pray for transformation, political and societal and economic; and we prayed for personal transformation, for conversion, so that people might be driven by inner conviction rather than by political expediency.

We pray also because we believe passionately in the power of prayer. Prayer changes things, Christians say, and that is true. It is that conviction, you will remember, that inspired us in 1985 to call for a day of prayer for the downfall of the apartheid regime. We prayed then in the midst of a storm too, and we were viciously condemned by all who felt themselves threatened by a God who listens to the prayers of the oppressed. We were vilified by those whose interests could not abide the changes we were praying for. But the thing is, God heard our prayers, things changed, and apartheid is no more. And you could come home.

You call the Newlands gathering 'sectarian', 'exclusive' of those who were not white, or 'coloured' or Christian. But that is manifestly untrue. Are you saying that Christians in this country are only 'white' and 'coloured'? That black people are not Christian, or not interested in prayer? Or even worse, were not invited? But they were there, in their thousands, calling upon God to do what God has done before: give deliverance, respond with love and compassion, work liberation for God's people. It may well be that the Langa rally was so sparsely attended because so many of the people expected there were at Newlands!

In fact, the utterly undesirable distinction between 'whites', 'coloureds' and 'Africans' was not made by the Christian gathering, but by you. I hope it is not intentional, for it is so much against what the ANC professes. It certainly is very much the antithesis of the Christian faith and what was the reality on Wednesday. God's liberation for which we prayed is not just for 'Christians' but for all in need, for all those oppressed by poverty, injustice, fear and violence.

And it is not as if this is something new. We have always believed this. God is a God of liberation and those deeds of liberation can be seen throughout history, beginning with the liberation of the people of Israel from slavery. And Christians have shared this faith with others in this country for as long as anyone can remember. My own participation in the struggle for liberation in this country was based on, and inspired by, my faith in Jesus Christ, but that fact never gave rise to the desire to be exclusive of others. The very first time I was arrested by the apartheid regime was in 1979 on the bridge to Gugulethu, and as we marched to be arrested I was flanked by two Muslims: Hassan Solomons and Faried Essack. We did not then think in terms of exclusivity because I happened to have marched with a Bible in my hands. Nor did we think it exclusive when Muslims met on Friday and prayed in their mosques while I was not allowed to enter even when in interfaith services Sheik Gabier spoke in my church from my pulpit. Throughout all those years we never thought that Muslims or others were 'wrong'. We just knew we could not live without Jesus. And that we could not live without publicly acknowledging that.

What you saw on Wednesday, Minister, was not an exhibition of Christian exclusivity, but the continuation of a long tradition within the Christian church, who believes the words of Jesus, 'Pray, and you shall receive.' Without this passionate belief in the power of prayer, without our faith in Jesus the Messiah, Christians would never have been able to join the struggle and to make the tremendous contribution they did make. Through all those years of struggle we were not inspired by slogans and speeches and vague dreams of 'freedom' and 'democracy' which, for millions, even today remain largely unfulfilled. Neither were we driven by philosophical concepts many did not even understand. We were, simply and wonderfully, inspired by our faith. So we did what we did, in the name of Jesus. It did not then offend our comrades of other faiths. Why should it now? We were not ashamed of our faith then. Why should we be now?

When we marched and demonstrated for the exiles to come home, for Nelson Mandela to be released, for the detainees to be set free, for the banned to be unbanned, we prayed and we believed. When we were tear gassed and beaten, set upon by dogs, detained and tortured, arrested by the apartheid police in our churches, publicly humiliated and scorned; when we lay bleeding, dying and afraid, we were inspired, not by Marx or Lenin, but by our faith in Jesus of Nazareth. We faced the viciousness of the regime and we took the pain, *not* because we strove for ideological perfection or were lured by the false dream of some worker's paradise, but because Jesus said, 'Do not be afraid, I have overcome the world.' We did not then ask if Mandela was a Christian, whether the exiles were Communists, atheists or agnostics, or whether those detained shared our faith. We prayed and his love sustained us and drove us to act.

Now today, there are millions who feel that what we have fought for has not yet been realised. They are deeply disturbed that our new democracy is threatened by crime and violence, by corruption in high places, public and private, by injustice in the courts, and by relationships poisoned by hatred, racism and class consciousness. They are concerned by the abuse of women and children, by an ever growing gap between the rich and the poor, and by a casual indifference, a frightening carelessness by those who have the power to make a difference. They come together to pray because they are deeply convinced that transformation that is only social, economic and political, however indispensable, is not enough. They believe that we need the power of God in our lives so that transformation can be fundamental. Let me be bold, Minister: South Africa would not be free today if there were not such people, and South Africa needs them today more than ever before. As you reflect on the history of South Africa, as you did last Wednesday, please do not forget this. More than anything our struggle was sustained by prayer and faith. I know. I was there. Denying this historical truth will only exacerbate our already grave situation.

According to the newspaper, you said that 'The ANC is different from the Christian gathering. We do not care what race or of what faith you are. We do not celebrate Human Rights day like those people. We celebrate it with joy and with love. We do not exclude anybody.' With all respect, Minister, that is a statement of stunning ignorance. First of all, at the heart of the Christian faith is the belief that 'there is no Jew or Greek, bond or free, male or female, but all is one in Christ'. The universality of the work of Jesus of Nazareth was one of the most revolutionary characteristics which marked the movement that took his name. That Western Christianity and racist churches in this country denied this for so long does not make it any less true. And in Goodwood prison, certainly, on Wednesday prayers were offered in English and Afrikaans, in Xhosa and Sotho, and even in Arabic.

Second of all, I would venture to say that one would have to go far to match, never mind beat, the unbridled joy that reverberated around Newlands Stadium on Wednesday. It is a joy that is not affected whether a speaker turns up or not, or speaks well or not, or says the right things or not. It is a joy that stems from the truth that Jesus has the power to save and change lives. It is a joy that surpasses all human understanding, so that even in prison on Wednesday we sang and danced and worshipped, not because we knew we were going home that night, but because we knew the truth about Jesus and about ourselves, and that truth has set us free. It is the same joy that sustained us even when the apartheid regime breathed fire and destruction. And I remember the songs that filled the air when we confronted the riot squads in the streets of our townships and when they surrounded our churches. It was the joy of knowing the man with the gun in the hand cannot at the same time hold onto our freedom too, and that if he wants to hold his own freedom he will have to lay down the gun.

We are told you are upset because the day of prayer looked like a Democratic Alliance rally. Please do not give the DA more credit than they deserve. Whether or not the DA leadership in the Cape were there because of political opportunism is not the issue now. The point is rather: Where were the ANC leadership? Those who are members of the ANC and Christians must wonder about that. Why were we not represented? Why are we afraid to be associated with prayer in public? Wednesday's celebration was a celebration of prayer, a heartfelt cry on behalf of *all* South Africa's people to God who promised us: 'If my people who are called by my name humble themselves, pray, seek my face, and turn from their wicked ways, then I will hear from heaven, and will forgive their sins *and heal their land.*' We should have been there, not to speechify or pontificate, but to pray.

Like you, I am distressed that some used the prayer gathering as an occasion to launch an attack on homosexual persons. You are right: that *is* against the spirit of Human Rights Day. It is also, I believe, against the spirit of Jesus of Nazareth. Many, many Christians, of whom I am one, do not agree with them. We differ fundamentally on our understanding of the Bible on these and other issues. I find the condemnation of homosexual persons, many of whom are committed Christians, wrong, lacking in compassion and distasteful. On this point, conservative Christians share the same views as conservatives in other religions. I want to ask the forgiveness of all those who attended, or listened or watched, who wanted to share in the spirit of the day and were profoundly hurt by those remarks. But let us not try to score political points off the ignorance or pain of others. Instead of making this a point of condemnation, we should use this as an invitation to open discussion and honest conversation, also within the Christian church. On the whole the issues that unite us are more, and of greater import, than those that divide us. Our differences can be overcome.

So far from attacking the Christian gathering, the government should applaud it, support it, embrace it. True transformation shall not come to South Africa through new laws only, or more money for the police services, or more new prisons. It is clear to me also that politics alone is not the answer. For all the lofty political language our politicians from all sides now habitually employ, for all the Constitutional guarantees we are believed to have in place, for all the talk of a 'rainbow nation', we know something fundamental is wrong. The vision of our politics has become the victim of our politics, our communal life has become confused, cheap and endangered, our public conversation through our politics and our media has long been, and still is, superficial, mean spirited and uninspiring. Our nation is in danger of losing its soul. Nothing less than the restoration of our covenant with God and with one another will save us. For Christians, that God is the God of Jesus whom we call Christ. What we need is a change of heart, a revolution of the spirit, an understanding of ourselves more than mere propaganda to make us feel good, and certainly more than the sectarian, hapless despair that so often poisons our public debate. We need a conversion of the soul. That cannot be done by parliament although what happens in parliament can reflect it. It cannot be done by politics although our political discourse and actions may be fundamentally changed by it. It can only be done by a spiritual force greater than ourselves, more powerful than our speech, more lasting than our dreams. That is what Christians are trying to do: submit ourselves to that greater power which is God, so that we may be used by God for the good of our nation.

The vision that our politicians speak of seeking cannot come from those on high. The father of my own Reformational tradition, John Calvin, has warned us that those in power rarely have the vision to use power for the sake of goodness. That vision has to be born amongst ordinary people, carried within their hearts, warmed by the fire in their souls, nurtured by their acts of selfless love. That is what this call to prayer is all about. I cannot imagine that anyone in government could be against that. Let me assure you: what has happened last Wednesday, and what will continue to happen in South Africa is much bigger than petty party politics, and cannot be exploited, manipulated or stopped by it.

I hope you will think again about your words. Let us not fight. Not on this issue. No good will come of it. History is littered with the debris of once powerful regimes who thought they could take on God and the church. The National Party government in South Africa is only the most recent example of such utter foolishness. That is a fatal mistake born of the arrogance of power. The ANC must not make that mistake. Let us not fight. Let us rather take hands and together fight against the forces that seek to destroy our nation and the future of our children. Christians will continue to pray. We invite you to join us. If you cannot pray with us, please do not stand in our way.

I hope fervently that you are not scandalised by my writing to you. Things have changed and many are desperately embarrassed to know me now and I apologise if I do cause such embarrassment to you now. The stain of leprosy which prison brings has added deeply to the pain of the last seven years. Now is not the time to discuss the reasons why I am here. Like so many others, I am sure you do know why. But I am a Christian, one who knows God's forgiveness and mercy, and although I am, in the eyes of the world, 'fallen from grace', I have found that God's grace is sufficient for me and that his mercies are new every morning. That is the promise upon which I dare to stand and in which I continue to rejoice. Although, as St Paul says, I am truly the very least of all saints, this grace was also given to me to bring to all God's children the boundless riches of Christ.

I am also well aware that I have, in the normal sense of things, no 'mandate', that precious stamp of legitimacy the ANC prizes so highly, so that you may be tempted to put this letter aside. I hope you do not, for my mandate comes from Christ, whose servant I still am. I am in chains, but the Word of God is not bound. And it is to that Word I seek to be obedient. I am in prison, but Christ, in his mercy, is not ashamed of me, and therefore I am called not to be ashamed of the gospel of Jesus Christ and it is to that gospel and to that Name I now give witness. I come to you with nothing more than this. And with nothing less than this.

Please allow me to end with another word from Paul, who had failings and fears like all of us, but who through the grace of God has left a marvellous legacy of Christian faith and witness, for us all to follow: 'Now to Him who by the power at work within us is able to accomplish abundantly far more than all we can ask or imagine, to

Left: Straining to hear journalists's questions outside Victor Verster prison. Would Mandela finally be released?

Middle: Studying media speculation about Nelson Mandela's release in1989, making this, for the first time, a definite possibility as result of the constant pressure from the resistance movement inside the country.

© Greg English

Leading the Peace March in Cape Town with Archbishop Desmond Tutu, Cape Town Mayor Gordon Oliver and trade unionist Zola Malindi, 1989.

© Oryx Media

With Rev Jesse Jackson and assassinated Prime Minister of India Rajiv Ghandi in Namibia in the building up of pressure for Namibia's independence. .

March with ANC leaders Chris Hani, Walter Sisulu, and Cheryl Carolus, 1992, to celebrate the unbanning of the liberation movements and the return of the exiles.

Things to Buy or Do

Thus wfmason36@eric   Re Thurs ✓
                                                        golf
1. CMasa 440 338 3573
2. • call 847 507 0191 re PI
3. • Pack bags
4. • cosponsors for testschref Seminar + receptn
5. • Tim Breen Host Center
6. • E Muir re: Host Dept consult   Peter Hamp
7. • Switch center Hendrix
8. • 9ets
9. • call D Burrell (NDr)
10.
11.
12.
13.
14.
15. • 7 - Blackhawks
16. • NBA
17. 6/4 -13 Yerman / Cahn / Cat Fmy
18.
19.
20.

Alan Boesak   As SB day of atonement

disdain for the poor reigns in S Africa

Tenderness of Conscience

Can I (we) come for a year to work in
Institute of Theology & Public life?

Sabbatical Projects
   Belgium - VG + HN   two fisherman
   Cambridge - "conversion"
   2 wounded Healers

WIPF *and* STOCK *Publishers*
199 West 8th Avenue, Suite 3 • Eugene, Oregon 97401
Tel. (541) 344-1528 • Fax. (541) 344-1506
Web site: www.wipfandstock.com

Emil Ray

CASCADE *Books*
PICKWICK *Publications*
WIPF & STOCK
RESOURCE *Publications*

Dear Kenneth,

Greetings from Wipf and Stock Publishers! We trust this note finds you well.

Here are your presentation copies of *Ministry on the Edge: Reflections of an Iinterfaith Pioneer, Civil Rights Advocate, and the First Bioethicist.*

Your book is ACTIVE and available for order.

Retail price: $31.00

Cost to you with 50% author discount: $15.50
(Note: Books purchased at the author discounted rate are non-returnable.)

To receive your author discount you may place an order directly to our customer service department. Please inform them that you are an author ordering your own book and provide them with your account number, **16584.** Online orders are not set up to calculate author discounts.

How to contact us:
Phone: (541) 344-1528
Fax: (541) 344-1506
Email: orders@wipfandstock.com
Jennifer Horning: Jennifer@wipfandstock.com

When the title is made ACTIVE it will be available via:
W & S Customer Service: Immediately
Wipf & Stock online: in 2 weeks
Amazon: in 6–8 weeks
Ingram: in 4 weeks

Thank you for your partnership in publishing this book.

On stage at a rally with Nelson Mandela in the run up to the 1994 elections in Paarl.

With American singer Paul Simon at our home in Constantia in 1992. We were celebrating our successful cooperation during the apartheid struggle and Simon pledged his continued support for me, now participating in the new politics of democracy.

Left: My return to the ministry at Piketberg Uniting Reformed Church, 2004. Looking on are Archbishop Njongonkulu Ndungane, and co-pastor Walter Philander.

Below: Joyous moments for Elna and me, with Archbishop Emeritus Desmond Tutu at a celebration of the presidential pardon at Bishop's Court, 2003.

© Oryx Media

© Oryx Media

Him be the glory in the church and in Christ Jesus to all generations, forever and ever.'

May grace and peace be with you,
Nkosi sikilel' iAfrika!

Yours faithfully,

Allan Boesak

P.S. Because of the public import of the issue at hand I shall treat this as an open letter.

13

AT THE RISK OF CHASING RAINBOWS: Race, Reconciliation and Justice in the Rainbow Nation

'This reconciliation thing ...'

They knew I was coming, and they must have been waiting for me, although 'lying in wait' might have been just as apt, considering the way they ambushed me with their opening gambit. In late 2001, a well-known American foundation with a proud record of doing great work in South Africa invited a number of persons, all with impeccable struggle credentials, to a brainstorming session in Johannesburg. The purpose was to determine how, after ten years of involvement in this country and with the new political situation unfolding, the foundation could still help, and how their work could be even more focused.

The venue, quite appropriately I thought, was the Apartheid Museum. It was going to be a memorable evening for me, and not just because of the discussions inside. They were waiting at the entrance, five of them, all young people. As I entered they greeted me and the spokesperson stepped forward. Without preamble, he said, 'Comrade Boesak, we've been waiting to speak to you. This reconciliation thing, it's not working.'

Somewhat stumped, I asked, 'What do you mean?' One of them explained. They had been watching 'this thing', he said, 'this thing' being the process of reconciliation. While it seemed to have been very good for white people, for black people, 'in the townships where we live', nothing had come of it, and nothing was seen of it. Besides, and here the back-up chorus from the others could be heard, they had the distinct feeling that white people just 'don't care' and, what was worse, had not shown that they understood at all what black people had gone through and what it had cost to offer the hand of friendship and forgiveness which, they felt, 'was being slapped away'. Then came a telling phrase: 'We are being wasted.' Not 'the process', not 'reconciliation' or 'forgiveness', but *we*. We, our past, our struggle, our feelings, our willingness to make it work, our faith that it can and must work.

By this time, slightly recovered, I had my thinking cap on and wondered if I could push him a bit. 'But what about Mr Mandela?' I asked, hoping that the invocation of *that name* would change the direction of the conversation, as it always seemed to be able to do. Would a bit of 'Madiba magic' perhaps change the minds of these youths? It was not to be. 'What about Madiba? If I were made president of the country and given his millions, I would also forgive everybody.' They laughed, but the humour was not heart-felt. I was saved by someone taking my arm and leading me inside. It took a while for my mind to focus on the conversation once inside.

Now, seven years later, this is a subject of serious discussion and reconsideration in black circles. Now, not just young people with limited education and limited opportunities, with anger and frustration at the unchanged life in the townships, but those of us with a strong educational background, excellent opportunities in a different South Africa and recognised intellectual abilities, are asking the same questions.

'What actually happened? and 'Was it worth it?'

Someone of the caliber of Dr Mamphela Ramphele speaks soberingly of 'a miracle that never was'. And even Archbishop Emeritus Desmond Tutu expresses his frustration that it has not all worked out as he had so fervently hoped and worked so hard for. Speaking of the government's inexcusable sluggishness with regard to the 'urgent reparations' the TRC had recommended, Tutu asked in an interview with a Boston newspaper in 2003:

> Can you explain how a black person wakes up in a squalid ghetto today almost ten years after freedom? Then goes to work in town, which is still largely white, in palatial homes. And at the end of the day, he goes home to squalour? I don't know why those people don't just say, 'To hell with peace. To hell with Tutu and the Truth Commission.'

Indeed. There is a growing anger at this failure of government, and it couples with waxing discontent with the very work of the TRC itself and the fact that we know more about the truth that still lies buried than the truth that was allowed to be heard. The main players themselves did much to undermine the legitimacy of the process: Mr De Klerk's successful court action to block publication of certain documents, his unashamed defence of apartheid as a policy that would have worked if given the proper chance and his offensive 'let bygones be bygones' rhetoric. The angry response of the ANC to certain aspects of the TRC process; the baleful resistance of Chief Mangosuthu Buthelezi or P.W. Botha, who has gone to his grave unrepentant, unreconciled and unforgiven by most of the country. The failure of the TRC to bring to book those who should have taken political responsibility for apartheid: the political leaders, the generals, big business. There is cynicism also at the way reconciliation has become a lucrative business for some on top of the profits they raked off apartheid, and at the world's persistence that South Africa is a model of reconciliation. Black South Africans know better, even though we continue to speak hopefully, if sometimes naively, of the 'rainbow nation'.

'De Nile is not just a River in Egypt'

The above expression has become a standard joke in black political circles, but the serious undertone is coming through more and more when we talk about racism in South Africa. It is very much like the joke about the journalist from abroad who travelled throughout South Africa and ended up perplexed that he could not find one person who had supported apartheid. But the denial of the existence of racism, our failure to acknowledge it and hence our failure to deal with it is no longer a joking matter.

This denial started with our unwillingness as a nation to recognise our past and the awful shadows it casts over our present and our future. We buried this past under an avalanche of selective forgetfulness all covered with the excuse of the need for reconciliation. Forgetting that reconciliation is not possible without honest confrontation with the past, that papering over the cracks cannot stop the walls from crumbling and, worst of all, forgetting the warning of Dietrich Bonhoeffer from his experiences with Hitler's Germany, that 'grace is never cheap', we decided that honest recognition of racism, its insidious tenacity, its endless ability to mutate, its scary tendency to hide itself in the guise of rational argument, was too explosive, too disturbing. So we decided to bury that past, hoping that our collective gratitude for the miracle would not just make us forget, but could actually change us.

At the preparatory conferences for the big UN conference on racism in 1998, we began to realise our mistake. We could hardly speak on the subject and therefore could not prepare properly for the conference. The debates were emotional and sometimes almost hysterical. Hours were spent debating 'where to draw the line', whether to include colonialism and slavery, and whether colonialism and apartheid could even be mentioned in one breath. Our own government was so scared of the slavery issue (and reparations!) that it battled hard to keep it completely off the agenda, and to keep its own relationship with the erstwhile slave-holding Western nations safe. Some wanted to speak only of 'apartheid racism', meaning 'Afrikaner racism' but not of 'white racism'. I remember Charles Villa-Vicencio of the Institute for Justice and Reconciliation responding furiously to a veritable tirade of denial by Dene Smuts of the DA: 'Now *that* is a South Africa I do *not* want to live in!'

Now of course our discourse is overshadowed not by theoretical debates but by a reality of racism as shocking in its ugliness as in its vehement denials. Today, those people who in 1994 called Nelson Mandela a 'kaffir' and who for racist reasons voted for the National Party and F.W. de Klerk, its white leader, still cannot live down their shame. I write out the dreaded 'K word' even as I shudder, for the sense of shock and shame should not be ameliorated by the niceties of editing.

Today, something like a 'Native Club' exists, in which 'Natives' are 'black Africans', and 'coloureds' and 'Indians' are told that they are not welcome. Disguised as 'intellectual endeavour', this club completely disregards the fact that the first 'natives' of this country were the Khoekhoe. Today there exists a climate in which a white employee who suffers sexual harassment from her black boss and then lays a charge is accused of racism. This same climate allows the abuse of the provisions of the law regarding affirmative action to create caveats like 'ethnic African' or, in total oblivion of the needs of the country, to place skin colour above all else, skills included. Such actions do not even try to serve the interests of the country; they serve the needs of instant gratification, the culture of entitlement and seek to make only one point: the race point.

Of course there is the argument that black people (all of us) cannot be racist because racism only manifests itself in relations of power. In the Black Consciousness days that argument was used, but then it had more substance. It was argued then that racism is not mere feelings or attitudes; it is systemic and structural, and finds expression in the systems of society. It is so dangerous because it is linked with power – political, social and economic. All of that is true. But Black Consciousness never argued that racism is *only* structural. Proponents of Black Consciousness knew too well the myriad ways in which black humanity had been assaulted and undermined and destroyed outside of the structures of power. How else could they have been so hurt by the Cape Flats attitude to one of the greatest leaders in this country's history? Besides, that point is surely moot now. Since at least 1994 governmental power, in the many devastating ways it can be manifested, has been in the hands of black people. And that this power has been used for racist ends cannot be disputed.

Today, we must speak of the white farmer who 'punished' his black worker by dragging him behind his tractor until he died and of the magistrate who imposed a fine of R30 000 on the farmer; of the young boy who was shot because it was thought he was a 'baboon'; of the young girl in Limpopo who was 'caught stealing' and covered with white paint. At least this is an improvement on such incidents as that which occurred in 1973, when an eleven-year-old black boy was captured by three white men when he attempted to steal a few pieces of coal in the dead of winter. They stripped him and forced him to sit down on the hot boiler of their steam locomotive. Four weeks after the incident a doctor who examined the boy's buttocks described the burns as of 'the most severe degree'. According to the Afrikaans Sunday paper *Rapport* on 16 December 1973, the magistrate who heard the case sentenced each of the men to six lashes and three years imprisonment. He then suspended the prison sentences. Thirty years ago such injustice did not matter. It matters now; but to whom?

Today the racism that 'doesn't exist' manifests itself in the casual callousness of youth, those who went to school after 1994, 'Mandela's white children': the three white kids who kicked a vagrant to death while he was seeking shelter for the night on the porch of a suburban church; the 'Waterkloof Four'; the Reitz residence incident on the campus of the University of the Free State; the young white man who drove all the way to the black township called Skierlik and killed four residents, including a four-year-old girl.

But here's the thing. In these instances, the first, most spontaneous reaction from certain sections of the white community was not outrage and condemnation, but denial and justification. There was shocked response – not at the horror of the killings, but at the possible judicial consequences. There was justification: white youth are angry and disillusioned (with our society? with government? with democracy?). Should anger at affirmative action justify murder? This reaction from the same community howling for the death penalty because of the crime and violence haunting South Africa. It is almost as if most of the white community still do not believe it possible for a white person to go to prison (let alone be hanged!) for killing a black person.

This attitude is perhaps best, if painfully, demonstrated by the reaction of an Afrikaner friend immediately after the incident on the Free State University campus. This man is not at all a person who is clinging to the past, disgruntled with a black government, or with secret longings for the old days when 'everything worked so much better'. Yet even he, in his response to my public comments on the incident, instinctively turned defensive. Why, he wanted to know, did I not pronounce myself on the racism 'from both sides', condemning the 'racism in reverse' of the black students in their reaction to the incident? For me our exchange was a lesson in the realities of the rainbow nation. He did not try to justify the vile acts of those four white students, but he tried to trivialise them by placing the reaction of the black students on the same level as the acts of the white students and in this way argue that both were racist. Somehow a greater tolerance, an almost super-human willingness to forgive, was expected from the black students. Thus it was their 'racism' we were expected to concentrate on. I wrote back:

> How on earth is this possible? Nothing those black students had to say was nearly as bad as what the white students had done. I wondered what white people had to do to get the reaction of righteous anger and indignation from the white community that other despicable criminal acts receive. A reaction not sugar-coated with psychological or political excuses.
>
> Racism is pathologically denied, any reference to the past is angrily rejected; meaningful reconciliation based on justice is not acceptable and our shallow reconciliation is held up as the ideal. We are subjected to a curious inversion: apartheid was 'good' because everything 'worked better'; racism does not exist but 'racism in reverse' does. Racism is redefined: racism is affirmative action and sport quotas; in fact, the whole transformation project. Somebody who drives into a black

township killing innocent people is 'a boy with problems'. Racism is black economic empowerment, and when someone like economist Sampie Terreblanche brings statistics to prove that white people have in fact benefitted more from BEE than blacks, that their wealth over the last 15 years has tripled and that the median income of white households has improved 20% over black households, the newspaper has no room for all the angry letters and SMSes. They call him 'crazy' and 'unbalanced' and claim that 'real' economists do not take him seriously, thus we had better not too.

White people's self-obsessed politics allow no other reality than their own. The only pain worth speaking of is their own, and it is the pain of loss of power, the fear of losing land, as if we [black people] had never lost anything, and the fear of real equality: that pain of sharing fewer opportunities and privileges. The pain of hunger, of real hopelessness and the illnesses and pestilences that only inflict the poor, of human degradation and humiliation that only the poor know – all this does not count, or has to be subjected to the luxurious suffering of whites. Our claim to equality is experienced as a direct attack on what is still seen as white privilege. Even the perverse equality of the suffering because of crime is experienced as if whites alone are the victims. The real inequalities – the economic ones – are still normal. Let me immediately say that this is not all white people's fault. Jody Kollapen pointed to the sore place. We, in our urge to make 'reconciliation' work, and to secure the economic position of the new elite, 'stuck out the hand of reconciliation too far'. The chairperson of the Human Rights Commission says that our government, in leaning over backwards to please white people, has taken our own people for granted, and has in the process neglected their deepest needs, longings and rights.

As a Christian I can never say that reconciliation 'goes too far'. But what I can and will say is that we have not taken reconciliation seriously enough, that we have abused that evangelical reality for the sake of selfish politics, and in the process abused our people's Christian convictions regarding forgiveness and reconciliation. That is the reason for the reproach we have been hearing all week from black people all over the country, that blacks have reached out to whites in forgiveness and friendship and that that hand has been rejected with disdain. We both know: our country has reached a crossroads.

I draw attention to this letter here because I think the issues raised in it are more representative of our current situation than we would like to admit. Even as I write, I still wonder whether I should include these harsh words here. But at this point I am more afraid of the consequences of not saying them, for at the heart of it all the disturbing question remains: are we for real, or are we chasing rainbows?

We certainly will be if we do not change our attitudes on the race issue; if we drown ourselves in rivers of denial; if we do not bring rationality, honesty and integrity into our discourse on race. We need to realise that racism is a monster we have not yet faced, and that in facing it we have to face it together, as a people, looking each other in the eye, creating new bonds of trust and holding onto the faith that together we shall, in recognising and acknowledging racism, define it, fight it, overcome it. Amanda Gouws, political scientist at Stellenbosch University wrote about the 'Waterkloof Four'. She concludes: 'If we teach our children that they are not part of the nation, they will act as if they are not part of the nation.'

Chasing rainbows?

South Africans' experiences with race matters are not divorced from our experiences with the reconciliation process. The questions we have been raising with growing urgency have everything to do with how we have understood reconciliation and how this understanding has shaped our expectations.

South Africa's Truth and Reconciliation Commission's (TRC) work has left a huge legacy, and South Africa and the world are still in the process of evaluating it. I think it is fair to say that its success is mainly reflected in the fact that we have been able to create a platform to break the silence around all those unspeakable things that happened during the reign of apartheid, giving some victims, to some extent, the opportunity to speak out and bare their souls to a nation that by and large was willing to listen. It is true, as some were quick to point out, that in fact very little of the truth about human rights abuses actually did come out, but nonetheless enough of that truth was heard to make us understand the horrific nature of the beast we had been saddled with for so long.

Furthermore, the TRC did create a context for the hard work of political accommodation, the breaking down of barriers and the building of pockets of trust, which otherwise would have been almost impossible to achieve. Whatever the difficulties we may now face, and these are both legion and profound, the foundations for nation building laid down in the work of the Commission are infinitely better than the situation that would have existed had the expectations of violence and mayhem post-1994 been fulfilled.

More than ten years of grappling with these issues have raised a host of questions as fundamental as they are unavoidable, and I am not sure just how ready we are to recognise and face them. Of course, hindsight brings also awareness of complexities once not seen or even expected and hence not taken into account.

But we have been warned. Early on Ibbo Mandaza of Zimbabwe pointed to what he considered one of the main problems in Zimbabwe: the requirement to succumb to what he called the 'ideology of reconciliation'. He warned South Africa not to ignore political and economic realities for the sake of political acceptance in the international community. And Mahmood Mandani, like others of us, expressed concern that South Africans continued to speak in terms of 'victims' and 'perpetrators' of apartheid. The focus is too narrow, he argued. There were some whites who perpetrated the system of apartheid, but *all* whites benefited from it. This was how we should address the question of guilt, repentance, reparations and restitution. He was right. We were focusing on what he called 'the fractured elite' (perpetrators and victims) instead of on society as a whole, on individuals instead of on the systems of injustice that apartheid essentially was, so that justice never became a demand for systemic reform of society as a whole. We did not seem to get beyond the single perpetrator or the single victim.

This narrow emphasis spawned a further injustice. It created the impression that Afrikaans-speaking whites, the most active 'perpetrators' of apartheid, were the only guilty ones. English-speaking whites, who benefited hugely from colonialism and apartheid, both denied and escaped all blame. Generally speaking, English-speaking South Africans' arrogant denial of their guilt in this matter remains one of the most stubborn stumbling blocks to genuine reconciliation in South Africa today.

For me, personally, as for many others who take reconciliation seriously, the moments of genuine remorse and repentance that did occur, followed by genuine forgiveness on a very personal level, though rare, were priceless. These moments represent that crucial spiritual element without which reconciliation is not possible and without which pure political accommodation remains a singularly insecure foundation for our common future. But despite this, and despite our gratitude for the work of the TRC, we have to admit that there have been major failures. I offer a broader context for my argument in my recently published *The Tenderness of Conscience: African Renaissance and the Spirituality of Politics*.

Understanding reconciliation

At the outset, the ANC government had set for itself the goals of 'reconciliation, reconstruction and development'. These, the 'kernel of the social transformation project' could be reached by the 'attainment of the twin goals of socio-economic justice and the restoration of moral order in our society'. This is according to Johnny de Lange, currently deputy minister of justice in the South African Cabinet. The government regarded our TRC as 'unique' because the aim was to achieve both justice and reconciliation, not just one or the other. De Lange refers to justice in the 'broadest sense' as 'collective justice, social justice, a restorative justice … aimed at nation building and reconciliation', which focuses on the future rather than on the past, on understanding rather than vengeance, on reparation rather than retaliation, on ubuntu rather than victimisation. De Lange rejoices in our success, because we have moved 'beyond' punishment and justice is not only done but 'seen to be done'. It is restorative justice, but also contains essential elements of retributive justice in that the truth is told, lies are exposed and the perpetrators are becoming known. It may not be perfect justice, De Lange concedes, but then perfect justice does not exist, and 'compromises have to be made for the greater good'. All this is to achieve an even greater goal, namely 'to heal our nation, to restore the faith of those in our country and the international community in our common future'.

For the limited purposes of this discussion, I shall briefly approach the issue of justice from three points of view. First, I shall speak of justice as the restoration of integrity, second, as the restoration of human dignity, and third, as the restoration of human contentment. The restoration I speak of is not a restoration of the status quo before the ravages of colonialism and apartheid. I speak of the restoration of the intentions of God as they are spelt out in the announcements of the prophets, in the longing of the songwriters of the Old Testament, and in the life and work of Jesus of Nazareth. The relevance of these insights of faith shall be immediately clear to all, I hope.

Justice as the restoration of integrity

Even taking into account De Lange's natural propensities as a lawyer and a politician, one must consider his understanding of justice to be far too narrow, especially as he wishes to place it within the context of reconciliation. De Lange goes even further, adding these majestic words to his exposition: 'Our call for a truth commission did not come from the Constitution or any law, but from our morality as people who want to heal our nation, and restore the faith of those in our country and in the international community in our common future.' This language is common in our politics, and spells out the abiding dilemma of South Africa's politicians. They strive furiously to define our political developments as a secular process, as matters of law and the Constitution, the demands of realpolitik and the vagaries of globalisation. But they cannot escape the intrusion of morality, the appeal to conscience, and the presence of spirituality which are such inalienable elements of South African politics.

This apart from the fact that they have chosen as the link between our political processes and nation-building and socio-economic development reconciliation, that unrelenting, demanding evangelical reality which bears no evasion.

De Lange's, and the government's, dilemma is that even in their narrow definition, justice has not been done, or seen to be done. Their intentions were that the perpetrators of human rights abuses be exposed, and if they willingly told the truth, be given amnesty. The victims would have the satisfaction of 'having heard the truth' and of 'reparations' by the government. Those perpetrators who did not disclose the full truth or did not come forward would be prosecuted through the 'normal' channels of the law. De Lange was counting on the integrity not just of the TRC process but also of the justice system. He was counting on the integrity of the 'perpetrators'.

The fact is that the number of perpetrators who came forward was relatively small. The justice system did not offer much hope for justice as seen in the failed trials of Magnus Malan, Minister of Defence under P.W. Botha, and the apartheid scientist Dr Wouter Basson. They both refused to apply for amnesty and their trial costs were borne by the state. De Lange complained that the legal system 'at the time' suffered from a 'serious crisis of credibility, legitimacy and efficacy' and, as a result, 'competent, honest, professional investigations and prosecutions could hardly have been expected'.

The problem is that the trial of Basson took place six years into the new democracy and the government had to face the same realities regarding the legal system even then. The new minister for justice,

Bridget Mabandla, at her first public appearance, bemoaned the 'untransformed nature' of the justice system, and today there is open tension between the government and the courts because of the efforts at 'transformation'. My point is that De Lange's 'imperfect justice' is still around, and he is not the one who is paying the price. The government's handling of the matter of reparations is nothing short of scandalous and the insult inflicted upon the victims of human rights abuses does not inspire trust in the integrity of our systems.

The issue of accountability is a problem all South Africans know about, but find hard to address. Those who were called to account for their misdeeds were mostly the foot soldiers, ordinary security policemen and soldiers who carried out orders and who were told that they should do what they did 'for the sake of God and for their country'. But the generals, of the police as well as the armed forces, the scientists and the technicians of apartheid, the politicians who made final decisions, were all left aside. That whole episode left an unhealthy odour hanging in the air.

We are also left to wonder about the 'truth' we had heard. Journalist Terry Bell and Advocate Dumisa Ntsebeza present a strong case on this particular issue in their book *Unfinished Business*. The question is not only how much truth was eventually told but also, even more pertinent, how much truth *survived* to be told. 'In little more than six months in 1993,' they tell us, '... some 44 metric tons of records from the headquarters of the National Intelligence Service alone were destroyed'. That is, shredded, wiped out and incinerated. They conclude that 'the undeniable reality is that many of the principal perpetrators of apartheid were never called to account, but all too often remain in positions of power'. In 2007, for reasons not altogether pure, the government decided to prosecute apartheid police minister

Adriaan Vlok and three others for the attempted murder of Reverend Frank Chikane, and a plea bargain ostensibly ended the matter. The unexpected and courageous act of remorse and confession made by Vlok to Chikane, one-time secretary general of the South African Council of Churches, and Chikane's consequent forgiveness of Vlok (which seemed to have prompted the prosecution), has shone an entirely new light on reconciliation in South Africa. It occurred completely outside the official process. It may not have completely turned the tide by itself, but it has set a benchmark for integrity and genuine reconciliation that the country has not experienced from senior politicians and it now leaves them exposed, if not ashamed. It is also a singular testimony to the power of the Holy Spirit in the life of a person and an example of genuine reconciliation inspired by the example of Christ. Yet in light of the tardiness in the prosecution of apartheid criminals in general, I fail to see how Vlok's late and isolated prosecution could in any way serve the process of genuine reconciliation.

Adding to the problem of Vlok's prosecution is the fact that significant sectors which in their own way represented the full weight of apartheid injustices were not called to account, or were called and simply refused to cooperate. I am referring to the media, government agencies and the judiciary. The distressing rows around racism on the Bench, with accusations not coming from the general public but from judges, proves the reach of the consequences of such lapses.

If justice is the restoration of integrity, South Africa is suffering from a failure of justice, and it is mostly the weak, the poor and the vulnerable who are paying the price.

Justice as the restoration of human dignity
No Future without Forgiveness, the title of Archbishop Emeritus Tutu's

well-known book, expresses his firmly held belief and conviction. He calls forgiveness a 'gospel imperative' which Christians cannot seek to avoid. At the amnesty hearings of the TRC Tutu insisted that 'the victims of injustice and oppression must ever be ready to forgive'. Tutu exerted his authority and the stamp of a Christian understanding of reconciliation was firmly impressed on the TRC proceedings. Whether this was right is not the issue. It happened.

Many were unhappy about this. They claimed that victims of apartheid human rights abuses were placed in an atmosphere where the strong impression was given that forgiveness was the only acceptable response. The hearings were structured in such a way, said Philip Wilson, that any expression of a desire for revenge would seem out of place: 'Virtues of forgiveness and reconciliation were so loudly applauded that emotions of revenge, hatred and bitterness were rendered unacceptable, an ugly intrusion on a peaceful, healing process.' Wilson, who attended the hearings, took this to be a kind of emotional blackmail.

Even worse, Audrey Chapman, another interested observer, has charged that at the Human Rights Violations hearings over which Tutu presided, more emphasis was placed on eliciting forgiveness from the victims than on securing knowledge of wrongdoing from the perpetrators. Under these circumstances there was hardly any possibility for the restoration of human dignity. Once again justice was denied. The TRC did not succeed in creating a context in which the perpetrators of human rights abuses ever felt the need to show genuine remorse and repentance in response to the offer of forgiveness from their victims. And there are distressing examples of policemen acting out remorse and then joking about it in the crudest terms to journalists immediately outside the room.

Now I know the argument here is that the legal brief of the TRC did not require remorse, confession or repentance from such perpetrators. It only required telling the truth about an incident. But then it remains extraordinary just how much pressure was put on the victims to forgive, even if forgiveness was not asked for or humanly possible. But then why call it 'reconciliation'? We have not begun to consider the damage that was done, layered upon the pain of the past in addition to the pain of retelling without hope of any resolution, closure, restitution or restoration. In this regard a young woman is quoted as saying, 'I don't know if I will ever be able to forgive. I carry this ball of anger within me and I don't know where to begin dealing with it. The oppression (of apartheid) was bad, but what is much worse, what makes me even angrier, is that they are trying to dictate my forgiveness.' I think this is unforgivable.

Forgiveness is indeed a 'gospel imperative', as Desmond Tutu says. But forgiveness is a *willing response* as an expression of our obedience to the prayer of Jesus that we should forgive 'as our heavenly Parent has forgiven us'. Forgiveness is always freely given. If forgiveness is given when the perpetrator sees nothing that he or she should be forgiven for, and there is no remorse or confession, this is extraordinary and an even greater cause for thanksgiving. But forgiveness can never be forced on anyone. No one should be coerced into forgiving, however subtly. Forgiveness is in itself an act of such sensitivity, such sacrificial self-giving, such enormous love that any attempt to coax it out of people robs it of its intrinsic value. It can never be taken for granted and is always the prerogative of the victim. Clearly most human beings need help to come to that point. But there is a vast difference between help and subtle pressure, especially in public, and especially on national television.

There is a place for rightful anger, and the Commission should have given it that place. It is impossible not to be angry at what happened to people under apartheid and it is grossly unfair to act as if that anger is an offence to God. That anger must not be denied, managed or manipulated. It must be given respectful hearing. Just as the victim has to hear the truth and the words of contrition, it is necessary for the perpetrator to hear the words of anger. The perpetrator has to *see* and *hear* the consequences of the wrongful deed in order to understand the depth of the wrong that was done, as well as the depth of the forgiveness given.

The miracle of God's grace is not that we manipulate the anger of the young woman into forgiving by making her feel guilty about her anger. Rather, it is that she is moved to overcome her anger, to willingly forgive, and as she remembers what has been done to her, she thinks back not in hatred or bitterness or despair, but in gratitude at having been able to reclaim her humanity and in the process that of her torturer, in order to create both a new humanity and a new beginning for both of them.

Inasmuch as the TRC denied people this, it denied its own mission. It subjected the victims of apartheid to the pain and humiliation of 'story telling' and victimised them again in that they were denied the freedom of righteous anger and the opportunity to challenge the perpetrator on the basis of equality. Within the context of apartheid and its aftermath, it is the expression of anger that brings the first level of equality, which then frees us for the equality of love. Only in the freedom of rightful anger can one find the freedom for that anger to be overcome, which in turn can lead to the freedom of forgiveness and the joyful liberation of the way of reconciliation.

In not being nearly as insistent about prescribing the response of the perpetrators and beneficiaries of apartheid as with the victims on this point, the TRC perpetuated the powerlessness of the victims because it exploited both their faith and their powerlessness to exact remorse. The same was not done with the powerful, who were too protected by the institutions of power: parliament, the courts, the media, government. The same is true for the powerful institutions themselves. The TRC chose to make the radical (Christian) interpretation of reconciliation the litmus test for the victims, especially those who are Christians. Inasmuch as the TRC failed to apply that test universally, it failed both the victims and the gospel.

There are more issues than the confines of this book allows me to discuss, vastly painful areas the TRC was not able or willing to cover and which are virtually ignored in the discussions on reconciliation, perhaps partly because of our pathological need 'to move on'. It is one thing to forgive the enemy, even though that is hard enough. But how does one forgive betrayal by one of your own: the security policemen, the informers, the torturers who lived in the black communities? Blacks have been asked to forgive white people who gave the orders, and the whites who benefited from their deeds. But what about the restoration of those black communities? Truly awful things happened there. There have been moving acts of reconciliation between blacks and whites, but hardly any between blacks who in the struggle stood on either side of the political divide. I fear that we have hardly scratched the surface.

Justice as the restoration of human contentment

I have borrowed the phrase 'human contentment' from John Calvin's sermon on Deuteronomy 24. It is a sermon that epitomises the radical Calvinism I have come to admire and embrace. It is about poverty and justice, about the rights of the poor, the quality and meaning of labour and the quality of community. In the question of economic justice, it is not just personal satisfaction that counts. It is the systemic transformation which extends justice to the *other* that helps society to function better. Calvin radicalises the notion of the 'neighbour' to undermine selfish economic tendencies as well as uncaring politics. And then there is that sentence that shifts not only the paradigm of fighting poverty but also, dramatically, the measure of our success in fighting poverty: 'It is not enough to know that the poor person has work or receives charity; it is necessary to know if the poor person is content.'

In de-linking reconciliation and justice, the TRC and the whole reconciliation process has completely missed this crucial point. And this is what we mean when we apply it to the political and socio-economic ramifications of reconciliation as we understand it. It is not when government or big business or the media moguls are satisfied that justice has been done and that reconciliation 'works'. It is when the poor, the wounded, the vulnerable, are content. To be content is to be fulfilled, in body and spirit. It is when the fulfillment of one's human potential is taken seriously, when one is allowed to flourish, when one's rights are recognised, honoured, respected and upheld.

The TRC has taken issue with the government on the question of reparations for the victims of human rights abuses. The sum of around $4 000 per victim, which the government finally seems to have agreed to, has hardly enhanced the dignity of the victims, the process or, for that matter, the government itself. But the issue goes somewhat deeper. The TRC failed to make big business accountable for their part in the creation and maintenance of apartheid. It did not see, and did not take up the challenge of, the *causative* role played by the systems of white political dominance, racial capitalism and apartheid over a considerable period of time. It did not, argues economist and historian Sampie Terreblanche, 'face the problem of those systems, in a deliberate and systemic way, bringing about and sustaining white wealth and white privileges on the one hand, and black poverty, black deprivation and black humiliation on the other'. In short, it let big business off the hook.

This presented a second problem. The TRC, failing to call big business properly to account, retreated to the shifting sands of charity, appealing to the business community to *voluntarily* compensate black people for their suffering under apartheid. Yet the exploitation of blacks did not happen voluntarily. It was compulsory and systemic. It was based, Terreblanche reminds us, on an economic and political system embedded in a network of compulsory legislation and justified by ideologies that were propagated as self-evident truths. To expect that big business would be prepared to compensate, and to the necessary degree, for the injustices committed for almost a century is not only totally idealistic but also hopelessly naive. And in truth, the issue here is not charity but economic justice, and it is a tragedy that the TRC did not see or insist upon the relationship between reconciliation and socio-economic justice.

The socio-economic injustices that plague our society are symptoms of the deeper malady that ails us: we are far from the reconciled society we claim to be. Those who disagree argue that South Africa is already experiencing a 'rapid de-racialisation of capital'. But that is patently untrue. The most recent studies show an alarming growth in the levels of poverty, and the gap between rich and poor in South Africa is widening, as is the gap between the wealthy, new, black elite and the poor masses. A recent study by Eighty20, a South African think tank, reveals that up to 60% of the population has to survive on less than $3 per day, while not less than 15% are trying to make a living from less than $1 a day. This is utterly shocking.

In 2003, Black Economic Empowerment deals amounted to over $7 billion. But that staggering amount was divided amongst basically the wealthiest and most powerful six BEE groups in the country. That is not 'de-racialisation of capital' at all. That is pure myth-making. All it means is that the tight circle of the new, empowered black elite have joined the white rich and powerful and the rich are still getting richer.

There is also growing evidence that per capita income growth will diminish as a result of increasing dependency ratios, increased burdens on health systems, constrained investment in productivity and reduced labour forces, because of, among other things, the impact of AIDS. In South Africa, the rate of infections has gone up – there are almost 5 million daily – and AIDS deaths have now reach the staggering total of 900 per day with almost 200 of those children.

All the talk of reconciliation, all the slogans about the rainbow nation, will remain empty unless reconciliation means compassionate justice done to these, the least of the family of Jesus.

Reconciliation: love and compassionate justice

'A just and well-regulated government,' said John Calvin in a sermon on Psalm 82: 3, 'will be distinguished for maintaining the rights of the poor and afflicted.' What is required is not charity that would leave systemic injustices untouched. Calvin is not impressed with superficial morality or political piety of either the wealthy or those in positions of political power. And nor should we be impressed. We cannot be satisfied with programmes and slogans that keep the poor chanting and dancing but leave them hungry. The measure for good governance is not how we please the G8, but our conduct towards the poor. In other words, conduct measured by political and economic policies that guarantee justice and are driven by compassion. And it begins by recognising the rights of the poor.

A social situation is just, argues North American philosopher and theologian Nicholas Wolterstorff, when the rights of people in that situation are honoured. He speaks of rights as 'ground requirements'. These rights, aside from being grounded in justice and in the love of God, also mean that 'we are not beggars in life'. Put differently, it is the *right* of the poor not to be beggars in life, not to be poor, but to be content. Reconciliation is about confession and confrontation with evil; it is about conversion and forgiveness; it is about personal and societal transformation; it is about restitution, restoration and compassionate justice.

There are those who fervently disagree, from politicians like Thabo Mbeki to theologians like Charles Villa-Vicencio and academics like Jakes Gerwel. For them, reconciliation in South Africa should be seen as political, a purely secular process of the accommodation of socio-political and historically determined realities. They think all talk of the 'neighbour', of rights and compassionate justice is 'romanticising', 'excessive spiritualisation', 'asking too much', and hence creating expectations that in the real world cannot be fulfilled.

It all depends where one stands. And in the black Reformed tradition in South Africa we have formulated this in the Confession of Belhar adopted by the erstwhile Dutch Reformed Mission Church in 1986. In Article Four, Belhar proclaims God as 'the One who brings justice and true peace, and that in a world filled with injustice and enmity God in a special way is the God of the destitute, the poor and the wronged ... That the church as possession of God is called to stand where God stands, namely against injustice and with the wronged.' It is this confession out of the African context that has reshaped our expression of faith and infused us with a new spirituality without which, we know

now, the church would not have survived.

As South Africa's transition unfolds, it continues to show us not only how far we have come, but also how much we have still to do. Our work towards genuine reconciliation has just begun, and by divine irony it is revealed in both the systemic distortions, the cries of the poor and the conversion of Adriaan Vlok. A new door for genuine reconciliation has been opened. We have an opportunity to do it right. And if we do this, our horizons established by our vision of justice, our strength renewed by the hopes of the poor, our faith rooted in the belief that it is possible to do what is right, we will rediscover our voice, re-establish our belief that the world can be changed.

If this is chasing rainbows, so be it.

14

'STANDING WITH GOD IN HIS HOUR OF GRIEVING': CHRISTIANS AND MUSLIMS LIVING TOGETHER IN SOUTH AFRICA

A togetherness of long standing

When the question of Christian-Muslim relations is asked in the coloured communities in and around Cape Town, it is usually treated with a sense of bored wonderment. After all, is the feeling, we have lived together for so long, have been neighbours, schoolmates and friends for as long as anyone can remember, have been dumped together in the same neighbourhoods under apartheid's Group Areas Act. Together we have suffered the same humiliating apartheid racial classification and were allotted the same social and political standing in the ethnotocracy South Africans for so long experienced as an inescapable, if totally unwanted, part of their lives. This, among other things, is what makes a place like District Six, as memory as well as symbol, so special.

On holy days we rejoiced together, sharing gifts, good wishes and food on Christmas and Eid, praying for each other during Lent and Ramadan. Friendships formed at school were, in my experience, genuine, lasting and largely free from ethnic, racial or religious tensions. Intermarriage between Muslims and Christians has over the years been frequent and family ties are as strong or as weak as the families themselves want them to be – in other words, normal. Family names are shared with no sense of embarrassment at all, but it is when one stumbles across a name such as Achmat van Heyningen or Fatima Viljoen that one realises how thorough and truly delightful the mix has become over the years.

These communities were aware of and sensitive to the diverse nature of South African society long before their white counterparts, who really only began to understand South Africa's diversity, with some sense of shock, after 1994. The sense of shock came with the realisation of the need for the essential equality of all religions before the law, and more importantly the wholehearted respect for other religions besides Christianity. It also means an acute awareness of the hybrid nature not just of the Cape communities but also of South African society as a whole. Most in these communities were rejoicing in the rich mixture of culture, colour and traditions long before the important studies of Hans Heese on the genealogy of South Africa's diverse people brought home forcefully just how ridiculous the notion of 'pure whiteness', had always been in South Africa. Recent DNA studies are making this fact even clearer.

This is not to say, of course, that coloured people were blissfully unaware of the considerable differences in our faiths, rituals and outlook on life. And despite all the familiarity with each other's way of life, there remained significant areas cloaked in religious mystery. The mysterious did not easily become the suspicious, however, and whatever tensions may have arisen from not knowing or not completely understanding one another's religions were evidently not considered important enough to threaten the basic togetherness that these communities seem to have experienced. Each seemed to be willing to accord the other the measure of respect and distance that are always necessary to make genuine diversity work.

But family ties and good neighbourliness, as important as these may be, cannot be the only reasons for the remarkable relationship Christians and Muslims in this country have maintained for such a long time. Other compelling factors ought to be considered.

First among these, I suppose, is the shared history of slavery in the Cape, the shared realities of suffering and oppression, the shared efforts at resistance and the shared longing for freedom. The slaves who were brought to the Cape from Malaya, the Indonesian Archipelago and other areas brought Islam with them and formed all sorts of alliances with slaves imported from Africa, and with the slaves and indigenous people who had been baptised into the Christian faith. These alliances had an enormous impact on life in South Africa: from the formation of the 'coloured' people to the birth of the Afrikaans language and the expressions of culture and music so peculiar to the Cape. And much else besides.

The revival of interest in the history of slavery and the ramifications of that history for South Africa, after conspicuous neglect and deliberate marginalisation over the last decade or so, are destined, I predict, to bring a new dimension to the role these communities are seeking to play in the life of the country today. That is, if they themselves understand this history and want this role in South Africa. The denial of slave history by many in these communities has come to an end and new understanding brings new forms of commitment and engagement. The shared sense of history also brings a shared sense of political identity, beyond the forced identity of the 'coloured' label in the political vocabulary and social order of South Africa.

In 1902, before the Union of South Africa was formed in 1910, the first formal, political organisation amongst black people came into being. The African People's Organisation (APO), which came before the African National Congress, was the first attempt to mobilise South Africa's oppressed people into cohesive, effective, political resistance to the racial and economic oppression that were the mainstay of colonial politics in South Africa. The Transvaal Vigilance Association and South African Native Congress followed in 1903.

The importance of the APO is only now in the process of being properly assessed, but I should like to make a few preliminary remarks I consider pertinent to our discussion. First, the fact that the person who succeeded the first leaders of this movement (W. Collins and J.W. Tobin) and who is most frequently associated with this movement, Dr Abdullah Abdurahman, was a Muslim, was not in any way a hindrance to recognition of that leadership by a very broad section of the Cape communities and beyond. Abdurahman found followers in the Christian communities who judged him not on the basis of his religious affiliation but on the soundness of his political convictions and moral stature. In fact, they admired the way in which his spirituality helped in formulating a political philosophy that embodied so many of the values they claimed for themselves. That is remarkable for the age, and for a community in whose life religious faith was, and still is, central.

Second, and I know there is not universal agreement here, in the very name African People's Organisation, and even in the change of name later to the African Political Organisation, we can discern the one major factor that has always been crucial to the progressive politics of the black communities of the Cape, namely non-racialism. They instinctively knew two things: they were part of the broader context of *African* politics and they knew to claim their Africaness. And they knew this fact to be integral to the practice of politics, to the integrity of their activism, even though it would prove more difficult in practice than they had perhaps imagined. Within the constraints of the time, the South African Native Congress agitated for 'Native rights' and the APO at first concentrated on the improvement of 'coloured education' and the 'coloured' franchise, and it is this piece of realpolitik, this bowing to the pressures of the times that has caused friction between Abdurahman and the younger, upcoming, more progressive leadership. But if blame is to be apportioned for racial emphasis in politics, one should then blame all black political organisations of the time. There are reasons, besides historic ones, why the ANC became a formal non-racial organisation only in the 1980s. It might not be spurious to argue that at the time, because the ANC saw itself as an African, meaning *black* African organisation, the APO thus found it necessary to claim the roots and sense of African belonging for the people of 'mixed blood', who also suffered under the racist oppression of white South Africa. When it looked as if the moderate approach of the APO could not be the answer to growing racist oppressive politics, there arose a more radical movement which drew its inspiration from leaders such as John Gomas and James la Guma, falling back on what it knew to be the most authentic expression of the politics of the Cape. But to be fair, by 1907, in light of the push towards the formation of a Union of South Africa, the understanding of the power of a united, non-racial movement took firmer hold. Eighty delegates of black political organisations from different parts of the Cape gathered in Queenstown, including representatives of the APO, and resolved that federation was preferable to unification and that the universal franchise of the Cape should be the basis of a federal franchise. That unity of action formed the basis of black politics in its resistance to a union that would eventually disenfranchise all blacks. In 1909 black delegates from all four colonies, again including the APO, met as the South African Native Convention in Waaihoek,

Bloemfontein, during which they passed resolutions objecting to the colour bar clauses of the draft act and decided to send a delegation to London should the (white) National Convention not heed their pleas.

Third, the strong, insistent current of progressive politics was picked up by Cissy Gool, daughter of Dr Abdurahman, Goolam Gool and Ben Kies. These three were the personification of the new radicalism and the persons who cast the final mould for non-racial politics, which were to be the measure for every political movement and politician henceforth.

I emphasis this piece of history because it is so important within the broader, current politics of South Africa. This insistence on non-racialism is the truest expression of politics in the Cape and this is the strain that runs through to the progressive politics of the 1980s. This is what makes the appearance of 'coloured politics', servile to a racialist agenda as manifested in the Coloured Representative Council and in the recently formed 'Bruin Belange Insiatief' ('Initiative for Coloured Interests'), so unacceptable. Harking back to the failed and bankrupt politics of 'reform' and 'accommodation' within racist structures, such initiatives never convinced nor found any significant support in these communities. The non-racial political insistence was a brand of politics far ahead of the immature, but nonetheless dangerous, racial obsessions of South Africa's white politics.

Non-racial politics is the legacy we have inherited from our ancestors, and this is what persons like me tried to give embodiment to in the struggle against apartheid. We took up that understanding and called for an awareness of self that was more than just individualistic self-definition, of a celebration of togetherness that was more than religious tolerance demanded by a secular constitution. And this is what helped to give shape to relationships between Christians and Muslims during that struggle.

Grieving with God

I am not trying to say that the view I am expounding was universally accepted. There were many on both sides who rejected this view out of hand. Conservative Muslims accused me of hijacking the pure Muslim faith, of undermining its efficacy in the struggle and contaminating the minds of Muslim youth with Christian ideology. Their attacks on young Muslim leaders, like those who founded the Call of Islam, were relentless.

Similarly, conservative Christians accused me of diluting our Christian witness, selling out our faith, and, in the words of one accuser from my own denomination, 'crucifying Jesus all over again' by my disobedience and defiance of 2 Corinthians 6: 14, which reads, 'Do not be mismatched with unbelievers. For what partnership is there between righteousness and lawlessness? Or what fellowship is there between light and darkness?' For them, I was the personification of that unholy fellowship and partnership. I remember well the outraged reactions when my friend and respected Muslim leader Sheik Gamaldien Gabier spoke in my church during an ecumenical prayer service for the release of political detainees. This led to formal charges against me from white colleagues calling for disciplinary action. The vilification from some in my own faith community was visceral, and the first discernable threats I experienced were ironically not from the security police, but from a radical Muslim organisation called Qibla.

Apart from philosophical and theological convictions, I had, in addition, real and meaningful experiences which helped to form my theological understanding in ways my formal seminary training here in South Africa could never do, and perhaps never intended.

In 1979, in a clash between youths and the police in the township of Gugulethu near Cape Town, police shot and killed three young protesters. I was asked by the parents and the community to participate in the funeral service. I invited some colleagues from my church and from the Muslim community to join us. On the day of the funeral, not one of my colleagues turned up, except for a minister of the United Congregational Church. But I was surrounded by a small group of about 19, representing Christians, Muslims, and one Jewish young woman. Among them were Imam Hassan Solomons and Maulana Faried Essack, a very bright young man. Both of them would go on to play important roles in the struggle in the Western Cape.

As we marched arm in arm across the Gugulethu bridge we were confronted with a road block of Casspirs and other police vehicles and a full contingent of armed riot police. The funeral, we were told, had been 'banned' by the government, meaning that only the closest family would be allowed to attend the service. This was of course anathema in the black community. No family is ever alone with their grief: sharing the pain of loss and affirming the everlasting bonds which bind is a thing for and of the whole community. As we were ordered to turn back, we linked our arms together and knelt down to pray. That day I experienced my first arrest by the Security Police.

But this is the important part: we were held first in Philippi jail, just a kilometre or so down the road. We were refused phone calls, visits or the food the friendly and concerned women from the area had sent us. Later that day we were transferred to Wynberg prison. Sitting together in one cell, talking about the meaning of that day, the shared moments of panic, the spontaneous civil disobedience act on the bridge, the one act of resistance that caught the attention of the surrounding community (hence the food!) we were drawn together by much more than a common prison cell. Faried suddenly asked, 'Shall we pray together? And Allan will you join me?' And so began one of the most transforming experiences of my life. We all prayed one by one, sitting in a circle, holding hands. The prayers were honest and emotional, unapologetic, intense. Unashamed, we spoke of our fears and the joy of being deemed worthy of this moment. For most of us, this was the first time we'd been arrested and imprisoned. We prayed for the struggle which for most of us was just beginning, for our hopes for our people, and for South Africa. Faried spoke words of meditation.

The hunger got worse. Robin Petersen, the other young Christian cleric and Rachel, the young Jewish woman, were the only ones who had come somewhat prepared. Robin had a sandwich, Rachel took out a chocolate: a lunch bar. I did not even bring a tooth brush – a mistake I would not make again. 'Why don't we share this?' Robin asked. Again we prayed, I broke the sandwich in smaller pieces, did the same with the chocolate, and we shared it amongst the group of prisoners. Communion in Wynberg prison, with Muslims and a Jew. I hope my inadequate words can convey something of the sense of awe and wonder that permeated that prison cell that moment, and my life, for a long time to come. Much later that evening we made bail. As we went home I knew: there were bonds stronger than blood, more meaningful than sitting in church together. This would remain one of the most unforgettable, and the most formative, moments of my life. It changed me in ways that continue to have meaning even today.

One of the poignant features of that day was when we marched across that bridge, Hassan, Faried and I in front, linked, both of them wearing their clerical garb and I clothed in my preacher's robe (what the then minister of police Louis le Grange used to call my 'battle dress'), carrying my Bible. None of us was ashamed to proclaim her or his faith, to be seen praying in the middle of the road, acknowledging our dependence upon and faith in God and confessing our trust in God who for all of us is a God of justice and liberation. The fact that they prayed to Allah and I prayed through Jesus Christ did not cause us to turn away from each other in embarrassment or to seek the often contrived and unsatisfactory consensus of inter-religious blandness. We took each other seriously as who we were. I did not have to become less of a Christian to make myself acceptable, and they did not have to dilute Islam in order to gain my comradeship. And this acceptance and respect would become one of the hallmarks of the struggle right through the eighties.

I never made a secret of the fact that I was in the struggle not in spite of but *because* of my faith. That my participation in the struggle was not just part of my discipleship of Jesus; it was at the heart of my discipleship. In this way, too, I was a child of Luthuli.

What bound us together was not just the struggle, even though we knew only too well about the centrality of justice, the longing for freedom, the affirmation of our birthright, the meaning of sacrifice and, not less important, the power of having a common cause. But we understood, separately and together, that the struggle against the evil of apartheid could not be fought by ourselves alone, that we would not survive, nor live, by bread alone. We acknowledged, separately and together, our faith in God as the deepest source of our inspiration and strength. We realised that this inspiration was found, not in worn-out political slogans (even though we could make those slogans sound new and fresh as the struggle went on) or in political ideologies thought up by those who were already falling on the sword of their own failure to keep politics humane. We knew through respectful listening and speaking, and through experience, that however else we define God – as Creator, merciful, beneficent, Saviour – our God is a God of *adal* and *insaf*, that is, justice and righteousness. This emphasis is very much evident in the thinking and work of my very learned and passionate friend, Pakistani Christian theologian Charles Amjad-Ali.

To be sure, there were those who sought to break this solidarity by pointing to Christian justification of slavery, and apartheid as the vile creation of Christians, a 'Christian policy', as the white Dutch Reformed churches proudly claimed in those days. Apartheid, underpinned by a spurious theology and a fundamentally flawed interpretation of the Bible, was itself the inevitable outcome of colonisation, which in turn was a result of the Christian West's desire to rule the world. I found no one here with the persuasive power and mythic proportions of Malcolm X, but these were nonetheless strong arguments. But in the end, those who criticised the relationship between Christians and Muslims did not succeed in breaking the bonds of solidarity. How could they, when we, the inheritors and interpreters of radical black Christianity took on the responsibility to unmask apartheid as pseudo-gospel, a heresy and a blasphemy, and did not stop until the whole ecumenical world recognised it as such? I remember how, in explaining this action by the churches to a predominantly Muslim audience in a meeting in the Samaj Centre in Athlone one Sunday afternoon, my description of apartheid as *haram* called forth waves of affirmation from the hall.

How could they doubt us when we shared with our people the discovery that God is a God of love and liberation who executes justice for the oppressed, gives food to the hungry and lifts the poor from the dust of the earth? That we, *all of us,* are not defined by the vagaries of apartheid racism, but by our infinite worth as persons, created in the image of God?

Some might want to make the point that at least part of the explanation for this solidarity of faith might lie in the fact that people were brought together simply by their outrage at the suffering of their people, whose pain was so palpable. It would have been unseemly to split religious hairs while people were dying. Under these circumstances it was understandable that debate over religious matters should be shelved for later, when things returned to normal. Some might argue that the overpowering needs of the common cause dwarfed all differences.

I have no doubt that some might have felt this way. In 1974 I published the first comparative study ever of Martin Luther King Jr. and Malcolm X. I understood then how even in the midst of struggle, in what Malcolm called 'the wilderness of America', the common cause of racist oppression can prove to be a very watery glue. Malcolm X was an indefatigable enemy, not only of white America but as much of the black Christianity espoused by Martin Luther King Jr. and the Southern Christian Leadership Conference. In fact, he was more scathing of black people's Christianity than he was of white's, as he held that blacks never succeeded in breaking the chains of this 'slave religion' inherited from the white man. The common causes of blackness under white racist oppression, the longing for freedom and civil rights were clearly not enough to break down the animosity, until Malcolm's conversion from the contrived Islam of the Black Muslims (now the Nation of Islam) to the religion of the Prophet. Malcolm's understanding of true Islam brought forth a different person, a different philosophy of life, a far more effective method of struggle. What would have happened, I often wonder, to the civil rights struggle in America, and to the Christians and Muslims in America, had this genius of the black revolution not been gunned down far too early in his life?

No, there has to be more than just a common cause. From Dietrich Bonhoeffer, that great theologian and martyr of the resistance against Hitler's Nazis, I have learnt that in the discipleship of Jesus of Nazareth we must allow ourselves to 'be caught up in the way of Jesus Christ'. It is not our religion Bonhoeffer argued that makes us followers of Christ, but our participation in the sufferings of God. We are called to share in the sufferings of God at the hands of a hostile world. That, Bonhoeffer maintains, is what distinguishes us from pagans. Note: it distinguishes us not from people of other faiths, but from pagans. Bonhoeffer here criticises not the pagans but Christians for whom it has become more important to be religious than to be followers of Christ.

We are disciples of Jesus when we 'stand by God in his hour of grieving'. The grieving of God is not in the pain of God for God, but in the pain of God for the pain of suffering humanity. When Bonhoeffer speaks of the pain of God he does not look towards heaven but around him, at people. At the same time Bonhoeffer's argument means 'not in the first place thinking about one's own needs, problems, sins and fears, but allowing oneself to be caught up in the way of Jesus Christ'. That, I believed then as I believe now, is a spirituality of struggle worth having. And that is how I understood my working together with Muslims in the struggle against apartheid. So the question really was not whether Christians and Muslims could work together. It was whether we could together stand with God in God's grieving for the sake of God's people in pain everywhere. It was my endeavour to share the pain of God with others that made me confess my desire to follow, as publicly as I could, the 'way of Jesus Christ'. And not just to follow, but to be 'caught up in it'. Being caught up saves us from the paganism of careless injustice, prideful indifference, sinful intolerance and willful, arrogant exclusion.

Justice, inclusiveness, dignity

It is trite but true: the world has changed. Almost 15 years into our democratic experiment I must confess to a certain sense of disquiet.

The paradigms have not altogether failed, but they have shifted dramatically.

Globally, relationships between the Muslim world and the West have all but broken down. The language of reasonable diplomacy has been replaced with the vulgar discourse of accusation and threat. The United Nations, the forum where our common responsibility for the world should seek common consensus on our actions on behalf of the world, has been set aside in favour of unilateral actions that shamelessly flout international law. Wars of terror in Afghanistan and Iraq continue to call forth acts of terror in New York, London and elsewhere. The Middle East remains the place where the lives and hopes of the innocent are slaughtered on the altars of political expediency. In this most powerful of countries, intellectual debate on these matters has been poisoned by vague and inaccurate constructs such as Samuel Huntington's 'clash of civilizations'. Pakistani author Tariq Ali insists that the global relationship between the West and Islam is, rather, a 'clash of fundamentalisms', but such is the mood that even conservative scholar Andrew Bacevich speaks with concern of a new American militarism that has Americans 'seduced by war'.

The United States, in its persistent search for an enemy to justify those frighteningly irresponsible defence budgets and maintain its unipolar hegemony, long before 9/11, found Islam. Through its global hegemonic drive it is dragging all of us into what President George Bush called their 'crusade against the forces of evil'. On the other side of the divide, Islamic militarists have immediately responded with calls for a holy war, not just against America but against all the 'Christian West'. It is in the White House and on Capitol Hill as it is on the hills of Northern Pakistan and in the valleys of Afghanistan: God wills it. Tariq Ali is right: it is indeed a clash of fundamentalisms. The true voice of Islam, as the true voice of Christianity, is completely lost in the cacophony of this war of words and guns. It is to be hoped that the policies of the new US president will help change these grim realities.

Hollywood has been relentless in its exploitative vilification of Islam, and the routine, stereotyped generalisations in the majority of the Western media are having effects we cannot even begin to imagine. Tensions in Western countries also home to permanent, sizable Muslim communities are always just below boiling point, waiting for the spark. As a result there is fear, suspicion, distrust and a proliferation of South Africa's own dubious contribution to globalisation, the 'laager mentality'.

Signs of hope seem to be coming from the realisation in religious circles that the gentler, more authentic voices ought to be heard. The Parliament of World Religions, the Conference for Religion and Peace, the United Religious Initiative, the World Council of Religious Leaders, the recent meeting of rabbis and imams held in Brussels are all forming what Rabbi Avraham Soetendorp of Amsterdam calls 'one single stream of rapprochement'. These, however, are the elite voices. We should support them in every way we can, but we should also impress upon them a sense of the urgency of the moment, and remind them that all the worldwide conferences will not mean a thing unless ordinary people on the ground, the ones most vulnerable to hurt and propaganda, the ones who *believe,* claim ownership of a new vision of peace for their own lives. They should also understand that unless religion addresses directly and passionately the issues of justice, it will remain a vehicle for useless rituals, and a source of power for fundamentalist intolerance and exclusivism.

It is as Charles Amjad-Ali says: 'Religion will have to transform itself into a powerful instrument of social transformation or remain a central ideology of the powerful with their use of God like any other tool in their arsenal. Religion has to be seen as a source capable of challenging the decrepit, false, and unjust social order, with its built-in socio-economic, legal, and political mechanisms of injustices which perpetuate the privileges of the powerful.' Cross-religious dialogue cannot be bogged down in debates geared towards past interpretations of sacred texts, neglecting the actual historical realities of religious communities. It should be directed at the dynamic of actual situations, seeking always to find ways of realising compassionate justice. Cross-religious dialogue should strengthen the quest for justice. The central focus of the prophetic traditions in the three monotheistic religions is this quest for justice, Amjad-Ali argues, 'to make possible what seems impossible'. For all three monotheistic religions it is a central truth that to know God is to know God in justice and peace.

Here in South Africa relations between Christians and Muslims have not remained untouched by the momentous developments in the world. Muslims here share the feeling that worldwide, Islam is under attack. The traditional solidarity with the Palestinian people which all of us in the progressive movement share is no longer the binding force it used to be. The protests on our streets over the wars in Iraq and Afghanistan have become almost exclusively Muslim. This is to our shame, since solidarity with the Palestinian people has a long and noble history among us, and the continued oppression and suffering of Palestinians under the inhuman Israeli policies makes that active solidarity today as necessary as ever. The new democracy has given Muslims more freedom to express themselves and they are, in this regard, far more assertive than so-called mainline Christians. Just as in the sixties and seventies we used to listen to smuggled-in tapes of Martin Luther King and Malcolm X, these days many young Muslims, I am told, listen to clandestine recordings of Osama Bin Laden and the eloquent young imams of militant Islam.

In South Africa, like in Latin America and elsewhere in Africa, for example, Christianity's remarkable growth is centred in an explosion of a new Pentecostalism. Mainline churches are stagnating, if not dying, but young people of all races seem to flock in droves to hundreds of newly established charismatic churches, many of them conservative, feeding on the fundamentalist theology of their American role models. They are enthusiastically and uncritically embracing and spreading the teachings that stream from the religious television channels originating in the televangelist culture of the United States. As a result, Christian fundamentalist American issues become our issues: the rejection of abortion but the embracing of war and the death penalty; the rejection of care and responsibility for the earth in favour of the 'rapture'; the propagation of Christianity as imperial religion and Islam as satanic; the condemnation of homosexual persons and the subjection and disempowerment of women as necessary for the 'proper role' and empowerment of men in a theology of 'sonship and dominion'. The list is long.

Moreover, since 1994 many Christians have felt disconcerted and disempowered by the loss of power of the church in South Africa. South Africa is no longer what they perceived as a 'Christian' country. Fundamental beliefs, they hold, are under attack and ancient teachings are being made suspect. For them, the certitude of radical conservatism is a far better hiding place than the dithering what-ifs of traditional churches. In the view of radical fundamentalist Christians, aggressiveness is boldness and 'fraternization' with other ('false') religions is an unforgivable sin. The hard-won ecumenical consensus on issues such as theological sensitivity in our common society, respect for the integrity of inter-religious dialogue and the value of interfaith action on behalf of shared values has become deeply suspect. To an alarming degree, the reasonable voices are becoming dangerously inaudible.

In light of all this, at least two questions arise. First, can we, Christians and Muslims, as people of faith, help South Africa to regain the spiritual values without which our struggle would not have been what it was, and in so doing help set a new vision for our country and its people, and help to give substance and direction to our floundering search for 'moral regeneration'? Second, can we, Christians and Muslims in South Africa, help turn the tide in Christian-Muslim relations across the world by regaining for ourselves that which was most worthwhile in the most difficult times, and offering *that* to the world?

This is perhaps our greatest challenge. Not to seek our refuge in exclusivist, accusatory extremism, but to face each other in the vulnerability of faith and trust. Not to join the strident voices of violence and despair, but to offer the gentle comfort of hope, solidarity and love. Not to be tempted by the flesh pots of imperial theology, but to be inspired by our faith to seek justice for the poor and destitute, the weak and excluded, wherever and whomever they may be. Not to uplift the foolish war monger and call him noble, but to acknowledge the nobility of the one who seeks true peace. To declare to the world not the chauvinistic triumphalism of our own beliefs, but to discover the presence of God, through our faith and together with others, in the pain of suffering humanity, and in that way stand by God in the hour of God's grieving. To put it differently, in the words of German theologian Jürgen Moltmann: to discover and revere God in the victims of our own violence. In the presence of God: no self-justification or self-righteousness, no boastfulness or pseudo-innocence. Only humility and joyful commitment.

For God is grieving still. In the hunger of the poor for food and for justice and in the humiliation and exploitation of women. In the victims of war and of acts of terror in the name of God. In the neglect of the AIDS sufferer and the loneliness of the AIDS orphan. In the denial of the image of God in homosexual persons and in the desperation of the powerless and the callousness of the powerful. In justice denied and dreams deferred, God is grieving still. Knowing this God, and standing by this God is the essence, and the redemption, of faith.

'Execute justice in the morning,' so speaks the LORD of the Hebrew Bible, 'and deliver from the hand of the oppressor anyone who has been robbed, or else my wrath shall go forth like fire and burn, with no one to quench it ... did not your father ... do justice and righteousness ...; he judged the cause of the poor and needy ... is this not to know me? Says the LORD.' (Jer. 22)

'O ye who believe!' is the testimony of the Holy Qur'an, 'Stand out firmly for justice, as witnesses to Allah, even as against yourselves, or your parents, or your kin, and whether it be (against) rich or poor; for Allah can best protect you both. Follow not the lusts (of your heart), lest ye swerve, and if ye distort (justice) or decline to do justice, verily Allah is well acquainted with what ye do.' (Holy Qur'an, 4: 135)

'The Spirit of the Lord is upon me,' were the words of the first public sermon of Jesus of Nazareth, 'because he has anointed me to bring good news to the poor. He has sent me to proclaim release to the captives and recovery of sight to the blind, to let the oppressed go free, to proclaim the year of the Lord's favour ... Today, this scripture has been fulfilled in your hearing.' (Luke 16: 18–19; 21)

Such is the prophetic language of the three monotheistic religions, and this is the call for all people of faith today. Jewish philosopher and theologian Jonathan Sacks said it well. 'My own view is,' he argues, 'that the world faiths embody truths unavailable to economics and politics, and they remain salient even when everything else changes. They remind us that civilisations survive not by strength but by how they respond to the weak; not by wealth but by the care they show for the poor; not by power but by their concern for the powerless. The ironic yet utterly humane lesson of history is that what renders a culture invulnerable is the compassion it shows to the vulnerable. The ultimate value we should be concerned to maximize is human dignity – the dignity of all human beings, equally, as children of a creative, redeeming God.'

I cannot resist mentioning Islamic scholar Reza Aslan, who reminds us, Muslims and Christians alike, that at the beginning of the revelation of the Qur'an, theology was not the main thing on the Prophet Mohammad's mind. 'At this point in his ministry, Mohammad had a far more urgent message. That message ... dealt almost exclusively with the demise of the tribal ethic in Mecca. In the strongest terms, Mohammad decried the mistreatment and exploitation of the weak and unprotected. He called for an end to false contracts and the practice of usury that had made slaves of the poor. He spoke of the rights of the underprivileged and the oppressed, and made the astonishing claim that it was the duty of the rich and powerful to take care of them. "Do not oppress the orphan," the Quran commands, "and do not drive away the beggar." (93: 9–10) ... Mohammad was not yet establishing a new religion; he was calling for sweeping social reform. He was not yet preaching monotheism; he was demanding social justice.'

These, it seems to me, are solid foundations upon which to build not just our relationships but also our response to the challenges of the

21st century. And we must do it as Christians and Muslims, people of faith.

Still, for all of us, a new testimony for the 21st century calls for a new kind of courage, beyond the captivity of a new Constantinianism and beyond an Umayyad Islam. It demands, says Charles Amjad-Ali bluntly, 'the removal of the idols, the tossing of the crowns in the air and the destruction of all thrones ... (for) these are the prerequisites for the sovereignty of God and the sovereignty of the people.' To this, I can only say 'Amen!'

15

The Trouble with Small Blankets: The ANC, SACP and Cosatu Alliance

The ANC of Polokwane

I have heard Matthews Phosa, general treasurer of the African National Congress and that most suave and charming representative of the new ANC regime speak of the 'new' ANC in a way that makes me think. Unlike most, Phosa does not refer to the ANC 'after Polokwane'. He speaks of 'the ANC *of* Polokwane'. This is not just a slip of the tongue, I think. Within the context of an explanation to a meeting of the Afrikaanse Handelsinstituut, Phosa talked about an ANC with a different style, a new awareness of socio-economic and political responsibility, an awareness of a social contract with the people that will honour promises and sacred pledges.

This new ANC is a symbol of renewed democratic space, responsibility and authority. It simultaneously represents a break with the immediate past – the ANC of Thabo Mbeki – and a return to the foundations of old, the fundamentals that shaped the character of the organisation throughout its long and honourable history, and which have been lost of late but will once again be made the pillars of the temple. The 'old'

ANC is the ANC of Thabo Mbeki and what he and his cronies made of it. The 'ANC of Polokwane' is the ANC of the people, of before the Mbeki era, returned into the hands of the people to whom it rightfully belongs. In this sense, Polokwane has become more than a conference, more than just an event. It has become the place of rebirth.

As events are unfolding at the time of writing, Phosa's version is of course exactly the point of dispute. Terror Lekota and those who left the ANC with him in 2008 view matters entirely different. For them, Polokwane does not mark a rebirth, but the beginning of a death of the movement as they knew it. For them, the ANC of Polokwane has deviated from the path of the fathers, degenerated into something unrecognisable, alienated from its own high standards, devoid of the attributes that gave this oldest liberation movement on the continent of Africa its greatness. Those very fundamentals which Phosa claims have been betrayed. Their view is that the very history that the ANC of Polokwane claims to have resurrected has since been held in a stranglehold of death. The Freedom Charter has become a lone, lost child.

What should not be lost amongst all the historic upheavals we are experiencing is the fact that the ANC of Polokwane is once again the ANC of the Alliance. After a long sojourn in the wilderness the South African Communist Party (SACP) and the Congress of South African Trade Unions (Cosatu) have reasserted themselves and claimed their ownership of the liberation politics of South Africa. The influence of Cosatu and the SACP at the conference in Polokwane made itself felt immediately and it is in large measure due to their determination and hard work that things within the ANC have changed so radically. They are ready, for the first time in years, to put their stamp on the nature of South Africa politics. Not the politics of the streets, mind you, but on parliamentary politics and on the policies of government. The sigh of relief in some quarters at the sidelining of these two Alliance partners during the Mbeki years has now turned into groans of exasperation and apprehension.

The Alliance partners want real power this time. They want to be in the driver's seat, not just in the *ventertjie* behind, hidden until they can be taken out, when the car is safely parked out of sight of the neighbours. This time around, the SACP will not be satisfied with being the 'intellectual guidance' of the ANC, and Cosatu wants to be more than just the volunteers working for an electoral victory for the ANC. As I see it, the agenda is not just to redirect the internal workings of the Alliance. It is to change the direction of the country, to put the 'National Democratic Socialist Revolution' firmly back in place, as well as on the governing party's priority list. If this is not so, I truly do not understand what the bloody battles are all about.

When I first wrote about the politics and intriguing intricacies of the Alliance in 2005, we were facing a radically different scenario. It was then that I used the saying referred to in the title of this chapter. It is a proverb amongst the people of the Afrikaans *platteland* and which my mother often used to describe a very difficult situation. She would say, 'It is like a small blanket in the cold': the attempt to cover your head uncovers your feet. You remain cold and distinctly uncomfortable. It makes for a long night in the winter of the Karoo. What, I now wonder three years and many momentous events later, remains of the reflections of 2005?

'The ANC governs'

At the height of the Mbeki reign the situation was markedly different. The Alliance amongst the ANC, Cosatu and the SACP had increasingly moved from the almost natural phenomenon it has become through decades of struggle politics to a political paradox whose strains, cracks and stresses could no longer be hidden from the outside world. In 2005 I wrote the following in *BY*, the Saturday supplement to *Die Burger*.

First, there were simply the questions, especially from Cosatu and the SACP, whether those comrades from the left in government positions would really be doing their job, namely to further and protect the 'leftist agenda' through exercising their power as Cabinet Ministers, Members of Parliament and other levels of government, bureaucrats with power to make crucial decisions that affect the lives of our people. The non-fulfilment of these expectations came as a severe disappointment, even a shock. Then there was deep concern at the abrupt abandoning of the Reconstruction and Development Programme, which was replaced by GEAR, the government's new Growth, Employment and Redistribution economic plan. This was an important moment, since it signified a shift away from what was seen as a socially sensitive economic policy to a more market oriented, neo-liberal economic policy. The SACP and Cosatu immediately expressed fears that GEAR was a more fundamental shift than government would want to admit, would not fulfil the promises made to the poor, and would therefore ultimately fail, but not before having done great damage.

Then followed complaints about the hardening attitudes of especially those ministers, members of the SACP, in the intermittent but increasingly bitter clashes between government and trade unions in the public sector when it came to wage negotiations and strikes. Public Administration minister

Geraldine Fraser-Moleketi and Labour minister Membathisi Mdladlana being a case in point. Meanwhile, public tongue lashings from both Mr Mandela and Mr Mbeki left the SACP/Cosatu group smarting, humiliated and extremely angry.

There were serious arguments about the failure of the Alliance to meet regularly, since this robbed the discontents of an internal platform to raise their concerns and, most importantly, to exercise influence over policy in the making. Being presented with policies as a *fait accompli* and therefore faced with a choice of either accepting them meekly or fighting their battles in public was not an option cherished by those who took the Alliance seriously. And that, of course, came to be the main concern: that the longer the ANC government was in power, the less seriously it took the Alliance. And, to be fair, that assumption was correct.

The point was made more than once: it is the ANC that governs. The Alliance is (merely) a political formation. In other words, the SACP and Cosatu are partners in politics, not necessarily in government, and those SACP members who serve in government are expected to carry out government policy as determined by the ANC. They are not there to pursue the separate agendas of the formations they come from. Those slogans on the posters, 'ANC Governs!' were not just slogans after all. This had all sorts of implications, not least for the 'mandate' from their membership and congresses these people are supposed to carry out faithfully, a sacred concept within the traditions of movement politics.

Apart from broad policy there were specific issues that raised the levels of concern and tension and among the most important are unemployment, housing, wage negotiations in the public sector, and the thorniest of them all: privatisation with its attendant job losses and huge political consequences. Rising food and fuel prices then as well as now became rallying points. All of this can be focused on one salient issue, namely poverty, and whether government is doing enough to combat it, never mind eradicate it.

'The Zanufication of the ANC'

Then came the bombshell that occupied the media for weeks and caused a great deal of upheaval within the Alliance, the notorious interview Irish journalist Helena Sheehan had had with Jeremy Cronin, foremost SACP intellectual and ANC MP. What created the sensation in the media were really two things: one, Cronin's accusation of the 'Zanufication' of the ANC, and two, the response of a KwaZulu-Natal leader of the ANC, one of Thabo Mbeki's henchmen, contemptuously slapping down Cronin as a 'white messiah' not needed by the ANC. These two issues struck, in different ways, a highly emotive chord in the South African political debate. Beyond the reference to Zimbabwe and the disaster Robert Mugabe was single-handedly creating there, this raised also the racial issue in South Africa itself.

I shall return to this article shortly.

'Cosatu's Power Diminishing' read the headline on the front page of the business section of an Afrikaans daily on 21 May 2007. It was a long piece, which included a thoughtful analysis by Prof. Sakhela Buhlungu, one of the most respected analysts of developments in the labour movement. Analysing the strikes coordinated by Cosatu over the last few years, and especially in response to the most visible bone of contention between the labour unions and the government, privatisation, Buhlungu came to the conclusion that Cosatu was losing its effectiveness and hence its power. Not being able to sit at the table when policy is being formulated, Cosatu has to resort to mass mobilisation in the streets. 'The weapon of last resort, mass power', then president of Cosatu Willie Madisha had called it. But at the peak of the tensions with the Mbeki government, Cosatu could not rally the masses as it had been able to do before. Even though the SACP threw its full weight behind those protests, the weapon was not nearly as sharp.

This, and the casual way in which the ANC was increasingly treating the Alliance, brought Buhlungu and his co-researcher Prof. Eddie Webster to the following sobering conclusions:

- Cosatu is gradually losing its organisational power, even though it still strikes fear into the hearts of the business community;
- The labour movement shows an inability to redefine the role of its own structures in order to fit in and respond to new, tangible challenges in the working place;
- Cosatu has to depend more and more on a shrinking pool of leadership, with women playing an increasingly insignificant role in that leadership in favour of a 'new balance of power: powerful men more and more inaccessible to ordinary people'.

They point out further that the loss of leadership in Cosatu has deeply hurt the labour movement. The September Commission which in 1997 wrote a report with far-reaching analysis and conclusions for Cosatu's future consisted of no less than twelve heavyweights from the leadership. 'Not a single one of them is still with Cosatu today,' the researchers say.

But Cosatu's power and effectiveness should not only be measured by its ability to get the workers on to the streets in protest. There is still the matter of its effect in the boardrooms. More and more companies evade or ignore labour legislation. According to Buhlungu, 'The number of fair labour practices reports that in accordance with the law have to be submitted to the Department of Labour decreases by 29% every year.' Even more serious is his conclusion that Cosatu is 'isolating itself from other community organisations'. Can it get more serious than this? From one point of view, yes. Buhlungu continues: 'In the years after the 1994 election Cosatu has allowed itself to be just as effectively drawn into the new leadership elite and became a role player in many institutions, from Nedlac and Parliament to local government.' This is 'unique', Buhlungu says, for 'nowhere else in the world has a labour movement succeeded in this after a liberation struggle'. Is this a good thing? I guess it depends. If I were a worker member of Cosatu, I would ask the question: What does all the participation in the 'elite leadership structures' mean if Cosatu fails where it matters most: in the making of policy by government and in the representation of its members' interests in the policies and practices of companies? Is the fear for Cosatu in the business community really limited to wage negotiations? Buhlungu's article ends by stating that Cosatu certainly has not yet lost all its power and influence. But Buhlungu asks: Is Cosatu's power more than just the legacy of its militant past?

I have spent some time discussing the above arguments because they highlight not only Cosatu's dilemma but also the dilemma of the SACP: beyond the slogans, what becomes of the issue of governance as it participates in the making of policy and the direction the country is taking?

We shall have to keep Buhlungu's report in mind as we return to

Cronin's finger and the sore point on which it pressed in that interview. I shall not spend much time on the 'white messiah' slur except to point out how sharply the lines can be drawn and how quickly a trusted comrade can become a white, vilified enemy. The choice of words was deliberately personally and politically hurtful, a sign of utter disdain as well as a warning. 'It shows,' I wrote then, 'the very intolerance Cronin had raised as a concern, something we are sure to see again and again as the situation worsens and more and more is at stake. But this is as true for the SACP as it is for the ANC. Criticism in general is not well taken. From within it is almost immediately seen as disloyalty, even betrayal.'

Here is the argument I made in 2005 in *Die Burger*:

> In saying what he did Cronin does not mean that South Africa is becoming like Zimbabwe and that the chaotic situation in that country will soon be duplicated here. This interpretation is more the desperate attempt of the mainly white opposition to score some political points, in the process showing once again how little they understood of the inner workings of the liberation movement. Cronin is speaking specifically of the ANC. Cronin is also referring to more than just 'bureaucratisation' – the tendency of placing more and more power into the hands of a small clique ('Mbeki-ites', he calls them) who would presumably drive through whatever Mr Mbeki wants against the will of the majority of the ANC membership.

> The main thrust of Cronin's argument is that Mbeki himself is becoming more and more of a dictator, a more sophisticated version of Robert Mugabe, if you will, stifling any criticism or critical debate with the ANC as well as in the Alliance, isolating himself from not only those within the leadership who disagree

with him, but also from the masses who supported the ANC. In Alliance jargon, Thabo Mbeki is displaying 'Stalinist' tendencies, a term Cronin uses quite deliberately in the interview. Apart from the irony that a leading communist is accusing Mbeki of being 'Stalinist', we would do well to take Mr Cronin more seriously here. If what he says is true, and I think it is, then the issue is not just a personality trait of Mbeki that is highlighted here. It points to a culture that is being created and cultivated in the ANC, a way of thinking, speaking and acting that does not only hold danger for the ANC as an organisation, but for the very essence of our young democracy. South Africans have to be far more alert to these developments.

There are serious undertones to this attack that have precipitated the ANC's angry reaction. In the same interview, Cronin speaks dismissively of Mbeki's vision of an African renaissance, the African Union and the New Plan for Africa's Development (Nepad). Cronin writes this off as 'a kind of fluffy, feel-good third-wayism for the African continent'. It is a 'voluntaristic' (which in this context means 'opportunistic' and therefore politically meaningless) promise of 'the African century', no more than 'an escape from the contradictions and difficulties of the present ...' With these plans Mbeki has proved himself to be no more than a 'lackey' of the West, a 'shop steward and conduit' of Western, neo-liberal capitalist ideas, and as such 'playing with a death wish on the global stage'. This harsh judgement continues, and Cronin is quick to point to the crux of the matter. Mbeki, he argues, does not understand that the issue is not a continental one, but a structural one. In other words, it is an ideological battle, not a philosophical one that is being fought, and on a global scale. It is not merely a matter of the development of Africa as a continent, trying to catch up with the West. Whatever Mbeki pretends it to be, says Cronin, the idea of an African renaissance is a 'threadbare notion'.

What Mbeki is doing is to use these 'vague' ideas as an 'escape route' because he is unwilling, or unable, to deal with the 'hard issues'. Cronin insists that 'there are more pressing points of focus like job creation and development'. The 'fuzzy' idea of an African renaissance can easily become an escape mechanism from dealing exactly with these issues.

One does not have to agree with Cronin's assessment of Mbeki's personal political agenda to see that the issues he raises here are crucial. Indeed, the African renaissance can draw attention away from what are desperate needs here at home, and it may well be that the success of this venture will depend on the success the government achieves right here on those very issues Cronin is so concerned about.

Looking at the events of the latter half of 2008, Cronin was prophetic. And he, better than those surrounding president Mbeki, saw the ideological fault lines within the Alliance, fault lines along which not the Alliance, but the ANC itself would crack and split. The sword which Mbeki then used to cut Jeremy Cronin down to size (he was forced to apologise for his remarks) was the very sword Mbeki fell upon.

The critique from the side of the SACP on Mbeki's African experiment is not new. Around the launch of the African Union in May 2005, Dr Blade Nzimande, SACP General Secretary, slated the idea that multiparty democracy be made one of the criteria for good governance in Africa, something that Mbeki insisted upon. 'It is not the be-all and end-all of everything,' he said. 'Good governance,' he asserts, 'has to do with service delivery to the poor, responding to the real needs of the people etc.' Of course Blade Nzimande is correct in claiming service delivery to the poor and responding to the needs of the people as core values of good governance. But is this an either/or situation in which a demand for democratic diversity automatically excludes social justice? In other words, does it matter less how we are being governed or how democratic our governmental institutions are, as long as there is 'service delivery'? Or is it simpler still: that Nzimande truly believes that a communist dictatorship is better able to respond to the needs of the people than a democratic government? However this is read, it means at the least that the well-known ideological fundamentals of the SACP are still firmly in place and that the SACP's design is not just for South Africa but for the continent as a whole. Cronin's views on the African renaissance and Nepad confirmed this. For many ANC members it was galling that a party that could scoff at such elemental building blocks for democracy should accuse the ANC of being 'Stalinist' and 'undemocratic'.

I did not agree with Cronin's assessment of Thabo Mbeki's African Renaissance then, and I am still of the opinion that without such a renaissance, a revival, if you will, economically, politically and spiritually, Africa will not be able to fully take its rightful place amongst the nations. I believe that in this matter, Mbeki was not simply driven by 'colonialist tendencies' or 'swollen-headedness' but by the sober realisation that historically and globally Africa now has an opportunity seldom seen in the last century or so. Also, and I agree once again with

Mbeki, South Africa cannot be an island of wealth in a sea of poverty and backwardness. I continue from my 2005 article:

> The continent cannot be left to its own devices: the swell of economic refugees to this country should make South Africans see the need for development all over the continent. The concept of economic security is of necessity a continental and global one. Africa's development cannot take place without a firm commitment to genuine democracy. Whether that democracy should also of necessity take on the form of a 'market democracy' worshipped by the USA and *as such* wedded to globalisation, is indeed another, serious, matter, and on this point I do differ fundamentally from the Mbeki ideology.
>
> To be sure, I believe that our government's uncritical embrace of the Washington Consensus and the neo-liberal capitalism that drives globalisation is a mistake, and one that we will regret sooner rather than later. I believe also that the government has to take much more seriously our own priorities at home, and that issues of unemployment, housing, food security, land and wealth distribution are rightly raised by the trade unions, churches and others as of fundamental importance. I am convinced that our people's desperate poverty is a time bomb that could blow every plan for our common future sky high. I believe with the United Nations Development Programme, moreover, and I say this at every opportunity I get: Poverty cannot just be alleviated; it can now in fact be eradicated.
>
> So Cronin's and the SACP's attack was not merely an accusation of 'Zanufication'. It went to the heart of what president Mbeki and the ANC see as their vision for South Africa and the continent. It is a vision the left do not share, for it is not built

on socialist principles. They had no part in its formulation, had no opportunity to influence its direction, and do not care for its outcome. It is a vision the left see as a fundamental departure from traditional Alliance policies, a betrayal in fact, not only of the Alliance, but of the people. This state of affairs, in my view, has the makings of a permanent rift. If the SACP wants to continue to be seen as a 'party of principles" it does not really have too many choices left.

'So pregnant with promise'

The final argument I made in 2005 went as follows.

But this, as important as it may be, is not all. In my opinion the tensions run even deeper. Let's put them in a row:

- The fact that the ANC in government sees itself as not bound by the ideological positions of its Alliance partners, however dearly held or sacred, is of fundamental importance. Here lies the deepest level of frustration for Cosatu and the SACP.

- The historic role of the SACP within the Alliance has therefore irrevocably changed. SACP intellectuals, with their ideological analyses backed by the socialist project and the overwhelming presence and power of the Soviet Union during the Cold War stand-off and the ANC's needs, no longer have the power they used to wield. Hence their complaint of being 'marginalised'.

- Also, in the words of Jeremy Cronin, they know that 'the paradigms have failed'. The ANC under Mbeki has moved swiftly to exploit that failure. They have chosen a path which does not correspond with the 'worldwide socialist revolution'. SACP members in Cabinet cannot change that and some of them, like Jeff Radebe, are in fact driving that process, and quite vigorously so. Throwing them out of the party's leadership structures makes a point, but no more than that.

- For all intents and purposes these people, and the leadership from Cosatu now in government, are helping to do what the left itself says it fears most: the 'stabilisation of the capitalist project' and the affirmation of 'capitalist hegemony in the rest of the world and in South Africa'.

- In the interview, Cronin takes heart from the fact that the broad membership of the ANC, he believes, is in support of the ideological positions of the SACP. They see the SACP in 'a moral sense as some kind of guarantor that the revolutionary, radical credentials of the ANC haven't disappeared, haven't debacled'. But the recent policy conference of the ANC with the SACP and Cosatu broadly represented, has debated all the sensitive policy issues including privatisation, and the ANC have reported 'agreement' on these policies that have caused so much dissent. This was borne out, the ANC argues, by the embarrassingly low turn-out for the strike called by Cosatu and the SACP.

- The new Cosatu leadership have not yet found a way to mobilise the masses around the issues they deem so important. They have not yet found a way to persuade people that the ANC is an 'enemy'. Neither have they been able to spell out clearly what is at stake. It must have been very disturbing to hear workers say that they ignored the call to strike because they 'don't understand what is happening here'.

Now, three years down the line, earth-shaking events have taken place and the ground beneath the feet of the ANC is shifting dramatically.

While the impact on South African politics, especially with the re-call of Thabo Mbeki, has been considerable, the impact on Alliance politics has been no less so. In my view, the split in the ruling party is by far not the last the ANC will see. Even though the mainstream media are full of dark foreboding and apprehension about the 'leftist takeover' at Polokwane, sober reflection advises caution.

In my 2005 article, I offered some thoughts on what I thought were the options for the left within the Alliance. I thought then that:

> there is more than enough reason for the left to make a decision about the Alliance, especially for the SACP. For them, as I see it, there are three options. First, they remain in the Alliance and accept the policy direction of the ANC, accepting also that the ANC has succeeded in domesticating the left. Second, they remain in the Alliance and continue to be the 'conscience' of the ANC. But that too comes with a price. Already there are accusations that SACP/Cosatu Members of Parliament are there only for the MP salaries and the perks, not protecting the leftist agenda, not having any influence on government. Cronin has admitted as much: 'We are now losing at the level of policy formation.' There is also the element of honesty. Again, Cronin: 'Being an MP would be a useful way of being an ANC person rather than being marginalized as just the SACP.' In other words, he knows that as a political party the SACP cannot draw as much support from the people and for reasons he would rather not mention. On this point the ANC would be able to call their bluff almost any day. But it is exactly this paradox in the individual that causes the strains in the Alliance as a collective. Besides, there is a whiff of hypocrisy here too. Third, the SACP could break away, form their own political

formation and fight the ANC in the next election. We have already pointed out the dilemma. It is not just a matter of numbers, but also the persuasive power of the political and ideological beliefs the SACP continues to cling to.

I for one do not believe the SACP needs to stay in the Alliance in order to be the 'conscience' of the ANC. There are more than enough radical democrats in the ANC to give that guarantee, if they will only rediscover their courage and begin to reclaim the ANC we had fought so hard for.

So, have we arrived at that moment with the new formation led by Terror Lekota and has the left really captured the heart and mind of the ANC? I do not think so. Despite the breakaway of the Lekota group the inherent contradictions within the Alliance remain, and will continue to plague, the ANC in its post-Polokwane existence. Even as Blade Nzimande claims a 'victory of the left' at Polokwane, the ANC leadership has been assuring the business communities across the world that there will be no substantial change in economic policy and as I write Jacob Zuma is in Washington in the dying days of the Bush administration reassuringly explaining exactly why they have asked Finance Minister Trevor Manuel to stay on in Cabinet. In immediate response to the mid-term budget (October 2008), president of the African Monitor's anti-poverty campaign Archbishop Njongonkulu Ndungane, has severely criticised its inability to fundamentally address the worsening situation of desperately poor people, almost 50% of our nation.

A new generation of intellectuals of the left are similarly sober about events after Polokwane. In an enlightening article in the October/November 2008 issue of *Amandla!*, ('South Africa's new progressive magazine standing for social justice', it describes itself), Wits sociologist Devan Pillay writes about 'working-class politics or populism: the meaning of Zuma for the left in South Africa'. I quote him here substantively as he represents, I think, the fresh kind of thinking that clearly sees beyond present calamities or victories and offers insights worth considering well into the future.

'The dramatic events of September 2008 which saw Thabo Mbeki and several ministers resign,' Pillay begins his article, 'are seen by some on the left as a victory against neo-liberal economic orthodoxy.' He questions this. The Zuma camp is 'an alliance of class forces' which had a common antipathy towards the relatively aloof leadership style of Mbeki, and the Polokwane victory 'certainly looks' like a triumph of the left. But can it be more than just a 'battering ram' for the creation of a 'predatory black bourgeoisie', and actually become an instrument for the 'advancement of a holistic development programme'? If former SACP treasurer-general Philip Dexter's assertion that the current ANC National Executive Committee 'has more business people in it than the previous one' is correct, is this committee not similarly captive to 'the new black elite'?

Pillay asks a question that I raised in my discussion of the Cronin interview: Is what we see working-class politics or 'the politics of patronage'? Both the membership of Cosatu and its leadership are 'insiders', that is 'beneficiaries of the post-apartheid order vis-à-vis the unemployed, informalised workers and the working poor majority who remain unorganised'. Cosatu has 'failed to organise informal workers within the formal sector (except in retail), has no interest in the informal sector (street traders, home-based workers etc.) or the vast numbers of unemployed (almost 40% of the workforce of the country)'.

Pillay goes further, substantiating a point made earlier in my discussion on Cronin: 'Cosatu no longer engages in meaningful action in community struggles (for example around water privatisation) and keeps a safe distance from most new social movements ...' Instead, Cosatu is caught up in 'business unionism and incorporated political unionism where mass action is wheeled out every now and then ...'

Pillay is just as critical of the SACP, which according to him has between 15 000 and 30 000 members 'and few critical thinkers'. Members seem more content 'to follow the line of dominant leadership with a strong tendency towards a hybrid Stalinist populism'.

Pillay also considers the opinion that argues that the SACP, under Blade Nzimande, has 'indeed masterfully succeeded in asserting its hegemony over the ANC and the Alliance, through the figure of Jacob Zuma'. In fact, Zuma might be so indebted to the left that he 'will have to follow their agenda once in power'. That might be so, says Pillay, but he asks the question, 'What agenda?' That agenda, Pillay asserts, 'is not the participatory-democratic, socialist politics of the working-class movement since the 1970s'. Instead, recent rhetoric and practice within the SACP and Cosatu 'suggest that a more reckless, intolerant, neo-Stalinist politics is emerging, under the guise of democratic working-class politics'. Independent, critical voices have been silenced or purged 'quite ruthlessly', not heeded. As for Nzimande himself, he is 'steeped in a vanguardist tradition of politics where "independence" only has meaning if these bodies bow to the will of the party'.

'The new situation,' Pillay writes, 'allows for a realignment of forces, if not for the 2009 elections, then for the next one'. Whether Kgalema Motlanthe and others can radically alter the character of the ANC remains a possibility, but is highly unlikely, 'given their patent inability to deal with the power of Big Capital (and nascent capitalist interests within its own ranks)'. What is needed now is a 'non-sectarian, participatory-democratic and eco-socialist left pole of attraction' to present an 'alternative to the working class to which they will orient when the time is right'. The article ends on an up-beat note: 'The political situation in South Africa has not been so pregnant with promise since the 1980s.'

It is not necessary to accept all of Pillay's reasoning, though he makes a compelling argument, to see clearly that acute problems within the Alliance persist. What Pillay and others are seeking remains in fundamental opposition to what the Alliance proposes as economic policy, and those differences cannot be papered over for much longer. I am not speaking of who has the 'right' to bear the title 'left', or 'revolutionary'. These labels have become almost meaningless in our ever more confusing political discourse. We should examine policies rather than labels, slogans or intentions. Thoughtful opposition to the present neo-liberal fundamentalism will grow as churches and other faith-based communities, as well as organised civil society, come more and more to understand the call to fundamental justice, equity and compassion.

Already, it seems that 'Alliance leaders have been speaking with widely differing voices about the direction the economic policy will take after next year's election,' according to an article in the *Argus* of 15 October 2008, reporting on the very first Alliance economic policy consultation after Polokwane. While Jacob Zuma, just before leaving for the USA for talks with business leaders and the Bush administration there, told metal industry workers that the ANC will remain 'a disciplined force of the left' (whatever that may mean), Matthews Phosa was assuring the business community in Johannesburg that the ruling party had 'no plans to abandon the recognisably prudent, economically conservative' policies of the last 14 years. And while one part of the ANC leadership agreed with Trevor Manuel that South Africa's fiscal policies have helped to 'keep us safe' in the midst of the international financial storm, Cosatu general secretary Zwelinzima Vavi argued that the route the ANC government had taken 'had left South Africa defenceless against this senseless panic'.

This kind of confusing message will destabilise the ANC more effectively than will the Lekota breakaway. What will become increasingly bothersome is not just the confusion but also the question of fundamental honesty. If the SACP is convinced that the majority of South Africa's poor people are on its side, why does it continue to hide its light under the bushel of ANC obfuscation? I am one of those South Africans who think that more honesty in our political debates as well as in our alignments is essential for proper democratic functioning. I do not want to wake up one morning after elections, having voted for the ANC, only to find that we have voted into power an SACP with not just a vague and confused 'socialist revolutionary' agenda, but with 'neo-Stalinist populist' tendencies to boot! An ANC that has not been overcome in honest battle, but conquered by stealth on the backs of voters who thought they had voted for something else. South Africans who have fought hard and sacrificed for democracy, and even those who have not 'been in the struggle trenches', deserve more respect than that. Political honesty is an essential part of such respect. So the SACP should nail its colours to the mast, reveal what it really stands for and give the South African people their choices and alternatives. The longing for clarity on these matters might just be a bigger factor in the choices offered by the Lekota faction than we might be inclined to think. But however all this turns out, it is clear to me that the blanket that we have woven to cover our fundamentalisms, confusions, perplexities and hidden agendas parading as the tolerance of a 'broad church' (yet another slogan as incongruous as it is meaningless) has become too small. The cold is creeping in.

This kind of politicking is detested by the 'thinking left'. What Pillay and those who think like him have in mind lies far beyond sloganeering on the one hand and appeasement on the other. What they have in mind also lies beyond the 'neo-Stalinist populism' Blade Nzimande's SACP represents. In rejecting the idea of the working class merely being turned into a 'battering ram' for the creation of a 'predatory black bourgeoisie' waiting to pick up the spoils after the bloody battles have been fought and won by the poor, the 'thinking left' places on record its determination to fight for something entirely different. The search for an alternative already signals that whatever is in the pipeline in the Alliance as it now exists and works in the ANC of Polokwane cannot satisfy those who, in their view, seek genuine transformation of South African society. Hence the expectations in a time 'pregnant with promise'. The real division awaits.

The heart of the matter: whose revolution?

There is, perhaps, a deeper philosophical issue at stake here. The Alliance speaks constantly of the 'National Democratic Revolution', a term to which much emotional and political value is attached. Up to now it has been a term which seems to have resonated with the masses, although there is increasing doubt as to whether its meaning is clear to all. In doubt, too, is the attractiveness of such terms for a younger, post-struggle generation whose terms of reference are the globalised realities that shape their lives. In their most honest moments, representatives of the left will explain that the National Democratic Revolution is the project through which South Africa was to be turned from what it was to a successful socialist state such as envisaged from the earliest days.

But all of this has come under intense scrutiny and nothing can be taken for granted anymore. And it shouldn't.

The question has become a crucial one: exactly what is that revolution, how are we to understand and interpret it, and ultimately and most importantly, who is the true custodian of that revolution? The revolution that was held before us – the revolution the ANC propagated into the 1990s, for which countless young people, beguiled by the siren songs emanating from beyond the borders and the safety of London surrendered their hopes and their life – that the ANC will triumphantly enter Pretoria á la Fidel Castro into Havana, flags waving and AK 47s punctuating the victory by shots fired into the air – was a pipe dream. For those hopeful and fervent youngsters, that revolution died when they and their dreams were devoured in the Quatros of this world under the heavy hands of the Commissars. No, I'm putting this wrong. The revolution did not die for them; they died for the revolution. More precisely, the revolution devoured them as revolutions have always done since the Jacobins. No wonder that by the time the revolution reached Pretoria it was too fat, too bloated, too gorged, too de-revolutionised to bring with it any meaningful change. That revolution did not storm into Pretoria. It waddled in.

The ideological revolution that would usher in the 'socialist project' here and for the continent is precisely the revolution whose 'paradigms have failed'. It failed because it was not able to face the real important questions, argues Philip Dexter in a recent article, 'such as whether or not socialism was a real and imminent prospect, the nature of the electoral system, the character of the national liberation movement and whether it should transform itself into a political party'. Dexter also mentions something called 'Thermidor'. For the sake of the uninitiated like me, Dexter explains: 'Named after the new calendar month in the French Revolution, Thermidor was the month during which the revolutionaries turned on each other, leaving a trail of blood and a collapsed revolution. As in all such periods, good sense and unity were the victims. So too in our Thermidor.' Ours began with a systematic programme to protect Jacob Zuma from alleged abuse of power: unless those from the '1996 class project' (the Mbeki-ites) could be stopped, Zuma would be 'devoured by the revolution'.

'But now in office,' Dexter continues, 'are comrades such as Jacob Zuma, Kgalema Motlanthe and Gwede Mantashe. They have failed us all in that they have done nothing to stop the vilification, humiliation and purging of many cadres both prior to and post Polokwane, culminating in the removal of the President of the Republic from office.' As with many, if not all revolutions before, 'the Thermidor was upon us'. In this manner, Dexter takes us to the heart of the matter. 'The new realities of the post-apartheid period of the oft-referred to National Democratic Revolution (NDR) are that personal and class interests are at play in the actions of all political leaders. The complexity of the class fractions that now dominate the liberation movement cannot be dealt with here. Suffice it to say that the elites that occupy political office are a central driver of the competition for resources and power that fuels the Thermidor. Merely claiming to be selfless, super-revolutionaries, dedicated to the struggle for the interests of the poor, the marginalised and the oppressed is no longer enough.'

From my point of view, though, the origins of Dexter's conclusions lie further in the past, and I mentioned this in my 2005 article: 'The ANC under Mbeki's leadership have resolutely chosen a different path, with a determined bias for the neo-liberal capitalist model as directed by the G8. However, while the ANC is pursuing these economic policies, they continue to use the language of the 'democratic revolution'. But clearly this 'revolution' had been redefined. Its contents and goals are radically different from those held dear by the left. But Mbeki has been able to capture the phrases and the slogans while radically exchanging their contents with something the left thought the ANC would or could never do. It is a revolution perhaps best captured by Thabo Mbeki's determined neo-capitalist economic policies on the one hand, and his easy and comfortable handling of the "revolution" phraseology on the other'.

The battle for ownership of the National Democratic Revolution seems to have been won by Mbeki's ANC. They have captured the revolution. But in my view the real revolution still has to be fought. The revolution I speak of will not have the agenda of the left nor of the new bourgeois revolutionists, in whichever 'camp' they might now find themselves. What we have seen in this first phase of our democracy has been the revolution of values, hopes, aspirations and dreams that have all gone under in the wave upon wave of fake revolutionary fervour on behalf of class and group interests. The real revolution should have everything to do with those matters that should have been building blocks for our democracy but which have become stumbling blocks: humanity, justice, peace, integrity, equity, reconciliation. The question then is not when the SACP and Cosatu will 'recapture the socialist revolution' but rather when will the people, in the restoration of our spirituality of struggle and in the rightful claim upon our power, reclaim those values in the only revolution that will matter.

This revolution cannot be 'captured' by any of the power-hungry factions now clamouring for the seats of power. It was never a revolution that had to be imported or even 'brought home'. It is a revolution the people have always guaranteed, not owned, for it can never 'belong' to any one generation, let alone one faction or political formation. It is the revolution that is inherently claimed by any genuine democracy itself, the kind of democracy, as John Quincy Adams has said, whose true character 'is iconoclasm'.

What that peerless journalist and modern philosopher Bill Moyers has said of the United States of America is equally true of South Africa. I freely paraphrase him: The most fundamental failure of our young democracy is the failure to embrace a moral vision of South Africa based on the transcendent faith that human beings are more than the sum of their material appetites or their allegiance or usefulness to ideologies; our country is not the private possession of ruling elites and freedom is not licence but responsibility – the gift we have received and the legacy we must leave behind.

With Greek philosopher Plutarch we reaffirm the ancient truth that 'the imbalance between rich and poor is the oldest and most fatal ailment of all republics'. Before him the Hebrew prophets through Isaiah of Babylon knew and called for the 'loosening of the bonds of injustice', the undoing of 'the yoke' and the liberation of the oppressed, to 'let them go free', and the breaking 'of every yoke' as the way towards humanity, real freedom and social stability. Isaiah knew that if you were 'to share your bread with the hungry, [to] bring the homeless poor into your house', to understand the unbreakable bonds of your common humanity, in the ubuntufication of our society – when we do that, 'then shall your light break forth like the dawn, and your healing shall spring up quickly ...'

The revolution I have in mind has to do with the 'tenderness of conscience' I have pleaded for elsewhere. It means allowing ourselves to be captured by the hopes of the poor, to be seduced by the dream of God for the world: humanity, justice, equity, solidarity, to be touched by the woundedness of God in the woundedness of humanity. This is a different kind of revolution. It releases us from the compulsory revolutionary fervour that binds us more to the dictates of the revolution than to the genuine compassion no real revolution can do without. It frees us from the stifling rules of the revolution and from the bureaucratisation of our minds, and opens us up to the liberating possibilities of fantasy and sensitivity in our search for the common good. It liberates us from the stranglehold of historical predetermination and sensitises us to the possibilities of human determination and courage in our protest against empirical reality. It helps us understand the freedom of not just fighting for power, but wresting power from the hands of the powerful, whomever they may pretend to be, and sharing it with those who have none. It helps us to make the transition from self-righteous justification, because we happen to benefit, to holy rage at the injustice which makes us benefit. In short, it blesses us with the freedom of humanising love.

Unlike the so-called national democratic revolution that widens the gap between the rich and the poor and uses the poor as a battering ram for renewed elitist interests, this revolution takes equity seriously as the principle source of global ethics: 'The idea of human vulnerability and the desire to alleviate the suffering of every individual to the extent possible,' as stated in the 2004 UNDP Report. 'Recognising the equality of all individuals,' the Report says, 'regardless of class, race, gender, community or generation is the ethos of universal values. Equity also envelops the need to preserve the environment and natural resources that can be used by future generations.'

This understanding is vital for all modern democracies, ours included, where, inspired by the victory rhetoric emanating from the United States, the ideal of equality, since the collapse of socialism, has been scornfully pushed out of our political discourse. One result of the current financial crisis, as hopefully we begin to understand the consequences of greed and human hubris (which the church calls idolatry), will hopefully be the renewed discussion on the meaning and necessity of equality. Without equality there is no freedom. 'Equality,' German theologian Jürgen Moltmann, writing expressly for secular audiences, notes, 'is not collectivism. It means equal conditions for living, and equal chances for living for everyone. As a social concept, equality means *justice.* As a humanitarian concept equality means *solidarity.* As a Christian concept, equality means *love.* Either we shall create a world of social justice, human solidarity and Christian love, or this world will perish through the oppression of people by people, through asocial egotism, and through the destruction of the future in the interest of short-term, present-day profits.'

And that hope I keep on speaking of is not some vague desire that things will become better all by themselves. It is the revolutionary hope I have learnt from African church father of centuries ago, St Augustine. He is the very one whose words I used against the apartheid regime: 'A government who lacks justice is nothing more than a gang of robbers!' This same Augustine says about hope: 'Hope has two daughters: Anger and Courage. The anger of hope means that one refuses to accept what is wrong, to put up with what is driving one to despair. The courage of hope means to have the firm resolve to pull oneself to one's feet and attack injustice, even though one has to pay the price for doing so.'

'Democracy requires a public aroused by the knowledge of what is being done to their country in their name,' writes Bill Moyers. 'We must resist the temptation to talk about problems, issues and policies, but we don't talk about democracy and about *people,* in whose name democracy is being shaped and driven. We must talk about what this democracy bestows on us, the revolutionary idea that it isn't about the means of governance but the means of dignifying people so they become free to claim the political and moral agency.' He is so right.

For the first phase of South Africa's democracy, our nation's story has been a false story. It has been a story of ahistorical determination, of arbitrary historical demarcation. It has been a story of heroism that excluded the heroism of the people, a story of victory that ignored the courage and sacrifices of the people, a story of a future that was shaped by a vision from above, by ruling elites rendered sightless by greed and the politics of self-obsession. It is a story of external messianism that denied the home-grown prophetic faithfulness of the people; a story of icons not cognisant of the iconic power lent to them by the people. It is a false story. The story of our freedom must forever be the story of faith, hope and courage of ordinary people who, when it mattered, did not hold their dreams too cheap, their hopes too illusionary, nor their lives too dear.

Philosophers now debate 'the moral status of future persons' (the coming, unborn generations): just how much claim they have upon us, how we can have duties to non-existent beings whom we will never know as individuals, how we can even tell with any confidence just what might benefit them. The debate is not an arcane art: it is dealing with realities and our understanding of our responsibilities now. It is what we teach our children about gender and the relationships we encourage in our understanding of the ways in which power works. It is the mind- and life-shaping habits we acquire, what Berkeley sociologist Robert Bellah calls 'habits of the heart'; the understanding of our oneness with nature and the earth, how we regard money and material goods, how deep are the levels of our respect for life. It is the choices of everyday life.

This revolutionary consciousness shall not find expression in the tired, worn-out slogans of Leninism that have no place in the democracy we are trying to build and determined to have. We shall be distinctly African, not in the impoverished, narrow ethnic sense that has become our burden despite all the revolutionary sloganeering, but first of all in the unbreakable embrace of all the people of this land in the wealth of diversities we represent, finding our many identities as well as our one identity in the single glorious garment woven of our past and our destiny as we celebrate and teach our children the immortal poetry which will be the enduring, compelling moment of Thabo Mbeki's legacy. But further, and therefore, it means that we shall rise up against any suggestion that we are unsuited for a dignified life, unfit to inherit the values of our parents and hence to bequeath them to our children. We shall reject the idea that we are irreparably damaged by the past and rebel against the notion that we are somehow naturally incapable of excelling or responding to that God-given destiny which is the essence of every human person.

It means that we shall not be sitting forlornly on the banks of our river of life, calling forth the pity of others, predators from without and within, eliciting their missionary zeal and messianic fervour to save us and remake us, and in the process having us conform first to the caricature in their own minds and then to the creature of their own warped imagination. In the predators' efforts to save us, we know from our own experience, they were really trying to save themselves, or saving us to better serve their own interests. Today, faced with the demands of 21st-century globalisation, we must vigilantly distinguish between self-serving activism and justice-serving commitment. What Amilcar Cabral said so long ago still remains true: 'The rice must be cooked inside the pot.' We, the people, are still the first line of responsibility in, and defence of, our own liberation.

In this distinctly African revolution, we shall have to understand, enhance, celebrate and enjoy the unique diversity of this continent and of our people. We shall have to celebrate Africa's will and ability to survive and yet not allow that to be an excuse for her to keep on carrying burdens not of our own making. In this too we will have to decisively deal with inherited and self-created problems of race, economic injustices, the adverse effects of globalisation and the mindless exploitation of the earth and her gifts. We shall have to have the nerve to unmask the disasters of our own making: the tenacious belief that violence is the solution to problems, our idolisation of arms and our worship of war; the ease with which we succumb to the lure of militarism, seemingly not understanding that that is by far the most glaring exhibition, and perpetuation, of the colonisation of our minds.

In this revolution we shall have to stand up against 'cultural' expressions of oppression as regards women, whose subservience is still necessary as compensation for some deep, bizarre male dissatisfaction with their personhood. And from our understanding of ubuntu we shall have to stand up, too, for the more than a quarter million children forced into armed combat in Africa, fighting the battles for greedy and bloodthirsty grown-ups and who at 13 years old have committed atrocities most of us are afraid to see even in our worst nightmares. And for the estimated 15 million Africans still sold and held as slaves of all kinds in Africa and other parts of the world.

We shall have to expose the abuse of culture for the exploitation, rejection and dehumanisation of others, and the abuse of power for the denial of human rights or the protection of corruption. We shall have to expose those who use religion to fan the fires of racism, intolerance and violence, and be firm in our resolve that they not speak and act in our name.

A distinctly African revolution would be a burning commitment to make our world a safer, cleaner, more just place. To help the world to see not only what is, but what could and should be. We must not, under the influence of a nebulous, non-committal religion called post-modernism be ashamed, or afraid of our inborn African spirituality. That deep, indescribable connectedness to our innermost selves and to the world we live in, to the earth that feeds us, the rivers that rush with our deepest emotions, the winds that whisper with the voices from beyond our imaginings, the life we share with every living and breathing thing. The knowledge that, surrounded by darkness, we walk in a light that darkness cannot overcome, and that our lives are held in the hands of a Being infinitely greater than ourselves but closer to us than the shadow at our right hand, in whom we find our being. This is what makes us unique, and it is our unique contribution to the development of humankind.

'What we possess,' confesses Notre Dame University moral philosopher Alasdair MacIntyre of the situation in the Western world, 'are the fragments of a conceptual scheme ... We possess indeed simulacra of morality, we continue to use many of the key expressions. But we have – very largely, if not entirely – lost our comprehension, both theoretical and practical, of morality.'

As American theologian and political activist Jim Wallis laments, 'Our most basic values of civility, responsibility, justice and integrity seem to be collapsing. We appear to be losing the ethics derived from personal commitment, social purpose and spiritual meaning. The triumph of materialism is hardly questioned now ... We are divided along the lines of race, ethnicity, class, gender, religion, culture and tribe ... Our intuition tells us the depth of the crisis we face demands more than politics as usual. An illness of the spirit has spread across the land.'

The spiritual resources Africans possess to combat this 'illness of the spirit' are vast and deep. It has been to our detriment and our shame that as a people we have suppressed this spirituality in our efforts to catch up with post-modernism. We know that without them we as a people would have perished long ago. It is exactly our spirituality that will offer a way out of the dangers our society is confronted with, and we must not be afraid to claim it unashamedly. We are undeniably, irrevocably, spiritual people. Therein lies our strength, and the reservoir of creative possibilities for ourselves and the world.

This is a revolution, if we take it seriously, that will turn our South African realities upside down, bringing justice and equity and creating the 'human face' for this country that Nelson Mandela is longing for. It is not the revolution we have been told to fight for; it does not need AK 47s or bombs, it has no need for the language of violence, fear and destruction. It is not dependent on the wearied and threadbare slogans of yesterday, nor on old pipe dreams dusted off and gussied up for an uncertain tomorrow. It is a revolution that is the inheritance of all South Africa's people. In this revolution the true story of our struggle and of our democracy will be told.

It is about hope and love and compassionate justice; it is about the power to dream and do. This revolution is the heart of the matter.

16

Was God in the Struggle?
Unremembering and the Role of Faith in South Africa's Struggle for Liberation

Unremembering as ideological tool

The role of religious faith and, subsequently, of the Christian church in the struggle for liberation in South Africa can hardly be in dispute. Or so one would think. It can be legitimately argued that if the church had not played a liberatory role, the challenge to apartheid would have suffered immensely and its demise would have been significantly retarded. Throughout the struggle for freedom and human dignity, religious faith was seen as central by the oppressed.

Yet, apart from the blandest of acknowledgements, there is no attempt at all to take seriously the impact of their religious faith on those who participated in the struggle. The church, not as a single, monolithic body but as the prophetic movement of believers who found in the gospel of Jesus Christ their inspiration for struggle and their thirst for justice, is hardly mentioned. Individual Christians are mentioned, only in terms of their political leadership or their celebrity status. Their leadership is almost always divorced from their faith and they are seen in, and used for, their *political functionality* rather than their prophetic faithfulness.

This is true for both academicians and politicians, as evident in recent histories of South Africa and the speeches of South African leaders. Not only is there an anxiousness to ignore history as it really happened but there is a conscious, and constant, effort to rewrite history by omission and commission.

In certain circumstances it is possible that people might strive to forget their history because the horrors of their past cannot bear further contemplation. Psychologists teach us that the pain of suffering is often (and easily) blocked out in a collective act of forgetfulness. The violence inflicted upon them can no longer be borne, and remembering is a way of carrying the memories with you. It is a victimisation that never ends. This can be true of the perpetrators too. They forget because they have an absolute need to forget. This goes beyond mere denial. It is then not enough to say, 'We did not know.' Complete obliteration of the past is what is needed.

But we are not speaking of forgetfulness here. We are speaking of a process I shall call *unremembering*. Unremembering is a deliberate political act for reasons of domestication and control in which a people's history, or their memory, is falsified, rewritten or denied. This process is not a confluence of accidental political factors, nor is it the result of inevitable political shifts. It is an act of appropriation. Although unremembering may also serve psychological ends – to succour 'exiles' to become central actors in the internal struggle or, as seen in the tendency of the ANC, to describe the church as 'a site of struggle' – as an act it is ideological and serves a political agenda.

Since the beginning of the 1990s a few remarkable things have been happening regarding the church and its role in the struggle. First, its role, and the centrality of religious faith especially, has been all but ignored by the academic community. Second, apart from a few well-placed pre-election remarks, the role of the church in the struggle has remained almost totally unrecognised by the leaders of government in South Africa. Third, the language of the church, to a remarkable degree, has been appropriated by the state. And fourth, space for critical, prophetic witness of the church is, although not denied, nonetheless dangerously constrained.

In the name of objectivity?

One of the foremost and most respected scholars of the left in the United States, Eugene D. Genovese, who writes explicitly as a Marxist historian, has raised the question of historians' acknowledgement of the centrality of religious faith in history in a recent study entitled *Marxism, Christianity and Bias in the Study of Southern Slave Society.* It is helpful to follow Genovese's thinking here.

'Until recently,' Genovese writes, 'we primarily had to contend with the illusion that a historian could proceed without a worldview and attendant political bias and somehow arrive at an objectivity that we might have thought only God capable of.' It may be possible to keep value judgements from distorting our most determined efforts at objective analysis, but if that worldview is the response to Max Weber's plea for ethical neutrality, that in itself should warn us against our own biases and admonish us to hold the inevitable distortions to a minimum. 'We must,' Genovese insists, 'rein in our prejudices if we wish to do honest scientific work [for] we cannot escape the intrusion of a worldview into our work as historians.'

As illustration Genovese uses his own work, *Roll, Jordan Roll: The World The Slaves Made*, a major study of slave life in the old southern United States and a book that in my view has few equals and no superiors. During this study, Genovese says he discovered that 'in contrast to my own beliefs', two central issues without which the question of slavery in the US cannot be understood. First, 'the vibrant culture under conditions of extreme adversity' which the slaves forged would not have been possible 'without the centrality of religion to that achievement' expressed in the 'unique features of the black religious experience'.

Second, there were the political implications of this religious experience, which tend toward the black nationalist interpretation of the black experience in the US, and thus the 'call for serious qualification of the rival liberal-integrationist interpretation'. It is striking, he notes, how many 'fine scholars' at least recognised the last, but have remained silent on the first, simply because it does not ideologically suit them to do so. (It is amazing, albeit not altogether surprising, how accurately Genovese's analysis reflects our South African situation).

For Genovese himself there really was no choice, although, by his own admission, he found the results of his study disturbing. 'The empirical investigations,' he confesses, 'disturbed a historian with the biases of an atheist and a historical materialist who had always assumed, however mindlessly, that religion should be understood as no more than a corrosive ideology at the service of the ruling classes.'

Contrary to his expectations, religion emerged as a positive force in the book 'indeed, as the centrepiece' – for, in the end, the conclusion was inescapable:

'For while much went into the making of the heroic black struggle for survival under extreme adversity,' Genovese writes, 'nothing loomed so large as the religious faith of the slaves. The very religion that their masters sought to impose on them in the interests of social control carried an extraordinarily powerful message of liberation in this world as well as the next.'

The slaves, exactly as their descendants, and their South African spiritual kin would do later, did this by developing their own interpretation of Scripture and the Christian faith and linking it with traditional African religious experience. We note that not merely religion, as in a vague, general religiosity, but 'the overpowering evidence of *religious faith*' aroused in Genovese 'a scepticism about the reigning tendency in academia to, as it were, sociologize faith out of religion – to deny *the reality of spirituality*' [my emphasis].

It is my contention that this is exactly what is happening in the writing of South African history and in the analyses of political scientists and politicians. Not only is the centrality of religious faith being denied by South African historiography, but as a consequence, the political implications of that faith are being ignored, because, in the words of Genovese, 'they contradict our (i.e. historians') intentions'. A historian, Genovese argues, has the duty 'to make those implications clear'. But simultaneously, they have the duty 'to resist the imposition of (their) politics on the empirical record by denying or ignoring the impact of faith on the political events and on the people who created them'. Says Genovese with characteristic bluntness: 'It is one thing to lay bare the political implications of our analyses; it is quite another to whore in some ostensibly worthy cause.'

These are worthwhile observations to keep in mind as we proceed.

Was God in the struggle?

In three of the most recent, respected and widely read histories of the South African struggle against apartheid Genovese's point is clearly illustrated. In these studies the church is variously described as a 'non-governmental organisation' and an 'organ of civil society' but there is no serious analysis or engagement of faith as a source of inspiration for political action or of the role of the church as a community of faith, conviction and action, such as attempted, and proved, by Genovese.

In his 1992 study of South Africa's internal political opposition against apartheid, Anthony Marx, an American student of South African politics, recognises only that Black Theology was a significant element in people's understanding of Black Power. His comments are revealing: 'Perhaps the way in which Black Power was most influential in South Africa was through the adoption of its derivative Black Theology by popular religious figures ...' However, he continues, advocates of Black Theology, inspired by the writings of African American theologian James Cone, 'emphasized spiritual rather than material oppression, and also healing'.

This I consider a statement of shocking ignorance. Marx seems to know nothing of the roots of Black Theology in South Africa, and has no knowledge of the inextricable link between Black Theology, Black Consciousness and Black Power. Nor does he know of Black Theology as a theology of liberation, demanding a radical choice for the poor and the oppressed. He does not seem to know that Black Theology seeks an ethic of radical transformation, and the change it looks for is a qualitative change of persons *and* society; that it deals with racism as well as classism. That Black Theology has never pretended to be satisfied with 'equality' with white people, but asks the question, 'What does equality mean in a racist, capitalist, misogynistic society?' When Black Theology describes racism, economic and political oppression as a 'sin', it is not a 'non-material' emphasis as Marx claims, but the understanding that sin is not merely personal but structural; that economic injustice, by the same token, is not just systemic exploitation of the weak and the poor but an assault upon the dignity of God.

What does it mean then, that Black Theology, made popular by 'popular religious figures', was spread among people who took their religious faith seriously, as black people did and the vast majority still do? What impact did Black Theology have on the thousands who came to church, listened to the sermons, heard the preaching at funerals and the speeches at rallies, read the books and pamphlets? What does it mean for a devout people when they are told that God is the God of the poor and the oppressed and that it is the call of the gospel for them to participate in the struggle for liberation, a matter of obedience?

Black Consciousness, as much as Black Power, was framed within the parameters of a Black Theological understanding of the struggle. To say therefore, as Marx does that non-violence was no more than a 'useful tactic' or even, as he later improves on his terminology, 'inconsistent with the (Black Consciousness) movement's basic ideological consideration', is to ignore the serious debate about the use of violence in the struggle in Black Theology that had raged from its inception into the 1980s when it seemed as if the unbridled brutality of the apartheid state could call forth only one response, that of justified retaliatory violence. At the very least, the continuation of the tradition of non-violence in the struggle in South Africa in the midst of a climate of violence from all sides should call for some reflection on the sources of this critical hesitation.

Yet Marx suspects that there is more to what he says than meets the eye. 'In this,' he says, 'there was a *conscious decision* not to follow Franz Fanon on violence and also a disregard of the tradition of Marxist thought.' Surely this begs the question. The allure of the violent ethic of Franz Fanon and some advocates of Black Power was powerful, packed as it was in the lyrical, poetic language Fanon and Stokely Carmichael could employ so well. How could black people not respond wholly and immediately to Fanon's ringing call to join the 'Wretched of the Earth' in their urge to experience in their own society the 'cleansing power' of violence? How could they resist the attraction of the romanticisation of the armed struggle by the liberation movements and their universal icon, Che Guevara?

What was it that made so many young people in South Africa withstand that temptation to react with counter-violence? Or to give in to the natural inclination toward vengeance? God knows the provocation was almost unbearable. Of course many of them did turn to violence, yet even with hindsight it is hard to simply condemn those who did. What is more astonishing than the sometimes ferocious violence is why there was not much more of it? But for some reason Marx does not ask this question.

We encounter the same problem with Tom Lodge, well-known and respected scholar of South African politics. In describing the context of black politics between 1945 and 1960, he begins by stating that the 1940s was a time when the proletarianisation and industrialisation that resulted from a socio-economic crisis in the countryside and the demands of a war-time economy created a vast new urban political constituency. The established political movements came to terms with it only hesitantly and in the meantime this new army of the urban poor dealt spontaneously with the immediate problems that confronted it. These new conditions, Lodge continues, combined to create a new political ideology, a fresh assertive nationalism, which drew on two separate sources of inspiration, ethnic romanticism and working-class radicalism.

What Lodge is saying is no doubt true, although I am not sure what 'ethnic romanticism' means. But once again the politics of black South Africa is cast in an entirely secular mould. In Lodge's view what inspired black politics was this 'ethnic romanticism' and 'working-class radicalism'. Seemingly nothing else. There is no mention of religion or the personal and communal convictions so decisive for public action that arises out of a radical understanding of the biblical message. There is no hint or acknowledgement of any source of faith, so natural in the black experience, inspiring people to take risks in their action against overwhelming, terrifying odds.

It is only much later that we get a hint that Lodge is not totally unaware of this. Writing about that decisive phase in the struggle, the Defiance Campaign of the 1950s, Lodge cannot avoid mentioning that in the period of preparation for that campaign, 'a mood of religious fervour infused the resistance. When the campaign opened,' he tells us, 'it was accompanied by "days of prayer" and volunteers pledged themselves at prayer meetings to a code of love, discipline and cleanliness.' *Manganos* (women's church groups) wore their uniforms, clearly identifying themselves as Christians, and as such participated in the struggle, and accompanied speeches with 'solemn hymn singing'.

There is a tone of bemusement, even embarrassment, in Lodge's observation. Even at the tense climax of the campaign in Port Elizabeth – where there were strong syndicalist undercurrents – people were enjoined on the first day of the strike to 'conduct a prayer and a fast in which each member of the family will have to be at home; and thereafter they attended nightly church services'. Those within the black communities would not have found this surprising at all. In fact, fighting the struggle *without* this inspiration would have been unthinkable.

This should have been a natural point of entry for a more meaningful discussion on the role of religious faith in the struggle for liberation in South Africa. Anyone who has read Gandhi or Martin Luther King

Jr. knows the crucial place of discipline and the power of love in the struggle. Both Gandhi and King knew that 'discipline' was first the discipline of spiritual commitment and second the discipline to be where one was needed, to resist, and rise above, the propaganda of the establishment, the threats of the state and the dictates of one's own immediate interests, which include such basic things as having a job, the need for food, paying the rent, and sending the children to school. Both also knew that love was not an empty, foolish, sentimental notion, but the power to withstand the urge to retaliate, to force the adversary to come to terms with your humanity and thereby recognise their own inhumanity.

Right through the 1980s we saw what that 'mood of religious fervour' meant and what it could accomplish. It meant a determined decision on the part of ordinary people that since this was a struggle for justice and liberation, and God was a God of justice and liberation, God was in the struggle.

What, one wonders, does Lodge think those people in the prayer services prayed for? What was said in those emotional outpourings of feeling so typical of the black church? What did they ask of God if not for 'the strength to love' as Martin Luther King Jr. would later put it? What did they plead for if not the boldness to face the powerful oppressor, his reprisals, his dogs, his prisons, his guns? What did they pray for if not for the strength to overcome this evil, to see victory? And what inspired them if not the certain knowledge that their Lord Jesus had already faced the 'powers and principalities' and had shamed, unclothed and overcome them?

Lodge therefore discovers that during the campaign, although some speeches were 'in the strident tones of Africanism, more typically [the verbal imagery involved] ideas of sacrifice, martyrdom, the triumph of justice and truth'. He discovers, in other words, the language of biblical radicalism. Not surprising, Lodge notes that these words 'set the tone for much that was to follow'. The gospel, in all its fullness, was and remained the inspiration for these people and they could not conceive of a God who was not with them in their struggle.

No wonder it was so utterly natural for African National Congress leader Albert Luthuli to say of this struggle, 'The road to freedom is via the Cross.' Luthuli employs a capital 'C' in 'Cross', leaving no doubt that he is not speaking of the general cross human beings sometimes have to bear. This is no metaphor. Lodge knows about Luthuli's Christian language and convictions and recognises that Luthuli's religious faith and training brought into his politics a principled belief in non-violence and a remarkable optimism about the ability of whites to undergo a change of heart. 'Unlike some of his predecessors and his fellow executive colleagues,' we are told, 'Luthuli still placed great faith in the moral impact of the African struggle.' In other words, Luthuli's faith led him to continue to believe in the spirituality of politics, in a politics fuelled not by greed for power but inspired by the gospel of Jesus Christ. But as to how his faith directed Luthuli and impacted his people as he led them – not a word. This despite the fact that Luthuli himself, like other leaders before him, did not hide their faith and unashamedly proclaimed it the very basis of their involvement in the struggle for justice.

Said Luthuli: 'It became clear to me that the Christian faith was not a private affair without relevance to society. It was, rather, a belief which equipped us in a unique way to meet the challenges of our society. It was a belief which had to be applied to the conditions of our lives; and our many works – they ranged from Sunday School teaching to road building – became meaningful as the outflow of Christian belief.'

Luthuli wanted to get 'into the thick of the struggle, taking my Christianity with me and praying that it may be used to influence for good the character of the resistance.' For Luthuli, and for the generations that followed, all those black Christians in the struggle, the character of the resistance was set firmly on the rock of biblical testimony and the example set by those whose faith in God became their very life: 'Laws and conditions that tend to debase human personality,' Luthuli proclaimed, 'a God-given force – be they brought about by the State or other individuals – must be relentlessly opposed in the spirit of defiance shown by St Peter when he said to the rulers of his day, "Shall we obey God or man?"'

Lodge knows all this, but chooses to ignore it completely, as his treatment of the invaluable contribution of Z.K. Matthews likewise shows. Matthews is not mentioned for the Christian convictions he brought to the struggle, but exclusively for his proposal for the summoning of a national convention at which all groups, on an all-inclusive basis, might be represented to consider the drawing up of the Freedom Charter, 'for the democratic South Africa of the future'.

Lodge makes one disdainful reference to the 'American derived' Black Theology, as one of the 'ideological stimuli which helped to distance black students from whites' in the years of Black Consciousness and immediately after the Soweto uprising. Apart from this negative and surprisingly superficial assessment there is nothing about the impact of Black Theology as a theology of liberation on the lives of black people during those crucial years. Lodge's only concern is the negative impact of black theology, in his view, on white-black relationships (proving Genovese's point about the denial of faith in social and political struggles). He is not able to resist the imposition of his own worldview on the empirical record, and tries to deny the reality of spirituality.

Lodge and Nasson, in their 1991 study, *All, Here and Now: Black Politics in South Africa in the 1980s*, refer to the South African Council of Churches (SACC) as 'a reinforcing factor in the revival of mass resistance ... a supporter of militant anti-apartheid activity'. But how, and especially why, it was reinforcing we are not told, although a simple perusal of the SACC resolutions at its annual conferences would have offered a wealth of information. Especially the debates on civil disobedience would have been helpful. Nor are we told in Lodge and Nasson what 'militant anti-apartheid activity' meant during the days of the state of emergency, at what costs such activity was initiated and maintained, and above all, what inspired such activism. The authors do not even try to explain their use of the word 'militant' or how one could be militant without being violent.

The *Kairos Document* is recognised by these authors as 'the most eloquent expression of the SACC position', wherein 'the god of the state' is exposed as anti-Christ, a call is made for rebellion against unjust laws, and God is proclaimed as the God of the poor and the persecuted who takes sides in the struggle against the powerful and for the poor and the powerless. The theology expounded in this document was in fact the classic position of Liberation theology which had been the staple of South African radical Christianity for almost two decades by the time the *Kairos Document* was written. There is no acknowledgement of this fact, of course. Furthermore, the *Kairos Document* was not an 'SACC' document at all, but the work of a wide range of theologians, the prime movers connected with the Institute for Contextual Theology. For a discussion of the political consequences of this document both within the churches and for the ongoing struggle in the last, harrowing phases of apartheid, one searches in vain in these books.

Two further omissions must be mentioned – the Defiance Campaign of 1988/9 and the Call to Prayer for the End to Unjust Rule in1985. Time does not permit full discussion of these events here, but allow me to make a few remarks.

The Defiance Campaign, initiated and guided by the United Democratic Front, was one of the most significant political events of the 1980s after, perhaps, the success of the election boycott campaign of 1983. The name itself was intended to call to mind the campaign of the 1950s, and it was much more than just an attempt to show the historical continuance within the tradition of the African National Congress, although that, too, was important.

For me, and for the thousands upon thousands of Christians who participated in this campaign, the religious fervour that was so fundamental for the campaign of the 1950s was once again the hallmark of our own participation over 20 years later.

The campaign to challenge the government by breaking banning and restriction orders, 'unbanning' banned organisations, desegregating hospitals and beaches, organising marches and demonstrations, embarking on actions of civil disobedience, defying unjust laws, and generally making the country 'ungovernable' through a non-violent revolution must be seen as a political breakthrough of major proportions. It was intended to break the back of apartheid through sustained, non-violent, internal resistance. And in a very real sense it did. Without it, it is quite possible that the ANC would still be in exile and the release of Nelson Mandela would still be just a demand on a placard. For radical Christians, it was a call to obedience to the gospel, to 'obey God rather than human beings' (Acts 5: 29), the text so prominently upheld by Albert Luthuli. It is no wonder that this campaign, like the one in 1952, started with a church service in the AME church in Athlone, Cape Town.

The campaign was a sustained, disciplined, non-violent mass action. And it mostly remained so, despite the most severe provocation. It emerged during the state of emergency, and the reaction of the apartheid state was never more brutal. The state's violence called forth counter-violence to a degree never seen before. Still, the non-violent heart of the campaign kept on beating and in the end it won. Throughout, the UDF clung to our ideals and these, too, emerged victorious: freedom, non-racialism, non-sexism, democracy.

Throughout these times the leadership given by Christian leaders was prominent and undisputable; their call on the people was based upon and issued from their faith. The many thousands who took their faith out of the sanctuary into the streets did so because they not only understood but believed. Their faith was deeply personal and therefore deeply political. And they knew: God is in the struggle. The political consequences of such a faith are awesome, and we have seen the evidence. That this evidence is so blatantly ignored is the kind of prostitution that Genovese has so mercilessly exposed.

The Call to Prayer in 1985 remains *the* turning point for the church in South Africa and the political consequences of the Christian faith, as well as for the relationship between church leaders and the people. At a very decisive moment in South Africa's history, the 'Call to prayer' called upon Christians to engage in a new level of opposition to the state. The call to pray for the downfall of the apartheid government presented the churches with a moment of decision quite unprecedented in the country's history. There was vicious reaction from the government, the establishment media (English as well as Afrikaans), and condemnation from church leaders. The call split the traditional 'anti-apartheid churches' down the middle, bringing forth, as theologian and member of the preparation committee for the Day of Prayer,

Charles Villa-Vicencio observed, 'the most convoluted and agonising statements' from their leadership. The debate on the Day of Prayer centred on the legitimacy of the government and whether Christians had the right to 'pray them out of existence', but the real issue was the *political consequences* for Christians in taking such a stand.

The Call represented a turn away from the theology of protest to a theology of resistance. The church became, in the words of Frank Chikane, 'a church of the streets'. While the white establishment found that turn terrifying, the young, black Christian activists embraced it with liberating joy. Both understood the power of such a stand, a power against which, once unleashed, the gates of hell would not prevail.

Such a faith, as Genovese found, had driven the slaves in the Old South, and such a spirituality was also the driving force in the politics of struggle in South Africa. The political ramifications of such a faith cannot be ignored. This is not a question of pleading for a more or less formal recognition of the role of faith and the church in the struggle. My point is more direct: there can be no understanding of the struggle itself if this salient fact is not acknowledged.

I am not saying that *everyone* who was active in the struggle was Christian or that there were no other factors that inspired people to resist. It may very well be that what drove those of no particular religious faith to act were indeed 'ethnic romanticism and working-class radicalism'. But to ignore the fact that millions of black people are Christians who take their faith seriously and who have discovered in the biblical story a powerful message of liberation, who believe passionately in God as a God of justice who in turn calls them to seek justice with all their might, is to distort the struggle, and is the height of both academic and political dishonesty. It is also a grave insult to those whose faith forms the heart of their life, including their political activity. Why is it so easy for academics to recognise the misuse of the Christian faith by oppressors of all kinds and at all times, yet they cannot recognise the power of the gospel as reclaimed by the oppressed, even if the empirical evidence is there for all to see?

Eugene Genovese makes the point: 'As we are tirelessly reminded these days, the history of Christianity has been strewn with blood, but, as we are rarely reminded, that same history has contributed a body of teaching that has made possible a line of resistance and counterattack.'

'Apartheid is a heresy'

In continuing the argument I must raise yet another issue, namely that of the moral basis for apartheid. There were basically three reasons why Christian churches, and Christians individually, could play such a significant role in the struggle against apartheid. One was the power of the biblical message itself as it pertains to the issues of justice. Another involved the convictions inherent in radical black Christianity and the political consequences of these. A third was the claim by the Afrikaner establishment that apartheid could be morally justified as a Christian policy, and the importance of that claim for both the political leadership and their followers.

The intimate, interwoven relationship between the National Party and the white Afrikaans churches, and consequently the relationship between the Afrikaner *volk,* Afrikaner nationalism and Afrikaner religion, are well documented. Suffice it to say here that this body of relationships made the Afrikaner more sensitive than most to charges that their actions and racial policies were unchristian and in conflict with the Word of God. But also, these relationships were such that observers have recognised that the highly religious orientation of

Afrikaner society *all but required* a theological basis to rationalise apartheid.

That theological basis was indeed given by the Afrikaner churches and became known as the 'theology of apartheid', a sophisticated theological construction that went far beyond the rather crude 'children of Ham' theology so prevalent in the discussions about race in the United States. And it was to become both the moral foundation and the cement that upheld Afrikaner nationalism and its most ambitious spawn, apartheid. Moreover, not only was the policy of apartheid the direct result of the mission policies of the white Dutch Reformed Church, but this church had done more than any other cultural or political body in the creation of apartheid.

Far more than merely a political philosophy and a socio-economic programme, apartheid became, to quote Reverend David P. Botha, an 'all-embracing, soteriologically loaded' philosophy, underpinned by a theological rationale second to none – in other words, a philosophy that pretended to offer a solution for the political as well as spiritual *salvation* of South Africa and its people. Indeed, apartheid, in its claims and pretentions, was not modest. This undisguised spiritual dimension functioned as a formidable cover for the atrocities of apartheid and acted as a haven for the conscience of white South Africa where their innocence could be protected. But it was, simultaneously, Afrikaner Christian nationalism's Achilles heel, because apartheid's call on the gospel opened, and made apartheid vulnerable to, the critique of the gospel. The more apartheid's Christian apologists misused the Bible to bolster their theological and political construction, the more this construction was vulnerable to the dynamic power of the Bible to blow it apart. And the power of the Bible was what Christians who took the Bible seriously understood so well.

Black Christians' sustained attack on the theology of apartheid and the 'heresy' declaration by the ecumenical movement worldwide effectively eroded the moral basis of that system and had a devastating impact on the Afrikaner's ability to continue to believe in apartheid, undermining their enthusiasm to defend it. H.W. van de Merwe ascribed the decline of apartheid in no small measure to the 'theological retraction' forced upon the Dutch Reformed Church by this victory over the moral and theological basis of apartheid.

Dr Andries Treurnicht, long-time DRC minister and leader of the Conservative Party, made the belief in the morality of apartheid clear: 'I know of no other policy as moral, as responsible to Scripture, as the policy of separate development ... If the Christian Afrikaner can be convinced that there are no principles of biblical foundations for this policy of separate development, it is but a step to the conviction that it is unchristian. And if we believe it is unchristian or immoral it is our obligation to fight it.'

We may not have initially convinced the Afrikaner on this issue, but we made it impossible for them to openly defend the legitimacy of their position. When the moral foundations of apartheid and its theological pretensions were stripped away, all that was left was the naked lust for power, utter rapaciousness and greed, and the exposed nerves of an isolated people with a siege mentality; a fearful, tortured conscience, and guns. To be sure, not many actually turned around and fought apartheid, but most had lost the will to *defend* it. As a consequence almost none were willing still to die for it. And it was the creation of this moral void that opened the possibilities for negotiations with the ANC.

'My power and the might of my own hand'

These words come from the book of Deuteronomy in the Hebrew Bible. The purpose of this discussion has not been to gain 'recognition' from the government or to extract 'payback' but rather to acknowledge the presence and the power of God in history, and the role of faith in the integrity of our democracy. The issue at stake here is *unremembering*.

The text under discussion is interesting and speaks forcefully to the issue. 'When you have eaten your fill and have built fine houses and live in them, and when your herds and flocks have multiplied, then do not exalt yourself, forgetting the Lord your God, who brought you out of the land of Egypt, out of the house of slavery, who led you through the great and terrible wilderness ... Do not say to yourself, my power and the might of my own hand have gotten me this wealth. But remember ...' (Deut. 8: 12–17)

The forgetfulness of which Deuteronomy warns is indeed the great temptation, and it is the calling of the church to make sure that the nation does not forget. Remembering where we have come from, and who it was who brought us here is the surest way of preventing us from falling into the trap of a new idolatry. Remembering the presence of God in the struggle will also help us to remember those closest to the heart of God: the poor, the weak, the voiceless and the defenceless, the powerless and the needy, the widows and orphans, the stranger, those with no name in the streets. To remember God is to remember those who are so casually excluded from the secular covenant between the power elites of this world. The more wealth the rich accumulates, the more the 'trickles' that come down to the poor.

But we must do this for yet another reason. It was the extraordinary moral courage of South Africa's oppressed people that gripped the imagination of the world through all the decades of struggle. But what really astonished people worldwide was the even more extraordinary magnanimity of our people when they succeeded in their largely peaceful transformation from apartheid to democracy. Nelson Mandela called for tolerance, forgiveness and reconciliation. And the surprising thing is, the people responded. In light of the horrific history of apartheid this was a most amazing thing.

How did South Africa's oppressed people do it, and where did Mandela find the courage to call upon them thus? He asked for this because he knew he could draw from the deep well of spirituality from which his people had drunk for so long. Mandela has a long history with his people in our struggle. He was there during the first Defiance Campaign and he saw with his own eyes the strength the people derived from their faith. He knows what and who inspired them to take those risks, face those dangers, make those sacrifices. That is why his language echoed so much the language of the church: forgiveness, reconciliation, peace. Mr Mandela also knew what was at the heart of the struggle as it continued for all those 27 years he spent in prison.

People spoke of the need for reconciliation even while they were in the midst of the storm, and this was not seen as a clever tactic to allay the fears of whites or conservative blacks but as an indispensable end of the struggle. What I tried to say about reconciliation and non-racialism at the launch of the UDF in 1983 – and the thunderous reactions of the crowd proved this – was that our way, based on our faith, was to offer forgiveness and reconciliation to white people even before they knew how much they would need it.

It is this legacy of spirituality that Mandela could call upon and which gave him confidence that his call would be heeded even by those angry young people who, not so long before, were exhorted to 'kill the Boer' as they sang and toyi-toyied. If this spirituality had not existed, there would have been very little Mr Mandela could have hoped for. Nothing in the legacy of liberal politics or in Marxist-Leninist ideology could ever have prepared our people for the call for reconciliation which for the Christian is rooted in God's reconciling work in Jesus Christ who 'emptied himself, and taking the form of a slave, humbled himself, and became obedient to the point of death ...' (Philippians 2)

Yet these are the very principles Marxism despises. Karl Marx, as he made clear in *The Communism of the Rhenish Observer*, violently rejected Christian social principles and poured scorn on the Christian concepts of love, forgiveness and justice. Christianity has done no good, he said, because it moves at a level of 'fantasy' and 'projection' which results only in justifying things as they are rather than changing them. Christian justice is warped, Marx argues, because even while 'speaking of justice they preach cowardice, self-abasement, resignation, submission and humility'; what the proletariat really needs, he says, is 'courage, pride, and independence, even more than it needs daily bread'.

No, it is not in the legacy of Marx, nor in the radically atheistic, working-class consciousness of the black proletariat that the political leadership of black South Africa found the astonishing willingness of South Africa's people to rise above themselves and deny their most basic human instincts for revenge and retribution. They found it in the rich memory of the powerful acts of God, in the truth of the prophets, in the life, death and resurrection of Jesus, and in the joy of discipleship.

They rejected the courage that Marx spoke of for the strength that lies in once again putting their legitimate aspirations on hold, deferring once again their dreams of justice, once again not claiming reward for their own sacrifices, thereby rising to a courage far greater than Marx ever dreamt of. By expecting and accepting this, all of us, the ANC, white South Africans, Mandela and Mbeki, have done what should be done only very sparingly and with great trepidation: we have taken upon ourselves the burden of asking too much of a people who have already given too much, and who yet are willing to give even more. This trust dare not be betrayed. It is at our peril that we now ignore this truth and act as if our transformation is the result of human effort only, or, as has been argued, of a peculiar, pre-determined set of historical circumstances which we as South Africans could not but obey.

When Thabo Mbeki calls on South Africans to perform 'new miracles' he is speaking to the very people who have already given more than their fair share. He knows it, too, for he calls on the 'spirit' of the people which inspired them 'to be willing to sacrifice everything for the common good'. Mbeki insists that he is not speaking of the supernatural world when he calls for new miracles. We should, he says, draw on the 'resources' which enabled us to maintain our humour during the brutal years of the apartheid tyranny.

It might de difficult for Thabo Mbeki to admit, but with all respect we must remind him that the resources he is speaking of are those very spiritual resources, faith, hope, and love, which gave us the determination to endure, to persevere, to sacrifice and to win – those resources he cannot seem to acknowledge. Yet without *these* resources and this *spirituality* we would not have been able even to survive, let alone fight and win. For millions in our country, those whom Thabo Mbeki recognises as the poorest of the poor, the weak and the excluded, it is still true what Sol Plaatje said in 1916: 'The only thing that stands between us and despair is the thought that Heaven has not yet failed us.'

So the remarkable transformation of South Africa, and the response which made Mandela an icon in the rest of the world, as well as the willingness to respond to Mbeki's call, are directly rooted in the tradition of spirituality which in turn is rooted in the faith of the oppressed people of South Africa. And *this* is what all of us are called to remember.

Unremembering is not an innocent lapse of fact, nor is it a temporary amnesia from which the nation will in time recover. Without remembering we deny the little people of God their rightful place in history, we belittle their heroic sacrifices, for their blood will have no binding call on our conscience. We will have merely served the rites of sacralised propaganda: 'watering the tree of freedom' of which only the rich and powerful will eat the fruit.

Unremembering denies the people not only the truths from their past, but also their hope for the future, for unremembering burdens us with a closed, predetermined history from which we can neither learn nor draw inspiration. American Church historian Eldon Ernst speaks of the study of history as a 'mind-blowing and heart-wrenching experience'. Without the recognition that people of faith can 'unleash forces that help to overcome evil in the world', history is empty, and ceases to be a source of hope.

We are a spiritual people – unashamedly so. This bent, this incorrigible faith, this search for the glory of God in politics, the unshakable belief that the 'handle that turns the wheels of the universe is in the hand of God' and because of that hand 'a new world is about to be begotten', as expressed by ANC president Reverend James Calata in 1938, is not just the fancy of one or two misguided people. Faith lies deeply rooted in the very soul of African people. It is indelibly written by every step of defiance, every march in protest, every act of love and solidarity and trust, every blow struck for freedom, and every single drop of blood shed for liberty. To search for the African soul and in the process seek to cut out that memory – the role of faith in the struggle – is to re-create a mutilated African.

Thus, to paraphrase what African American theologian Gayraud Wilmore said about black America: pride in what we have achieved as a people, pride in what we have to become as a nation, the dignity and freedom of the African soul – all this has no past without the religious faith of African people and the prophetic church, and without them these may well have no enduring and meaningful future.

17

Naked in the Public Square: The Politics of Struggle Funding

The root of all evil?

Every NGO knows it, and those who have worked in struggle times know it even better: you need money to keep afloat. During the struggle people's organisations were formed to respond to the needs 'on the ground'. To keep them alive and to do the work without which the struggle would have stumbled and fallen, we needed money. And that money, almost always, came from abroad. It was a reality that caused conflict within ourselves. I do not mean only fights about how and where to secure funds, and whether or what to accept from whom when offered money. Huge problems were created, for instance, when someone was suspected of having taken 'CIA money'. Rifts were caused that would never heal. Distrust, sometimes deliberately and skilfully constructed, destroyed once solid relationships, sunk carefully thought-out plans vital to our fight. We wrestled with our souls: were we, in accepting this money, even from well-intentioned folk, in fact selling precious little parts of our dreams, our hopes, our intentions and plans? Were we toning down what was really needed in the harrowing times and life-threatening situations in which we lived and worked, in order to make it palatable to donors? And wasn't that selling a bit of the soul of the struggle – a little bit of *our* soul?

At stake was not just 'the struggle'. For us that always meant dreams that had to be kept alive, ideals that could not be compromised, and most of all, lives that were at stake. The struggle was also people with names. At report-back meetings with donor agencies in those far-off lands the agenda would read 'Country report' or 'The political situation' or 'State of the organisation'. Bland and safely written, careful in the mentioning of names, for reports always got filed, always went higher up. The donors listened, sought for, and caught onto words and phrases they could handle safely and sell to their source of funding: the churches, well-endowed organisations and governments. The representative of struggle organisations would talk and think of people: struggling mothers, helpless, hungry children, angry youth, besieged communities. Parts of our work were alright: money for poor hungry children was not so hard to get for example. Even as we sat there, reporting, we would think of young people working underground, secret hiding places, safe houses and security, police files that got thicker, names that were added even as we spoke, detention and torture, plans for resistance. Other parts were trickier. How much of *that* could we tell? Even trickier: how much did the funders need to know? And trickier still: how much did they *want* to know?

The donors were mostly good-hearted people, genuinely disturbed by the vileness of apartheid. They were also deeply concerned by what they knew to be the complicity of their own governments and countries in the oppression of our people, and some of them understood the duplicitous nature of politics. We knew all that, but it was still hard to get away from the feeling that we were begging. 'Don't worry so much about it', a friend from the churches, a feisty old fighter from the Dutch resistance against Hitler, Rein Jan van der Veen, used to say, 'it's all money we have stolen from you guys in the first place anyway!' I would smile ruefully. In the bigger story of colonialist exploitation and skewed modern economic realities this was true. But I hardly saw myself making such an argument to politicians who saw themselves as 'progressive', and church 'aid agencies' who thought they were doing God's work but who in the normal course of events, found themselves in constant battle with their conservative bosses and even more conservative constituencies. And this would be crucial to remember: functionaries of funding agencies got paid for what they did. Helping us was their job, and some handled that better than others.

Sometimes, as the situation deteriorated, struggle organisations did two reports on their work. We had to. One was the official report in which the language was careful and politically correct, the agreed-upon items clearly spelt out. Then there would be the unofficial report, verbally given, where the truth of the crisis could be explained in greater detail, those same agreed-upon items interpreted, and plans and programmes placed within the context of strategy. The audience would be a carefully selected group, depending on the political mood prevailing in the donor country, and who were the trusted ones in the organisation with which we were dealing. In crucial situations and times of emergency we would work on the basis of mutual understanding and trust: the items in the publicised report could never cover the real work that needed to be done. Real names and projects would never be written down. And mostly the representatives of our donors, and even politicians who sometimes became personal friends, kept the trust. But then again, some did not.

It was inevitable that in certain circumstances funding was used to drive a domestic or internal party-political agenda over which the recipients had no control. It happened. Sometimes elections would take place in donor countries, the progressive government with whom we had worked and built relationships of trust would be voted out of power, and conservative governments would take their place. Overnight things would change. New politicians whom we did not know, or worse, whom we knew and did not get along with, would take over crucial portfolios. In Scandinavian countries, where this happened often, two of those crucial portfolios were foreign affairs and international development. Suddenly the rules would change dramatically. What could be funded was no longer the same. Items such as community mobilisation, political education, and advocacy had to disappear from the list. Anything that smacked of politics became suspect or worse, taboo. In those situations, descriptions of the ANC swung from 'liberation movement' to 'terrorist organisation' in one single election in those donor countries. Some friends in donor agencies and in the bureaucracies were creative and found ways around the new rules, some asked us to be patient until something could be worked out with the new ruling elite, others simply folded. Always, for us the consequences were considerable and sometimes disastrous. So apart from the ordinary vagaries of political funding, personal relationships and political differences, these were things that shaped our work in ways we could not always control and sometimes did not like. But struggle organisations in South Africa at the time had very little choice.

Here in this country, the politics of funding also could not escape the politics of race. Most of the organisations on the ground that did valuable political work could not, for various reasons, receive funding directly. Capacity was sometimes the problem, especially in rural areas. Sometimes it was because of prevailing political situations. But sometimes the feeling was raised (to me, many times, anyway) that overseas organisations did not fully trust black-run organisations. Just recently, the same point was made by a black participant in a conference between a donor agency and NGOs. 'The only good NGO,' this black person said, 'is an NGO run by white people.' Not much has changed since my days, I thought on hearing this. My point is that the struggle organisations were run by people obviously trusted and respected by the local communities. The issues involved were those identified by the communities. That they would be political, and sometimes intensely so, is without question. That they could not get funding directly, but only from intermediary organisations run by whites who became the conduits for and controllers and decision makers of funding to be used in the liberation struggle, was a point of great contention. Activists found those arrangements paternalistic, outright racist and disabling. It was one more humiliation we did not need: having to hold out the begging bowl to white liberals who themselves knew nothing of the struggle, were not in any way involved in it, had no interest in the outcomes we were seeking, but had the right, purely by their whiteness and privileged positions, to be trusted with decisions about our struggle, which, let me repeat, they never claimed as their own. Except, of course, afterwards, when 'everybody' was in the struggle, and 'nobody' ever really supported apartheid.

The sum total of these things made for a heavy burden and for explosive realities in communities and within and among organisations. It increased levels of distrust, created unnecessary competition, made for undignified scuffles for funding preference from donors, and distracted us from the all-important work we were called to do. Feelings were bitter. Most of all, it left us feeling naked in the public square. But we would be left exposed in other ways as well.

Am I saying that money, donor money, was the root of all our evils? I don't think so, and I hope no one thinks I am. And I hope these musings do not distract from the very real gratitude I have for those who helped to make our struggle and our liberation possible through their generosity and commitment. For, truly, without them we would never have been able to do what we did. Besides, it is the *love* of money that is the root of evil, the Bible says. South Africans were and are responsible for the evils of our society. But the feeling of having to surrender something precious whenever one has to take someone else's money persisted right through those years. It was as if we were somehow, delivering our struggle into other hands willing to give to us but not ready to bleed and become dirty for us; making ourselves vulnerable to reversals of political fortunes we could not foresee or control; having to entrust our hopes to people whose hearts might have been in the struggle but whose bodies never were.

It's all about politics

When I stood accused of having stolen donor money, my Scandinavian partners came to testify. One of the things that left me speechless and totally distraught was their testimony, especially that of Christian Balslev-Olesen from DanChurchAid in Denmark, that their donations should never have been used for political work. It was always meant for 'development' work, he claimed. I had, in other words, abused those funds, and subsequently lied to them about it. They said this despite the fact that the Trust Deed of the Foundation for Peace and Justice (FPJ), the organisation I headed, stated clearly that as a ministry of the Dutch Reformed Mission Church in Bellville, we worked on the mandate of our synod which declared apartheid a sin, a blasphemy and a heresy, and therefore were duty bound to work for the end of that unjust system. The FPJ, everyone knew, was a struggle organisation. All our work was geared toward that end. Every visit to these donor countries had been unabashedly political, with discussions occurring not only with the donor agencies directly but also with politicians, from the prime minister downwards, many of whom I knew personally, sometimes as friends. Furthermore, every single report was an analysis of the political situation and an interpretation of the political work in which we were involved. I was quite upfront with it all.

But rather than try to make an argument regarding the work of the FPJ, I have provided extracts from the reports of successive years from 1987 to 1994 to these funding agencies and let the reader judge for themselves. Copies of these reports are being kept in the Allan Boesak archives at Unisa. It's all about politics.

From 1987 to 1988

In this report I began by mentioning that the situation was worsening. The struggle newspapers *New Nation* and *Grassroots* had been banned. 'We must reckon with the fact that there will be no alternative press left at all.' I mentioned this because the FPJ had given financial support to these community papers. 'Large numbers of activists remain in detention of which the majority are children. The ruthless suppression of our people continues and the victims of apartheid continue to multiply. The banning of no less than 18 organisations and many individuals reveals the government's utter determination to stamp out all peaceful protests.'

Under the heading 'Activities' I reported: 'As can be expected, much of our funding goes to the victims of apartheid. This year, requests for aid have come from as far as Namibia. In Cape Town itself, the needs in our townships remain staggering, and especially areas like Crossroads and KTC still need special attention.

'Our cooperation with trade unions continues and we have been able to give assistance in various ways. This year we have had no specific request for mediation with management, but we have been frequently drawn into meetings with the workers themselves and our involvement here has taken the form of both giving advice as best we could and, even more importantly, providing pastoral care for those on strike.'

I then spoke of the struggle in the rural areas and how the establishment press was loathe to publish anything that was 'embarrassing' to the government. 'Resources there are few and far between and it takes a special kind of courage to work openly for justice …'

I ended the report with an appraisal of 40 years of National Party rule in South Africa: 'For the vast majority in this country (it means) forty years of apartheid, humiliation, suffering and festering injustice … Our daily involvement with the suffering of our people is a far more eloquent testimony of white rule in this country than all the self-congratulatory speeches that will be made over these very weeks … At one level it is true: the government seems more firmly in the saddle than ever before … they have been trying to "control" the situation, and they have gone to extraordinary lengths to do so. Yet the more they claim "control", the less they have it. Every time they seek to show their "power" by promulgating yet another state of emergency, tear-gassing a meeting or church service, detaining activists or killing another child, they strengthen our resolve to resist them. And so they never win. What many see as signs of power, are in fact signs of utter desperation. In fact, after forty years of apartheid, absolute white rule and ruthless, mindless violence, white South Africa in general, and the white government in particular, must face the fact that this most grandiose of all political schemes, this most idealistic of policies taking on all the characteristics of what the NG Sendingkerk calls a "secular gospel", is a shambles, a miserable moral and political failure.'

I then showed how at our schools, colleges and universities, at factories and in communities our students, workers and people had through their resistance and rejection of apartheid proved the failure of the system. 'After forty years this government is presiding not only over the demise of apartheid, it is also forced to watch the sad but inevitable disintegration of white politics. We are not saying that the fight is over, or that our suffering has already come to an end and that utopia is around the corner. But we are pleading for a different reading of the signs of the times, and for another way of understanding what makes for power, or for peace … The days of white domination are just about over and we had better prepare ourselves for this new reality, and for the final battle that will precede and usher it in.'

From 1988 to 1989

This time I fell in without much preamble: 'The battle must still be fought on many levels, and the Foundation has subsequently been involved in more issues than we can justifiably handle: from local struggles at base community level to national and international issues.' I then analysed how the changing situation in Europe, especially in the Soviet Union under the leadership of Mikhail Gorbachev, was impacting on South Africa and its internal politics. I took note of the pressures on white South African politics. 'On the one hand, one cannot say that the fall of the South Africa government is imminent. On the other hand, only the blind cannot see that the cracks in the granite wall are everywhere.'

I then spoke of the release of many political prisoners and the fact that although almost all of them remained under house arrest, their release was testimony to the results of our sustained campaigns. I wrote that we should see even this as an opportunity for renewed confrontation with the government: 'Instead of complaining that our comrades are restricted, we should see their restrictions as a new opportunity for a campaign that should further embarrass the government and heighten the sense of purpose of the democratic movement. We have subsequently made certain proposals which at this moment are being looked at by those directly involved, and I am hoping that in the next few months something will happen.'

I talked of Mr De Klerk and the political changes he might bring, the support he was getting from Britain's Mrs Thatcher and our continued efforts to conscientise the United States Congress on the question of sanctions. I warned that things would change: 'The Soviet Union simply cannot afford involvement in Afghanistan and Southern Africa. The cost, economically and politically, is too great. For glasnost to succeed, perestroika must be a success, and for that, economic assistance from the West is needed. It is therefore gratuitous for the USSR to aid what are called peaceful, negotiated settlements in areas of conflict …' I sensed that, as a result, pressure on the government and its friends internationally might have arisen. 'My understanding therefore,' I wrote, 'is that black South Africans would be extremely foolish not to take all of these matters into account. Lest we be caught unprepared (like SWAPO), we had better begin a serious programme of preparation for the possibility of negotiations in the near future. And it is with this scenario in mind that I believe that the Foundation should prepare to play a role in this phase of preparation …'

I reminded the partners of our work, locally and internationally, in the field of politics. I reported on large ecumenical gatherings in Europe and new groundbreaking work with the historic black churches in the USA, in order to gain greater support for the anti-apartheid movement there. 'We have worked very closely with the governments of the Frontline States on many issues and it is clear that this will continue ...' I reported on meetings with the Non-Aligned Movement, the Foreign Ministers of the Commonwealth and the Socialist International whose annual meeting I would be addressing the following June. I reported on speaking engagements abroad, including several international Forums on World Peace and a key-note address at a Leaders of the Future conference to discuss issues ranging from the environment to hunger and poverty, justice and peace. I mentioned the work we had done with trade unions and our political and financial support for the 'brave young people of the End Conscription Campaign who refuse to do military service in South Africa at this time'.

I spoke of the government's intentions with the so-called 'Foreign Funding Bill' as a 'hideous piece of legislation' sure to come into effect that year. I expressed the opinion that the FPJ, as 'an extended ministry of the Bellville NG Sendingkerk' should adopt the attitude that 'the government has no right whatsoever to dictate to the church how we should spend the funds we receive from other churches abroad. For myself, I would rather face trial than give up this principle.'

From 1989 to 1990

'This report is written at a time when it is extremely risky to put anything on paper,' I began, referring not only to the continuing dangers of the situation but also to the speed of political changes in South Africa. I spoke of the dramatic changes affected by Mr De Klerk and noted that 'international diplomatic isolation, economic sanctions, political pressure and internal pressure being given new life through the Defiance Campaign, were beginning to take their toll. The government could no longer afford to ignore these realities and realised that to continue the suicidal, childish politics of the P.W. Botha era would be ruinous – politically as well as economically.' I spoke of Mr De Klerk who had apparently taken good advice: 'It is to his eternal credit that he listened.'

I continued then to state what I believed should be our next move politically: 'Our view is clear: sanctions should remain in place until it is palpably clear that the process of negotiations is irreversible, i.e. free, fair and non-racial elections have been held to determine who will sit around the negotiating table; the legal process has been set in motion (through Parliament) to scrap the laws known as the "pillars of apartheid" (Land Act, Separate Amenities Act, Group Areas Act, Population Registration Act). It is in the power of the government to do so, even if, as in the case of the Population Registration Act, it requires Constitutional change. Then the government has the duty to at least announce its intention to revoke that law.

'We insist that Europe and the United States be consistent: in their relationship with Eastern Europe and Central America it was clearly understood that there would be no change in political attitude (including sanctions and, in the case of Nicaragua, war) unless there was irrefutable proof of movement towards democracy. That proof lay in the respective governments' willingness to hold free and fair elections which would lead to multiparty democracy. That was a simple, understandable, fair criterion. Our demand is that the same criterion should be applied to South Africa. Sanctions should not be lifted until the South African government meets this demand.'

Next I spoke of the ongoing internal struggle. 'Apart from sanctions, the single most important factor of influence over the past year must be the Defiance Campaign.' I was talking about the UDF decision to challenge the government by breaking restriction orders (exactly as I had proposed a year before): 'unbanning organisations ourselves, desegregating public facilities, beaches and hospitals, and most significantly, organising marches'. I called the decision a 'political breakthrough of major proportions' and mentioned how I was personally involved in just about every major march across the country. It was understood that the funding for much of these activities came from the FPJ, and activists even today will attest to that.

But then I found it necessary to explain my reasoning for campaigning so hard for the Campaign as a non-violent act of resistance.

- 'The Defiance Campaign underlined the sheer determination of our people to be free. The courage displayed by individuals in breaking their restriction orders, and by the masses in marches and demonstrations, was astounding.

- 'The Campaign was a sustained, disciplined, non-violent mass action. And it remained so under the most severe provocation, both from the State and the white public in general.

- 'The Defiance Campaign emerged during the state of emergency. The state of emergency was designed to prevent any kind of mass political upsurge, let alone any planned mass campaigns. The State's grim determination to bludgeon our people into subjection is now a matter of record: thousands were put in prison without charge or trial (over 30 000 in the first 18 months following July 1985, 40% of them children under 18 years). Many hundreds killed, indemnity for "security personnel", and wide, sweeping powers which gave rise to the most incredible brutality; no justice in the courts and a total breakdown of confidence in the legal system; the legal criminalisation of political activity and non-violent resistance; brutal, violent suppression of non-violent resistance; the silencing of the press and the persistent, day to day intimidation that became so much a pattern in our lives.

- 'At that point, all political experts were as one in their opinion that the South African government had finally found a way to squash the opposition. All were agreed that any form of defiance was self-defeating, if not suicidal. That people would find the courage to challenge these hard realities and build a campaign that would finally force the government to recognise the right to peacefully protest is a miracle of God and one of the most significant victories of the past decade; the other two being the formation of the UDF and the acceptance internationally of sanctions as a viable, effective political tool to pressure the South African government.

'We are grateful that we could play a small part in all of this. It was not at all easy to convince people that the best way (politically and morally) was a Gandhi-like, Martin Luther King-style non-violent revolution when everyone was convinced that the only answer should be a revolution based on counter-violence. The fervent belief in violence as the only answer in life was a chilling reality of black politics and frankly, seeing the state's brutalisation of politics, it *was* extremely hard to find arguments against this approach.

'Non-violent resistance campaigns work on certain assumptions: some legal space, at least one common basis of understanding (e.g. the Constitution), a sympathetic press. We had none of that. Yet the Defiance Campaign can be described as enormously successful and we have achieved much. Let me try to summarise:

- 'We have learnt the valuable lesson Gandhi put this way: "In politics the use of political power is based upon the immutable maxim that government of the people is possible only so long as they consent either consciously or unconsciously so to be governed". Martin Luther King popularised Thoreau: "Non-cooperation with evil is as much a moral obligation as is cooperation with good." We understood our own Steve Biko anew: "The best ally of the oppressor is the mind of the oppressed." The point is clear: we should no longer participate in the perpetuation of our own oppression.

- 'In defying unjust laws we are showing that "law and order" based on injustice is chaos, and that "order" in society is the result of justice, which in turn is the guarantee of order, because it is the guarantee of peace.

- 'It is possible, even in the most adverse circumstances, to claim the moral high ground. We did that and simultaneously exposed the illegitimacy of the South African government. The fact that, taking the whole of the population into account, the government drew only 6% of the vote in real terms is proof of this.

- 'Especially through the marches we have been able to live out our ideals of non-racialism. It was gratifying to see the growth of white participation as the Campaign went on. In contrast with the pitiful, grim, violent demonstrations of the far right, our marches were an anticipation of what South Africa could become.

- 'We were reclaiming the proud history of our people's political struggles since 1911. For the first time the younger generation began to understand that this too, not only the armed struggle which was forced upon us by an intransigent government, was part of the tradition of our liberation movement.

- 'For us, though, the most important element of this phase of the struggle was this: we were actively engaged in trying to save the soul of our nation. If this is to be done, we will have to learn to break the cycles of violence that are paralysing much of the country. We will have to challenge the culture of violence that is holding so many South Africans, white and black, captive. With what is happening in Natal this issue becomes more and more important; in fact, quite literally a matter of life and death. This is an area where the Foundation must of necessity continue to play a role and even enhance our activities … In the situation in South Africa at the moment, the time is long past where we address only the *use* of violence where that occurs. We must address the *belief* in violence as a solution at all. This means that we must raise this challenge to all groups involved – the government as well as the black opposition, white right-wingers as well as our own youth. We are called to address a basic political and moral flaw of which all involved are guilty: the glorification and romanticisation of violence as an acceptable, even necessary "solution" to political problems. Here lies a difficult, but nonetheless necessary task.'

From 1993

The 1991/92 report is a long analysis of the violence that was tearing South Africa apart at the time; the violence was especially incongruous, and dangerous, since it occurred during the time of Codesa and the struggle for a negotiated settlement. I then saw as our task also to continue to prepare our people 'for responsible participation in building a democracy and in safeguarding it' in the uncertain situation we were living through then.

During this period the FPJ played a vital role in providing funding for the ANC, salaries for some ANC officials, funding for the ANC's campaign in the Western Cape, including the expenses that came with visits of president Mandela, endless expenses for vehicle rent, and rallies far and wide. More importantly, however, as I mention in the previous paragraph, was our role during that most difficult period in the early nineties when negotiations were so uncertain and constantly threatened, and our country was flooded with new waves of violence. The facts say it all: during 1990, 3 600 people were killed while negotiators put together the Groote Schuur and Pretoria Minutes. During 1991, while Codesa I was meeting, 2 700 were killed. In May 1992, we saw the meeting of Codesa II. Meanwhile, 3 550 died. Just before the agreement on a new constitution was reached in November 1993, the number of persons killed was even higher: 4 450. In that fateful April Chris Hani was killed, we were on the threshold of civil war and I was asked to return immediately from the United States where I was trying to inform people there of the volatile, contradictory but important period we were experiencing, to help calm the waters. Again I was in the streets and spoke everywhere. All this happened in full light of day and donors were well aware of my activities, even as leader of the ANC in the Western Cape.

Listening to the State prosecutor claim during my trial that after Mr De Klerk's speech of February 1990 it was no longer necessary to do things clandestinely, that we were then living in a democracy, that the situation had 'fundamentally' changed, I thought that only the blind, the mischievous or the politically completely ignorant could make such statements. The point, however, is that the court accepted these arguments. All these activities were funded with FPJ money which the donors testified in court I had not intended to use even though the use of money was reported, and even though both Christian Balslev-Olesen and the Danish Ambassador Peter Bruckner had sat on the stage the day of my election as ANC leader and shared a celebratory dinner with us that night. When Advocate Mike Maritz, my legal representative, asked Balslev-Olesen whether it was his testimony that the struggle and especially my deep involvement with the sanctions campaign should not have been funded by the FPJ, he replied, 'Yes.'

I want now, however, to turn to an argument I made in the 1993 report which takes us back to the beginning of this chapter. At the urging of Beyers Naudé I had earlier written a document to overseas funders to make a case for continued, direct funding of NGOs despite the insistence of the ANC on government-to-government funding, which would seriously jeopardise the work of NGOs and community organisations. What follows is essentially a repetition of that argument in the report.

Speaking of the difficult task ahead of the new Government of National Unity I prayed that the noble ideals it had set for itself would be realised. I worried about the legacy of apartheid which was bound 'to play havoc with a Government of National Unity, its policies, decisions and its ability to deliver the goods'. I spoke of the challenges that came with poverty, lack of housing and the state of the economy. I then made the point that 'the challenges for the government will be enormous, but the challenges to the South African people as a whole and to the historically disadvantaged communities in particular, will be no less so'.

'In this context the role of non-governmental organisations, on their own, interlinked with one another and in cooperation with government will be more crucial than ever before. There is no way that the new democratically elected government will be able to respond adequately on its own to these challenges. NGOs therefore, will find their role enhanced rather than diminished in the fields of development, human rights and socio-economic and political empowerment.

'In light of all this, I want to re-affirm my belief that it would be a grievous mistake for the governments who have traditionally supported NGOs in South Africa to suddenly shift to government-to-government aid programmes. The continued independence, as well as the continued existence, of NGOs will prove essential to the process of developing democracy in South Africa. It may very well be that the democratic partners in a government of National Unity will have to depend more than it is now foreseen on the existence of genuine NGOs in order to carry out developmental programmes that could be beneficial to the community at large.

'Besides, the work of educating our people to participate fully and responsibly in the creation of sustainable democratic institutions in South Africa has only just begun and can, in reality, only be done by organisations firmly rooted in our communities themselves.'

For reasons of their own, and because the ANC insisted on complete control over civil society (and what better way than through control of funding?), funding agencies did not take us seriously, and I was certainly not the only one to make the argument. The result is that we are now facing a situation with a seriously weakened NGO sector, almost denuded of the leadership they had and had to concede to government at many different levels and selective support from government to the NGOs of their liking. Those who do accept government funding are increasingly uncertain of their independence, and weighed down by government expectations of an NGO sector that is decidedly apolitical, confined only, in the words of Thabo Mbeki, to volunteerism, *letsema* and *vuk 'unzele*. As it is, the prevailing ANC attitude is that civil society organisations should simply play a supportive role in government initiatives, and not be allowed to critically help shape both debate and policy, bringing to bear on those policies the weight of experience, conviction and moral authority on questions that cannot be answered by politics on its own.

Where the money went

I guess it's time to talk about that most painful period in my life: the trial, the conviction and my imprisonment, since most likely everyone reading this book still has those newspaper headlines in their head, 'The millions in Boesak's pocket'. The public story was the story of self-enrichment, monies stolen from poor children, betrayal of trust and the indelible shame I had wrought on the nobility of our struggle. For all these years I have not spoken in public about this except to maintain my innocence. On the day of my return to South Africa from the United States, I said that if I went on trial, the struggle would go on trial with me. That, too, caused some angry responses, as did Dullah Omar's public embrace of an old friend and struggle comrade and his explanation of how 'struggle bookkeeping' worked. Both his act of solidarity and explanation were met with derision and scorn, as if we had not just emerged from decades of struggle, situations of life and death, and as if our real experiences were no more than the myths of deluded minds created for self-justified glorification.

The (legal) reasons why I insisted I was not guilty as charged will be set out in the legal argument a legal team has put together on my behalf as part of my petition for presidential pardon. I am not seeking to make any inferences of political conspiracies or to call Judge Chris Nicholson as witness in any argument I might want to make. All I intend to do is to tell the story around the charge of which I was finally found guilty by the courts in hopes of reminding us all of the political contexts within which this happened.

This story began with no less than 32 charges of fraud and theft, with hundreds of sub-charges involving millions of rand I was accused of having stolen from my Scandinavian donors, DanChurchAid, the Norwegian Church Aid (NCA) agency, and the international development agency of the Swedish government, SIDA. In the Cape High Court, Judge Foxtrot found me guilty on three charges of theft, one of fraud, and refused leave to appeal. I had to obtain special leave from the Supreme Court of Appeal to approach that court. The legal details of this can be found in the annexure. At the end of both processes all but three charges had been dismissed, including all charges that pertained to funding from the Coca-Cola Company, SIDA, DanChurchAid and NCA. In a television interview with e.tv at the time, Balslev-Olesen, when asked, refused to admit that their accusations levelled against me (and in the process against my wife) were groundless and refused also to offer an apology. In this, the FPJ accountant, Freddie Steenkamp, was a better person than he. In court, Steenkamp had the courage to admit that he, in collusion with others, had stolen the monies from 'loan accounts', and that in fact more money had been taken than he was convicted for. He admitted that I did not know about this, and that they had completely abused my trust. Freddie Steenkamp apologised – in court and on record.

At the Supreme Court, I was convicted of three charges, two of which derived from one set of facts based on one donation, that from American singer Paul Simon. And that conviction, too, was based on an unattested letter which the Cape High Court deemed 'inadmissible' as evidence because no one was called by the state to testify to its authenticity or its contents. How that worked will be explained by others. So all 'the millions' had been cleared. I thought it important to place things in proper perspective after the very wide publicity over so many years failed to do so. I also need to tell the story of how I got involved with Paul Simon, what transpired and how the donation was made, and finally, what happened to that money.

The graceless powers of Graceland

By the middle of the 1980s American folk singer Paul Simon apparently found himself at a low point in his career. He then decided to come to South Africa, met with South African artists unknown at the time, learnt of the distinctive South African musical sounds, and returned home re-energised. The upshot of it all was an invitation to join Ladysmith Black Mambazo, trumpeter Hugh Masekela and South African music icon Miriam Makeba to join him in what became known as the 'Graceland Concert'.

At first it looked like a success story on all fronts. Unknown artists from South Africa all of a sudden found themselves on the world stage, something they could not have begun to hope for before, being black in South Africa at the height of apartheid. Miriam Makeba and Hugh Masekela, huge talents in their own right, lent lustre and enormous weight to the concert, and Paul Simon himself seemed to have found a new lease of life for his musical career.

But not all was as rosy as it seemed. The clouds were gathering. The powerful anti-apartheid movement in the United States, under the leadership of the redoubtable Randall Robinson of TransAfrica, which had the backing of some of the most illustrious names in US public life and wide public support, accused Simon of having broken the cultural ban on South Africa, of having 'stolen' South African sounds to revitalise his own career and of having 'used' struggling but talented South African musicians eager to make their name away from the stifling atmosphere of the apartheid state for his own dubious purposes. The United Nations Committee on Apartheid got involved and there was talk of putting Simon on the international cultural blacklist (the same as what happened with Frank Sinatra and others), and plans were underway to boycott and picket the concerts in the US and elsewhere. A planned world tour was suddenly in jeopardy. It was a dreaded prospect.

It was 1987, we were in the middle of the second state of emergency, violence had our townships in its grip and I hardly took notice of these things. It was only my regular contacts with the US that kept me somewhat abreast of these developments. But it was not a priority for me at all. Until I was approached by Paul Simon, who had sent a co-worker and friend as emissary to me. Jay Levy came to ask for my help on behalf of Paul Simon. He explained that Simon had not meant any harm, was innocent of the political ramifications of his visit, and thought that what he was doing was helping both South African artists and our music. All he wanted was for me to come to the US, to meet him and the South Africans and to listen to their side of the story. I went to the US and met them all. I was touched by the pleas from Ladysmith Black Mambazo: they, too, did not think it wrong, and this was indeed a great and wonderful opportunity for them, one they would never get at home. I was persuaded.

The result was that I ended up pleading Simon's case before the anti-apartheid movement in the US, meeting with them and the UN's Committee on Apartheid and its Chair, Ambassador Joseph Garba of Nigeria, several times. In the end it worked out well. Simon would make a public statement, such as the one Frank Sinatra had to make, the boycotts would be called off, the place of the South Africans on the tour would be secured and he would not be blacklisted. I had to do one more thing to help Paul Simon. In order for the public to understand that things were alright and Simon was both forgiven and accepted, I had to appear on stage with him and say a few words. I did that twice: in Madison Square Garden in New York City, and in Washington DC.

Paul Simon was very grateful indeed. In response to his question as to what he could do as a reward for me, I asked for support for our work in the struggle. He agreed. For security reasons I requested him to send the money through the offices of the United Presbyterian Church in the US, a church that played a strong supportive role in our struggle. I often wondered afterward whether I would have been safer had I simply taken the money as he originally intended: remuneration for a service provided by a professional. How would this whole thing have turned out then? But such wonderings are fruitless and frustrating, adding only to the many 'if onlys' we all seem to hold onto but which do not make our life, or our memories, any easier to deal with.

After some consultation with friends and comrades it was decided that we would use part of the money for the ongoing political work, and devote some to helping those children who had been severely traumatised by the violence of the previous few years. We would be able to get help with that. The money arrived in March 1988. The month before, in February 1988, the government had struck what it thought would be a lethal blow. Eighteen UDF organisations were banned. So were all sorts of peaceful activities as well as activists. Many were detained without trial, many had to go underground. When they were at last released after sustained pressure by the democratic movement, they were served with severe 'restriction orders'.

The government had taken the decision out of our hands, so to speak. There was no longer any question: the money had to be used to help deal with this emergency. With the help and under the guidance of struggle lawyer, trusted comrade and faithful friend Essa Moosa, we put the money to use. All of that money, after the portion decided upon for the Children's Trust was put away, was used in this manner. Assistance ranged from legal aid to emergency aid to continued funding for the new campaigns needed to combat the new oppressive situation caused by the state of emergency. Among those so assisted were trade unions and community organisations, families and individuals. The ANC of course knew all this but, like so many others, and much to my distress, decided to remain silent. This despite a promise that they would take 'collective responsibility' in this matter. A statement would have been made, and there was even talk of an advertisement in the papers. Nothing ever came of this.

In court, even though the state did not try to claim that I had taken this money for personal use, I was nonetheless found guilty. Judge Foxcroft would not believe that I needed and used money for my political work, and there was no 'proof' as to how this money had been used. With the liberation struggle scarcely behind us, the courts could not accept that I needed money during the struggle against apartheid under the all-powerful P.W. Botha. They determined that the money had been stolen, and for this I was sentenced to three years' imprisonment.

When a right became a cross

Over the years the question has repeatedly been raised: why did I not testify? If the court had heard my side of the story, surely the decision would have been different, some might say. I am not so sure. But it still is a valid question. Especially since the Supreme Court of Appeal held it explicitly against me: one reason for my guilt and conviction was the fact that I did not testify. I had thought that the Constitution guaranteed the right of silence and that that silence should not be taken as admission of guilt. The Supreme Court ruled otherwise. We sought help from the Constitutional Court on the basis that a basic human right had been violated. We argued that the Court's negative inference regarding my silence was a violation of my constitutional right to silence. The Constitutional Court dismissed the plea. That was the day I knew how easily, even in a constitutional democracy, a right could become a cross. I bear it to this day.

So I did not testify. Here's why. First, it was, and still is, the considered opinion of my legal team that the state had failed to present a *prima facie* case against me. There was never any direct evidence, no proof 'beyond reasonable doubt' and, besides, Freddie Steenkamp's testimony and admissions in court removed all doubt as to whether I had stolen any money at all.

Second, in my discussions with ANC comrades and leadership, especially an emotional one Elna and I had had late one night with Dullah Omar at his office in Plein Street, I did raise the prospect of my taking the stand. In order to explain the way we spent money during the struggle, and especially about the fact that we kept no 'proof', no 'evidence', no 'invoices' or documentation of any kind. We all knew that we were in a war, that lives depended upon trust and silence, that we had to keep the struggle going despite the draconian laws of the government and despite the frightening efficiency of the security police. All struggle organisations had to work this way, even though it was illegal, according to the law. All such work was not just resistance; it was regarded as seditious, treasonous. We were not sure how a court, still very much an apartheid-era court, would judge such matters. Former apartheid defence minister Magnus Malan had just been found not guilty in KwaZulu-Natal. Elna asked Dullah the question: 'Who decided to throw my husband to the dogs?' Dullah's response was simple, honest and not without emotion: 'Allan fell in the cracks of reconciliation.' Dullah Omar was one of the most righteous people I have ever known and our discussion that night will haunt me as long as I live.

I had been part of and had worked intimately with the Christian Institute and the South African Council of Churches, among others. We all, from time to time, had to work under such circumstances: no names, no documentation, no direct or indirect ways to help the security police find those who fought for our democracy. In order to persuade the court, had I testified, I would have had to call Nelson Mandela and Desmond Tutu, Beyers Naudé and Frank Chikane and many members of parliament who had administered or received monies for whatever reason in those dark and difficult days. Our democracy was young, not yet established, and there were fears of destabilisation. Some of those I would have had to call were in very delicate positions. Besides, I was told, 'there is no way they can find you guilty'. Well, they did. Even when Elna, after the Constitutional Court decision, told me that all was lost, I still could not believe it. Reality sank in when I was visited by Judge Siraj Desai who told me to see my conviction and imprisonment as 'my final sacrifice for the struggle'. I was shattered, and had it not been for the wisdom of Elna and Njongonkulu Ndungane, I would, in my utter desperation, have embarked on a hunger strike. But I still do not regret not having spoken or, afterward, not having sought public support through calling upon people's loyalty and stirring up emotions. Instead, I have kept my peace on this issue since 1994, when the Danes first made public their accusations. Others have spoken on my behalf.

Yet after all this time I still find myself asking, my comrades had known all this, and after seeing that I indeed had gone to prison, why did they do nothing? The issue is not why I did not testify but rather why they kept silent all these years. Why did no one volunteer to offer the information the public sought? Even after repeated pleas from and meetings with my wife. Even more important: Why was it so important for them that I forever be portrayed as a thief and a fraudster? More important still: Do I not owe it at least to my children to speak up now? Can loyalty to the movement go above loyalty to my children? My children, at least, deserve better. I know that legally I exhausted the possibilities years ago. Legal redress is no longer an option. President Thabo Mbeki gave me a presidential pardon, and I am grateful. The criminal record has been expunged, even though people's memories of what they think they know remain, and visits to visa offices are a recurring humiliation. But I think of the time we met in Mbeki's office at Luthuli House in the week of my appeal, and we talked of the case that was nothing more than a 'set-up', how it was not possible for us inside the country to work differently. He recalled how the young people who had to flee the country were turned into 'students' eligible for 'bursaries' on reporting lists so as not to disturb the donors and not to alert the security police. To my question as to what made Bulelani Ngcuka, as newly ANC-appointed director of the National Prosecuting Authority, support the order to prosecute, I received no direct answer.

Still, upon reflection, I must admit that my unease about my silence will not go away. Not for the reason that I had a case to answer. My legal team was absolutely right, but there is another reason. Why should I not have called my closest colleagues in the struggle, who had not been tainted by being charged with theft, to testify about the struggle situation, the way we had to work in those dangerous and life-threatening situations? How did the things we had to do to save lives so quickly become the target of scorn and the butt of sick jokes by those who knew nothing of our struggle and yet so soon sat in judgment upon it? Why would it have been wrong, or embarrassing for them to relate what the struggle was all about, what was necessary to protect activists, to feed their families, to save their lives and help them flee the country, and that all of this could be done without any regard for the frightening powers and relentless brutality of the apartheid regime and its security apparatus? Why would it have been a shame or not proper or politically incorrect to admit that we broke the laws of apartheid in order to seek and establish justice? As if they had done something wrong? Especially since, as Advocate Gumbi's investigation had found, and the courts confirmed, not a single cent had illegally found its way into my accounts? But it shows how vulnerable we all were to that strange and perverse inversion of reality as well as of values so quickly after 1994: our past, our struggle, apartheid, even in its state-of-emergency harshness – it all had to be sacrificed to the pressures of our desire to 'move on', to keep South Africa a 'good news story', to make our process of reconciliation 'work'. But why should it be against the spirit of true reconciliation to claim publicly what was necessary, honoured and respected a scant few years before, in a struggle against a system declared 'a crime against humanity', a 'blasphemy' and a 'heresy'? I think it remains true what I have said: when I went on trial, the struggle went on trial, and in many ways, that trial is not over yet. My ordeal was just a small part of it all. We have not yet begun to run against horses.

18

A Country not Destined for Destruction:
The Politics of Hope or the Politics of Delusion
Reflections 25 Years after the Launch of the
United Democratic Front

The address was given in July 2008 as the annual Ashley Kriel Memorial
Lecture in honour of a young MK activist who was shot and killed by
security police in the 1980s.

Revisiting the dream

What did we do, 25 years ago, when we converged in our thousands on
Rocklands, Mitchells Plain, to form a movement that would change the
course of history in South Africa? What did we believe in? What was it
that made us believe so much in the cause we stood for, in the promises
we made to ourselves and to our people? Why were we willing to take
so much risk, sacrifice so much, put our lives on the altar? Why were we
so captivated by a dream, and why did we believe that we could make
that dream come true in our lifetime? What did young Ashley Kriel die
for? Was it the politics of hope, or the politics of delusion?

Of course the obvious catalyst was the new constitutional plans of
the Nationalist Government; the idea of a tri-cameral parliament that
would exclude the vast majority of South Africa's people. But that was

not the only reason. We understood, instinctively and through careful analysis, what was at stake. We grasped that we had arrived at a moment of singular importance in the history of South Africa, and that the struggle for justice, its meaning and destiny, was about to be put on the scales of history against our integrity as an oppressed people. We had come not only to register our protest. We had come to fashion a dream, to spell out a vision, to make a promise. Hence we said, 'We are here to say that what we are working for is one, undivided South Africa that shall belong to all of its people, an open democracy from which no single South African shall be excluded, a society in which the human dignity of all its people shall be respected.'

We asked coloured and Indian people who were tempted by those proposals to understand that these were a hoax, a desperate search for allies by a government discredited across the world, a lure into a trap politically unacceptable and morally unjust. We spoke of black solidarity, our commitment to non-racialism and our dream of democracy. We said that 'all South Africans who love this country and who care for its future, black and white, Jew and Gentile, Christian and Muslim, have no option but to reject these proposals.' And the vast majority did.

We also said this: 'We are here to say that there are rights that are neither conferred by nor derived from the state. They are God-given. And so we are here not to beg for those rights, but to claim them.'

And then we spoke of 'three little words': *All, here and now.*

> We want *all* our rights. Not just *some* rights, not just a few token handouts the government sees fit to give – we want all our rights. And we want *all* of South Africa's people to have their rights. Not just a selected few, not just 'coloureds' or 'Indians' after they have been made honorary whites. We want the rights of *all* South Africans, including those whose citizenship has

already been stripped away by this government.

The second word is the word 'here'. We want all our rights *here,* in a united, undivided South Africa. We do not want them in impoverished homelands, we don't want them in our separate little group areas. We want them here in this land which one day we shall once again call our own.

The third word is the word 'now'. We want all of our rights, we want them here, and we want them now. We have been waiting so long, we have been struggling so long. We have pleaded, cried, petitioned too long now. We have been jailed, exiled, killed for too long. Now is the time!

The politics of delusion?

What were we speaking of? Was this the politics of delusion? The cynical politics of the past years, the arrogance of those in power, the shameful neglect of the dreams of, and our promises to, the poor seem to suggest so. But I remember that day too well. I remember the faces of those who came; I remember the joy and the songs, the determination and the steadfastness. I remember the years of struggle, the courage with which we faced the dogs, the teargas and the guns. I remember how we marched, were shot at, beaten to the ground, fell down, but stood up and marched again. I remember prison, and torture and pain. I remember the fear, and I remember the faith that overcame that fear. I remember death, the open graves and the tears, and I remember the strength of those who turned away from the grave to say: 'You can do what you will, but there is a fire we have lit in our hearts, and it burns for freedom!'

I remember all this and I know: this was not the politics of delusion; it was the politics of hope. I look at South Africa today and I see disappointment and disillusionment, anger and frustration. But I also see the resilience of hope, the refusal to give up, the strength that continues to dream. Our people are not looking for the politics of instant gratification and entitlement; they are longing for the politics of justice. They are not looking for the politics of self-satisfaction and self-aggrandisement; they are searching for the politics of hope.

When we spoke of 'all our rights' all these years ago, we did not speak of the rights taken from the pages of some liberal document and taken for granted in what is usually called a 'liberal democracy'. We spoke of the rights that would make a qualitative difference to the lives of our people. We spoke of the right to be free and the right to struggle for that freedom and the right to live in that freedom. The right to have the government of our own choice and the right to hold that government accountable; the right to fashion our own destiny and to participate in the shaping of our society. We meant the right not to be poor and destitute, not just the right not to be discriminated against but the right not to be wronged; not just the right to have rights but the right to be trusted with responsibilities, because we know how easily rights alone can fall victim to the ambivalence of paternalism or even worse, democratic despotism. By this I mean that kind of democracy where we have the vote, but are bereft of our voice, where our speech is not the speech of vibrant diversity but of controlled uniformity; where we are shown a manifesto but never a vision; where the dreams of the poor have become the blanket of the rich; where justice for the poor is a line in a slogan but not the song of our hearts.

Flirting with ethnicity

There is another aspect to the word 'all' that we must consider tonight. In 1983 we said, standing upon the incorruptible truth of the Freedom

Charter: 'South Africa belongs to *all its people*. That is a basic truth we must cling to tenaciously for now and for the future.'

We said that in defence of our view that in this new organisation we shall invite all to work together, white and black. We were severely attacked and some refused to cooperate with us on those grounds. But we knew that we were right: non-racialism is a central pillar in the political and social construct of South Africa, an essential part of our soul as a nation, and an unmissable gem in our system of values. We would not do without it then, and we cannot do without it now. So though in light of South Africa's history of racial enmity, hatred, discrimination and exploitation we understood how they felt, we nonetheless remained firm. What the UDF then became, in our prayer meetings and discussions and rallies, in our marches of protest and our services of thanksgiving, in the prisons and in the torture chambers, was the embodiment of the ideal of a non-racial South Africa.

We were not naively or romantically speaking of all white people, but rather of those 'who have struggled with us, who have gone to jail, who have been tortured and banned … those who have died in the struggle for justice.'

We were serious when we said that 'the nature and quality of our struggle for liberation cannot be determined by the colour of one's skin, but rather by the quality of one's commitment to justice, peace and human liberation'. We meant it when we said that 'in the final analysis, judgement will be given, not in terms of whiteness or blackness, whatever the ideological content of those words may be today, but in terms of the persistent faithfulness we are called to in this struggle'.

I believe this today as I believed it then. There are those who mockingly call us 'romantic' when we speak of this ideal today. They point to the 'reality' that South Africa is not a non-racial society. That in this we have failed miserably, and for all intents and purposes, we should forget about it.

I want to say tonight that those persons who argue thus have not been part of the UDF, never shared its values and its ideals and therefore would not know what we are talking about; they would not understand; or they have once believed but since then exchanged those values for selfish politics and lust for power. In their hearts, they still do not accept nor really believe that South Africa belongs to all who live in it. Hence they live in perpetual resentment that South Africa is no longer a white man's possession, or they have set their sights on claiming this country as a 'black man's land' or they hide in the draughty cave of 'coloured' politics. They still do not see the need to share the wealth of our country with all who live in it. They cannot share the vision of a common land, a common dream, a common future, because sharing that dream means sharing what you have, opening your hand to let go of what you have in order to accept what the other has to offer; letting go of the certitudes of today in order to take hold of the hope for the future. To the measure that they have excelled in their ability to accumulate, they have lost their ability to dream.

In January 1983, when I called for the formation of the UDF, I reminded the audience that South Africans' flirtation and fascination with ethnicity is an exercise fraught with danger. Ethnicity, I warned then, does not solve differences, it entrenches them. 'Ethnicity tends to emphasise group interests, keeps alive tendencies towards tribalism, white and black, and fosters narrow, ethnic nationalisms that can only aggravate an already volatile situation. Furthermore, ethnicity is inseparable from racism, however subtle it may be. The insidious nature of this evil is a warning that societies such as ours have enough problems without exacerbating their inherent racism by making ethnicity a basic, politically divisive factor.'

But this is precisely the tragic situation our country faces today. When one strays from the narrow path of non-racialism, one inexorably moves into the camp of ethnic nationalism. Or one is pulled in. When this happens, we lose sight of what is happening to all of us, because we see only what happens to us in our own little camp – to those who look like us, think like us, talk like us. We then begin to believe that the evil that strikes is targeting us and us alone, that the pain of betrayal is ours alone. We then begin to fear when there is nothing to fear.

That is why, before we know it, we begin to accuse and slander, to maim and kill in a xenophobic frenzy so utterly strange to the deepest heart of our people. That is why, throughout South Africa's painfully slow transformation processes, some Afrikaners find refuge in a new Afrikaner nationalism; they can think not of what we shall all gain if and when justice is done, but only of what *they* will lose if the disinherited get their due. That is why we saw that peculiar, but pathetic show of *boeretrots* with the De la Rey phenomenon, and they did not know how far they were removing themselves from the centre of this nation.

That is why there is a new movement for coloured people, seized by 'coloured' concerns and a new dream for justice for 'coloured' people. They do not see that if what happened in South Africa since 1994 is a betrayal, it is a betrayal not of coloured people, but of *all* marginalised, *all* poor, *all* destitute people. The problems besetting the coloured communities are problems besetting *all* poor communities right across the length and breadth of this land. The alienation they feel is shared by millions of other black people and the hope they long for is desired by millions more. If justice is denied one, it is denied all and it is not helping us when we give injustice an ethnic specificity. When Cosatu marches in the streets of our nation in protest against high prices and demanding compassion and justice, they do it for *all* poor, needy and neglected people who suffer injustice. And that is how it should be.

That is why there are those who call themselves 'African' to the exclusion of all other Africans, including the sons and daughters of the Khoi and the San who were the first to live on this continent and who gave birth to the human race; and of all those white brothers and sisters whose roots are planted in the soil of Africa, who share the lot and the dreams of this continent, who want to be known by no other name than African.

That is why there are those who seek to establish levels of suffering, levels of pain and levels of disadvantage and upon that falsehood try to build new levels of privilege. And no matter how they go about it, it always ends up with levels of colour. To narrow down our Africaness to an ethnic dimension, 'Africans' becoming 'ethnic' Africans is not only humanly degrading, but historically untrue and politically offensive. That is why affirmative action has in places taken on new forms of racial exclusion, ruthlessly and thoughtlessly throwing overboard the solidarity forged through years of struggle.

That is why even the ANC has succumbed to the subtle but pernicious temptations of ethnic thinking, has brought back the language of ethnicity into the speech of the movement and has as government brought back the hated system of racial categorisation. That is why today, everywhere we look, it takes but the merest provocation for the ghosts of racism to rise and haunt us, because we have buried them in graves too shallow and too close to home.

The flight into the imagined safety of ethnic mobilisation is understandable, but it is neither safe nor right. We shall regret the stoking of these unholy fires. The non-racialism we believed in, fought for and actually practised is in danger of disappearing altogether in our new democracy. The racial divisions and ethnic categories are back, and with them simmering tensions that are threatening to dictate the trend of our democratic discourse, the integrity of our democratic institutions and the quality of our life together.

We demanded all our rights 'here', in a united, undivided South Africa. Of course our immediate reference was to the bantustanisation of our country and the political realities these represented, the group areas and the political meaning invested in terms such as 'white South Africa'. Looking back we realise just how tenacious the legacy of apartheid has proved to be, and how we underestimated the pernicious permanency of such a system. We also underestimated just how agile apartheid was going to be in the mutations it assumed in its endless capacity to adapt to the new situation.

The homelands have been removed from the statute books and geographically no longer exist, but they are economically just as entrenched. They no longer exist in law, but they are persisting in the economic injustices and crippling inequalities inflicted upon the vast majority of our people. Likewise the group areas act has been scrapped, but separate areas have proved to be physically unmovable. Moreover, the group areas mentality seems to have been indelibly entrenched in the minds of many of South Africa's people. Too many of us live with that unbearable paradox: our bodies might be in the promised land, but our minds are still in Egypt.

That 'here' has in other ways become ambiguous. Apart from those who run away because they find it impossible to connect with a democratic South Africa, there are those who genuinely want to stay and make a contribution and are genuinely feeling that for them South Africa is a home denied. Those of us who truly believe in a non-racial, non-sexist, democratic South Africa must assure that South Africa *is* their home.

But it comes even closer. For many all over this country who gave their all in the struggle, for whom the UDF was the embodiment of their most sacred political beliefs, politics in South Africa have become a strange and frightening space. They have become alienated from those with whom they thought they shared dreams and aspirations, ideals and a vision for the future; forcibly removed from what they passionately believed in, tragically estranged from the movement they love. We must find the courage to seek, find and acknowledge the reasons for their sense of alienation; bring correction and healing, and call our brothers and sisters home.

A promise renewed

The UDF did not just make promises of freedom and democracy. The UDF was itself a promise to the people of South Africa, a glimpse of what we might become if we but believe; a vision of the destiny God had intended for us. And it was a promise for all of us, right here and right now. The people believed, and that is why we could do what we did. But the question put before us by the still poor, still destitute, still denied, but still hopeful people of South Africa remains: was it just the politics of delusion, or was it the politics of hope?

A promise deferred is a promise denied. A promise not fulfilled is a dream defiled. A promise reborn is a moment re-created. A trust once betrayed is a weakness one can understand; a trust twice betrayed is a deed that is not easily forgiven; a trust recaptured is a priceless treasure. Tonight is a reminder of that promise. We can renew it here, but the fulfillment of that promise must take place elsewhere: in the presidency and in parliament; in provincial legislatures and municipalities; in board rooms and in the courts; in politics and business, in schools and universities, in churches and mosques and temples, in hospitals and clinics, in the workplace and in our neighbourhoods; in our minds and hearts.

I am convinced that we now have an opportunity, a second chance as it were, to make real and give substance to the dreams we once had, to the promises we made, to the ideals we have held up to our people as they so bravely struggled for a better life than the one they had.

But if it is a time of new promise, it is also a time of new challenges. The reality is that in almost 15 years we have not nearly achieved what we had hoped for. Oh, make no mistake: we have done much. We have one of the most progressive constitutions in the world. We have put in place policies, processes and structures for the implementation of procedures for the transformation and development of our country. We have protection of human rights many countries still jealously seek.

We have democracy, but we lack the spirit of democracy. We have serious problems with the level of commitment of too many of our politicians. Internal strife and fighting for positions are far more prevalent than any desire to fulfill any promises of service delivery. Too many of those in power have become drunk with power and live in careless forgetfulness of their responsibility to their people.

We have not prepared for the alarming levels of corruption, for the growing gap between the rich and the poor, for the devastating results of our selfish economic choices and for the anger now spilling onto the streets. From across that dismal divide they now look differently at the rest of the nation, stunned and angry that their belief in what they hold dear has not been rewarded. We have made economic policies that favoured the rich, impoverished the poor even further and reduced their opportunities to almost nothing. We have taken the suffering, and the patience of our people for granted and now we find that the 'time bomb' is real, and ticking.

We live in a time when distrust in our democratic institutions is growing. Parliament, legislatures and local councils, the criminal justice system and the courts have not been able to completely win the confidence of the public. They turn to them not in faith, but in desperation. People harbour strong suspicions that those in power, if it suits them, will either ignore or manipulate our institutions, but have themselves not come to trust them as fully as they could.

We have been stunned, amazed and devastated by the senseless talk of violence by some of the present leadership. Not only is such talk totally out of place in our democracy, but it is a shameless abuse of positions of trust, and shows a lack of sensitivity for the task of rebuilding trust and respect the new leadership clearly needs to do. This is not the language we speak. But more than that, it is a cruel and thoughtless inversion of commitment. When Nelson Mandela testified from the dock in 1964, and spoke so eloquently of 'an ideal for which I am willing to die', he spoke of a willingness to lay his freedom and his life on the altar for the sake of the life and freedom of his people. His first thought was not taking the life of others, but giving his life for the sake of others. All of us who faced guns and threats of death could say that after him. But what we hear now, despite all the justifications, is not a willingness to die for the sake of others but a desire to kill for a cause that is not necessary to kill for, and that Jacob Zuma himself, I am sure, would not want anybody to die for. That is not the language of the politics of hope and liberation. It is the language of the politics of delusion.

Wake up from mourning

So where do we stand tonight? The answer lies within us. We can either succumb to the politics of delusion, or we can stand up for the politics of hope. We must begin by repeating what we said in 1983:

> 'This country is our country,' we then said, 'and its future is
> not safe in the hands of people – white or black – who despise
> democracy and trample on the rights of the people. Its future is
> not safe in the hands of people – white or black – who depend
> on economic exploitation and human degradation to build their
> empires. Its future is not safe in the hands of people – white
> or black – who need the flimsy and deceitful cloak of ethnic
> superiority to hide the nakedness of their racialism. Its future
> is not safe in the hands of people – white or black – who seek
> to secure their unjustly required privileged positions by violent
> oppression of the weak, the exploited, and the needy. Its future
> is not safe in the hands of people – white or black – who put
> their faith simply in the madness of growing militarism. So for
> the sake of our country and our children, whether *you* be white
> or black, resist those people, whether *they* be white or black …
> So let us not be fearful. We are doing what we are doing not
> because we are white or black, but because *it is right!*'

South Africa's problem is not an ethnic problem. Our problem is a
problem of betrayal of the poor, of a loss of faith in the people, of a
loss of vision for the nation. It is a problem of disconnectedness with
the people, of greed and hunger for power, of self-deceit and mindless
arrogance. Our problem is not believing in ourselves, not trusting
ourselves with our own dreams of justice and not claiming our heritage
of freedom. Our problem is forsaking our spirituality and forgetting
our faith.

And those rights we have fought for and think we have lost? It is time
to claim them with new intensity. All, here, and now.

Too many of us are despairing, mourning the loss of what we thought we had, bemoaning the state of our democracy, blaming others and forgetting our own responsibility. Let us be done with all that now. Remember during the struggle, when attending funerals, we used to say, 'Wake up from mourning!'

This is what we need to say to ourselves now. This is what South Africa needs to hear now. Wake up from mourning! We are a tried people, but we are not a broken people. We are a tested people, but we are not a failed people. We might be battered, and disappointed and disillusioned, but we are not defeated. We are a fighting people. We may stumble, we may fall, but we rise up again and walk! Let me say this to you tonight: I do not believe this country is destined for destruction, but for the greatness God has set aside for us.

We must say this, not to the politicians, not to the world, but to ourselves: to the parents and the children, the students and the workers and the professionals, the churches and the mosques and the temples, the organisations and the movements; to ourselves, all of us, the people of South Africa, *all* the people of South Africa, in all our rainbow brilliance: Wake up from mourning! Yesterday is behind the mist of night. Today is the gift of new arising. Tomorrow is the dawn of our awakening. The coming day belongs to us! Let us wake up from mourning and do what we know is right. Let us wake up from mourning and unite this nation. Let us wake up from mourning and take hold of our destiny. For ourselves; for our future; for our country.

Annexure 1

PETITION TO THE PRESIDENT FOR PARDON OF DR ALLAN BOESAK IN TERMS OF SECTION 84(1) (j) OF THE CONSTITUTION

INTRODUCTION

This is an application for a Presidential pardon of Dr Allan Boesak in respect of his conviction on one count of fraud (count 4) and two counts of theft (counts 5 and 31). Counts 4 and 5 arise from the same set of facts. This amounts to a splitting of the charges. The state alleged that its fraudulency misrepresented that he received an amount of R423 000 instead of R682 161 and stole the difference. Dr Boesak denied that he committed fraud or theft. His defence was that the amount of R423 000 was earmarked fro the children's trust and the difference was earmarked for his political work and expenses. Count 31, which initially compromised 100 amounts totaling R1 121 947 was eventually whittled away to compromise 3, amounts totaling R147 160.

Dr Boesak was initially charged with 32 counts of theft and fraud. At the trial court he was acquitted of all charges except 4. He was refused leave to appeal by the Supreme Court of Appeal (SCA). On petition to then chief justice, Ismail Mohamed, leave to appeal was granted. On appeal he was acquitted of further counts and the amount of 31 was substantially reduced. His effective sentence was 3 years. He has served his sentence and paid his debt to society. We might mention that advocate Gumbi who investigated the alleged charges leveled at Dr Boesak in the beginning was substantially vindicated by the courts of law. Mr President, we will in this petition try and show that she was completely justified in coming to the conclusion that she did before discussing the merits. We will deal with the principles of Presidential Pardon.

PRESIDENTIAL PARDON

The President is vested with the power to pardon. The source of this authority is to be found in the constitution. Section 84(I)(j) provides that the President is responsible for pardoning or reprieving offenders and remitting any fines, penalties or forfeitures. This power to pardon is not limited by any law and is only subject to the provisions of the constitution. The constitution does not regulate or limit such power of the President. The exercise of such power is subject to judicial scrutiny like certain limited grounds such as procedural irregularity, mala fides or illegality. Provided the President applies his or her mind to the question of pardon and comes to a bona fide decision, the exercise of such power cannot be challenged in a court of law. In the exercise of the power to pardon in individuals cases, it is difficult to conceive of a situation where a constitutional attack could be mounted against such an exercise of the Presidential power (President of the Republic of South Africa v Hugo 1997(4) SA1 (CC)).

The President has the power to pardon unconditionally or subject to such terms and conditions as he or she may in his or her discretion deem fit. It is not a prerequisite to the granting of such pardon that the person express remorse for his or her conduct or admits to his guilt. Where the law has taken its course and the person has paid his debt to society he can become eligible for Presidential pardon. A prisoner who qualifies for release on pardon is usually required to express remorse before he or she is released on parole. The exercise of such power is not an administrative act. It is a political act often granted to a person who has knowingly or unknowingly committed an indiscretion or an offence but who has made an invaluable contribution to the broader interests of society. Presidential pardon can be granted on political, social or humanitarian grounds.

The exercise and scope of prerogative powers were traditionally determined by the common law. It is now governed by the constitution. The manner in which it was exercised previously was not subject to judicial review (Sachs v Donges N.O. 1950(2) SA265(A)). This rule was however amended in Boesak v Minister of Home Affairs 1987(3) SA665(C) which recognized illegality, irrationality and procedural impropriety as grounds for judicial review. In Ex pan chairperson of the Constitutional Assembly in re Certification of the Constitution the Republic of South Africa 1996 the court held "that it has never been part of the general functions of a court to pardon and reprieve offenders after justice has run its course". The court stated that "the pardon functions is ordinarily entrusted to the head of state in many national constitutions where the doctrine of seperation of powers is strictly observed".

The concept of pardon emanates from the British legal system where royal pardon was granted. The Presidential pardon of the United States of America is to be found in its constitution. In both countries, clemency or pardon has been granted to its citizens from time to time. It is a common practice in the United States of America where the term of office of the President is due to expire. He or she pardons many of its citizens who have fallen foul of the law. The discretion in exercising such power is wide and virtually absolute. An appeal is made to the President to exercise his power of clemency to pardon Dr Allan Boesak.

MOTIVATION

Dr Boesak was convicted of theft and fraud of an amount of R259 161.00 arising from a donation made by singer, Paul Simon, to him (counts 3 and 4). This amount represented that portion of the donation that was allocated for his political work and certain expenses incurred by him. There is no direct evidence of theft or fraud. The conviction on both counts is essentially based on a letter allegedly written by Dr Boesak to Mr Simon acknowledging receipt of cheque from him via the Presbyterian Church. The admissibility of this letter was seriously challenged at the trial and correctly so. The letter was introduced by the forensic accountant who had no first hand knowledge of the correctness or otherwise of this letter. This letter was provisionally admitted, as it was the intention of the state to call Mr Simon to testify. He could have confirmed the receipt of the letter and the correctness or otherwise of the contents of the letter. It would then have become admissible as evidence. He could also have testified on the agreement between him and Dr Boesak. Such evidence would have proven whether or not Dr Boesak committed the fraud and theft as alleged by the state in counts 3 and 4. The failure of Mr Simon to testify seriously undermined and flawed the state's case in respect of such counts.

Mr Simon refused to come to South Africa to testify. The state applied for the appointment of a commission to take his evidence overseas but the trial court refused such application. The status of the letter was therefore suspect as he failed to confirm or refuse the authenticity or contents of the letter. The trial court placed very little, if any reliance on the letter when convicting Dr Boesak. On appeal, the conviction of Dr Boesak was not upheld on the basis of the conviction by the trial court. The appeal court convicted him on the basis of the letter in question. The state did not counter-appeal which would have permitted it to ventilate the appeal on a different basis. This was no doubt highly prejudicial to Dr Boesak.

Dr Boesak in his trial elected to exercise his constitutional right to silence. On the advice of his counsel and for political reasons he declined to testify. The advice of his counsel, in our view, was correct. The basis of such advice was that the state had not made a prima facie case against Dr Boesak for him to meet. This was vindicated on appeal as Dr Boesak was not convicted on the basis of the reasoning of the trial court. It is therefore axiomatic that no prima facie case was made for Dr Boesak to meet.

The SCA first admits the hearsay letter as evidence; second, concludes that it is authentic after comparing signatures and third, by inferential reasoning and in the absence of an explanation by Dr Boesak concludes that the whole amount donated by Mr Simon was earmarked for the children's fund. Whether those are the only reasonable conclusions, which can be drawn, are questionable. Firstly, at the time the letter was written the children's trust was not yet formed. The trustees of the children's fund never complained that they were changed. Neither did Mr. Simon. In the absence of direct evidence from Mr Simon or Dr Boesak what the actual arrangements were, to draw certain conclusions from the letter pointing to the guilt of Dr Boesak is highly unconvincing. It appears that Dr Boesak was granted a mandate by Mr Simon to allocate the monies and to form the trust as in his sole and absolute discretion. Hence no one queried how the funds were allocated.

The conviction of Dr Boesak on counts 4 and 5 can therefore be challenged on a number of legal grounds. They are firstly that Dr Boesak was convicted on the basis on which the trial court convicted him, despite the fact that there was no counter-appeal by the state. Secondly, the SCA convicted him on the 'letter', which was introduced under questionable circumstances, and on which the trial court did not rely. Thirdly, the authenticity of the letter was established on dubious grounds. Fourthly, the contents of the letter did not lend itself to the only conclusion that the SCA arrived at. Other interpretations or conclusions could also be justified. Fifthly, that no criminal intent could be inferred from the contents of the letter. Sixthly, that there was a splitting of charges and a duplication of convictions which arose from the same facts. Seventhly, that no prima facie was made out to put Dr Boesak to his defence. Eighthly, that without admission of the letter, the entire foundation of the conviction by the SCA would have collapsed. Ninthly, the adverse inference drawn by the court for Dr Boesak not testifying violated his constitutional right to silence as the state has failed to make out a prima facie case. Tenthly, the test of truth used in civil matters and not criminal matters where the test is beyond reasonable doubt. The fact that Dr Boesak's defence could be reasonable possibly true could not be excluded.

It is unfortunate that Dr Boesak had no right of appeal to another court in respect of the conviction on the 'new ground' SCA. The constitution provides for an accused to have a fair trial, which includes the right of appeal or review by a higher court. Dr Boesak's right to a fair trial was seriously impaired because there was no higher court than the SCA to which the appeal on the new grounds could be taken to. The constitutional court to which the matter was taken found that the issues were of a factual nature and not constitutional issues. If accordingly refused him leave to ventilate the matter in the constitutional court. The constitutional court alluded to the fact that there was a lacuna in the right of an accused to take a matter on appeal or review where the SCA gives judgement on issues in the first instance because it was the court of final instance.

It is common cause that the 32 counts on which Dr Boesak was arraigned, were formulated on the basis of the investigation by the forensic auditor, Dawn King. Most of her evidence constituted inadmissible hearsay evidence. The state failed to call witnesses to substantiate such evidence. This accounted for the fact that Dr Boesak was acquitted of most of this counts. The letter on which the SCA convicted Dr Boesak on counts 3 and 4 constituted part of such hearsay evidence. Dawn King was not able to dispute the fact that part of the donation was earmarked for the children's fund and that the balance was intended for his political work and expenses. The state at the trial conceded that the letter was hearsay evidence and did not rely on it for its conviction on the two counts. The trial court also did not place reliance on such letter when convicting him of the two counts. The trial court relied on other considerations for its conviction. On appeal, the SCA convicted Dr Boesak on the basis of such letter, giving its own interpretations to the contents of the letter and confirming its authenticity by its own observation and not by expert evidence or other acceptable evidence, and without Dr Boesak having been afforded an opportunity to challenge such observation, interpretation and conclusion. The state's conduct in conceding the inadmissibility of the letter and in argument before the SCA to rely on the letter is highly unconscionable and contrary to every notion of fairness. It was also highly prejudicial to the conduct on Dr Boesak's case.

The conviction in respect of count 31 was based on funds disbursed from the WARC account. This was a discretionary fund opened and used by Dr Boesak when he became the president of the World Alliance of Reformed Churches. Various monies earmarked or paid to him found its way to this account. When the WARC account was closed, two payments and the proceeds of Futura policies were paid of the Foundation for Peace and Justice (F.P.J). This constituted a loan to F.P.J by Dr Boesak. Later, payments were made to Dr Boesak by F.P.J and such payments were set off against such loan accounts. They were clearly legitimate transactions. The SCA found that Dr Boesak did not use the money in the WARC account for his personal purposes. In this regard reliance was placed on the evidence of Ms Sacco. Reliance on her evidence, which was contradicted by the evidence of six other state witnesses on these points, was misplaced. She left the employ of Dr

Boesak in February 1988 more than a year before the WARC accounts were closed and more than a year before the investments out of the WARC accounts were paid into the Futura policies. Ms. Sacco conceded that some the monies made into the WARC account belonged to Dr Boesak and some of the monies belonged to the struggle. Steenkamp who was also the bookkeeper, confirmed that the funds in the WARC accounts which included the Futura policies belonged to Dr Boesak personally. This direct evidence of Steenkamp contradicted any inferences drawn by the SCA to the contrary. Steenkamp confessed to theft of funds from the children's fund and the F.P.J.

Advocate Gumbi in her report concluded and we quote, "I went further and inspected Dr Boesak's accounts. There are no entries that suggest that the funds he allegedly misappropriated were deposited into this account. There is also no evidence to suggest that the funds were dealt with in another way. The trustees of the foundation, as well as Dr Boesak, failed to exercise due control over the affairs of the Foundation. Dr Boesak, as the executive director, should have spent more than he did working on the affairs of the foundation. This said in full appreciation of the role he played in the anti-apartheid struggle. Having said that, there is no evidence that Dr Boesak misappropriated the Foundation's funds as alleged." This conclusion is justified and he was acquitted of most of the charges. On the remaining charges he was convicted on legal technicalities. It is our considered view that Dr Boesak in the first place should never have been charged. This is borne out by the fact that that he was discharged on 29 of the 32 charges. The two counts (count 4 and 5) were based on the same set of facts. This amounted to a splitting of charges and duplication of conviction. On the remaining count (count 31) Dr Boesak initially faced 100 fraud and theft items. This was whittled down to 6 items by the trial court and on appeal was whittled down to 3 items by the SCA. The amount was whittled down from R1,2 million to R147 000. Both convictions are open to serious legal criticism.

Mr President to give a perspective of the involvement of Dr Boesak, a copy of the letter addressed by him to you and dated 11 June 2002 is annexed here to be read in conjunction with this petition. The letter sets out the charges, the circumstances relating to the theft of the funds, the circumstances relating to the donation by Mr Simon, his explanation for the allocation of the funds and his personal involvement in the church, in the struggle and in politics. Because of the comprehensive explanation and motivation of the various issues by Dr Boesak, it was convenient to annex it as an annexure to this Petition.

PLEA

Mr. President only you can right the wrong. We are not asking you to interfere with the judicial process and set aside the conviction and sentence. We are asking you to exercise your constitutional prerogative granted in terms of section 84(1) (j) of the constitution. Dr Boesak's case cries for Presidential intervention in the form of granting him pardon and clemency. If he was judged by his peers, the unfortunate fate which befell him could have been different. For the sake of the struggle, our people and our country, we appeal the President to exercise his power of pardon and clemency in favour of Dr Boesak. His contribution to the demise of apartheid and establishment of the new democratic order is invaluable. In appreciation and recognition thereof, he deserves to be granted such pardon and clemency. We hope and pray that you will be guided accordingly.

DATED AT CAPE TOWN THIS 8th DAY OF DECEMBER 2003

Annexure 2

11 May 1995

Rev Balselv Olesen
DanChurchAid

Dear Rev Balselv Olesen

REPORT ON THE FOUNDATION FOR PEACE AND JUSTICE

The Deputy President asked me to send you this report on the Foundation compiled by our office.

The report is based on the information available to us, which includes court papers in the sequestration proceedings against Mr F Steenkamp.

The Deputy President has not yet made the report public.

Sincerely

Miljenku Gumbi
LEGAL ADVISER

REPORT ON THE FOUNDATION FOR PEACE AND JUSTICE

DanChurchAid, one of the sponsors of the Foundation for Peace and Justice (the Foundation), ordered an investigation into the financial affairs of the Foundation. DanChurchAid appointed the law firm Bell, Dewar and Hall to conduct the investigation. The terms of reference of the investigation are not clear.

At the end of their investigation, the lawyers reached the conclusion that the trustees of the Foundation 'acquitted themselves of their duties in a cavalier and reckless fashion'. The lawyers also concluded that Dr Boesak put his own personal fate and that of the Foundation in the hands of subordinates.

The statement refers to the fact that all of the Foundation's and Dr Boesak's financial transactions were done by Mr Steenkamp, who was the Foundation's Bookkeeper.

Finally, the lawyers conclude that in the absence of 'pleasurable' explanations by Dr Boesak, the only conclusion that they can reach is that Dr Boesak has 'unlawfully appropriated to himself moneys to which he was not entitled'.

First of all it needs to be emphasised that the financial information relied upon by the lawyers is that provided by Mr Steenkamp, who has himself admitted misappropriation of the Foundation funds.

The only account from which it appears that personal payments, in respect of Dr Boesak and Mrs Boesak, were made, is the Urban Discretionary account. The only other allegations against Dr Boesak is that according to entries made by Mr Steenkamp in the general ledger, it appears as if Dr Boesak borrowed an amount of R95 799.13 (reflected as R1 139 439.00 in the lawyers report) from the Foundation, over a three-year period. For purposes of clarity the two allegations will be dealt with separately.

1. THE URBAN DISCRETIONARY ACCOUNT

    It must be stated up front that Mr Steenkamp, who kept all financial books to this account, stated that he has lost the cashbook, bank statements, cheques, deposit slips and most of the vouchers making up the transactions for this account. He has to date failed to make any of these documents available to either myself or Bell, Dewar and Hall. He instead offered to reconstruct the entries, from memory, I believe. This offer was accepted by Bell, Dewar and Hall and forms the basis of their conclusion in respect of this account. This account was opened in 1989 and closed in June 1993. The reconstruction account consists of nine pages, each with fourty entries. That means that we have 350 entries which are totally unsubstaniated. To draw any conclusion from these entries will be dangerous.

    However, if we accept Mr Steenkamp's good faith and accuracy of his memory, the following scenario evolves. An account of R851 401,34 of personal funds was deposited into this account. Mr Steenkamp does not deny that these are personal funds. He just states that he does not know where the money came from. Dr Boesak explained that whenever he received personal grants he would ask Mr Steenkamp to deposit them into this account. He also recognises some personal insurance policies which were cashed and deposited into this account. This reconstructed statement suggests that Dr and Mrs

Boesak misused R612 862.00 from this account. If he put in R851 401,34, it means the Foundation still owes him R238 538,34.

2. STAFF LOANS

A summary of staff loans prepared by the lawyers (Annexure K153), reflects Dr Boesak as having borrowed R1 139 499.00 from the Foundation. However, Annexure K1 to K8 shows otherwise. According to the entries made by Mr Steenkamp in the ledger, loans to staff members started in 1990, during the period in which Mr Steenkamp became a full time member of the Foundation staff. In 1990, there is no record of a loan to Dr Boesak. In 1991, there is an entry of R10 156.00. A life policy on the life of Dr Boesak, to the amount of R159 609.53, was used to 'repay' those loans (this is in addition to the other policies proceeds paid into the Urban Discretionary account). In 1992, an amount of R32 666.00 was entered and in 1993, R53 977.00. No entry was made for 1994. The total of these entries is R95 799.00, totally different from the amount of R1 139 439.00.

Two questions arise in respect of these ledger entries. The corresponding journal entries are either not made or are incorrectly reflected. This brings into question the reliability of those entries. Secondly, while other staff members are reflected as having paid back some portion of their loans, there are no such entries for Dr Boesak. This is explained by the fact that since Mr Steenkamp deposited Dr Boesak's insurance into this account he used this same account to pay some of Dr Boesak's accounts. Dr Boesak has consistently denied that he took loans from the Foundation. Unfortunately, Dr Boesak is not able to explain the entries because he did not make them and was not aware of them.

I went further and inspected Dr Boesak's personal account. There are no entries which suggest that the funds he allegedly misappropriated were deposited into this account. There is also no evidence to suggest that the funds were dealt with in another way.

The trustees of the Foundation, as well as Dr Boesak, failed to exercise due control over the affairs of the Foundation. Dr Boesak, as the Executive Director, should have spent more than he did working on the affairs of the Foundation. This is said in full appreciation of the role he played in the anti-apartheid struggle.

Having said that, there is no evidence that Dr Boesak misappropriated Foundation funds as alleged.

These findings were communicated to the law firm retained by DanChurchAid. They informed me that the body of their report also refers to these issues. I have myself confirmed that these facts and figures are contained by the body of the report, except for what may be additional errors in the lawyer's report. They further informed me that at the time they compiled their reports, Dr Boesak had not given them a full explanation. Dr Boesak denied this allegation. The lawyers also worked under a tight schedule.

Selected Bibliography

Allen, John, 2006. *Rabble-Rouser for Peace: The Authorized Autobiography of Desmond Tutu.* Johannesburg: Rider.

Ali, Tariq, 2002. *The Clash of Fundamentalisms, Crusades, Jihads and Modernity.* London & New York: Verso.

Amjad-Ali, Charles, 2006. *Islamophobia or Restorative Justice: Tearing the Veils of Ignorance.* Johannesburg: Ditshwanelo CARAS.

Arendt, Hannah, 1977 (1950). *Between Past and Future: Eight Exercises in Political Thought.* New York: Penguin.

Bell, Terry and Dumisa, Ntsebeza, 2001. *Unfinished Business: South Africa, Apartheid and Truth.* Cape Town: RedWorks.

Boesak, Allan Aubrey, 1984. *Black and Reformed: Apartheid and the Calvinist Tradition.* Maryknoll, N.Y.: Orbis Press.

Boesak, Allan Aubrey, 1987. *If this is Treason, I am Guilty,* Grand Rapids, MI: Eerdmans; Geneva: World Council of Churches.

Boesak, Allan Aubrey, 2005. *The Tenderness of Conscience: African Renaissance and the Spirituality of Politics.* Stellenbosch: Sun Press.

Biko, Steve, 1996 (1978). *I Write What I Like: A Selection of his Writings.* Johannesburg: Ravan Press.

Bonhoeffer, Dietrich, 1966, *Ethik.* Munich: Christian Kaiser.

Bonhoeffer, Dietrich, 1971. *Letters and Papers from Prison* (ed. Eberhard Bethge). London: SCM Press

Bonhoeffer, Dietrich, 1995, (1937). *The Cost of Discipleship.* New York: Simon and Schuster.

Bonino, José Miguez, 1983. *Toward a Christian Political Ethics,* Philadelphia: Fortress Press.

Calvin, John, 1956. *On God and Political Duty* (ed. John Mc Neill). Indianapolis: Bobbs-Merrill Educational Publishing.

Crawford-Browne, Terry, 2007. *Eye on the Money: One Man's Crusade Against Corruption.* Cape Town: Umuzi.

Dramna, Sabine, 2007. *Dietrich Bonhoeffer: An Introduction to his Thought.* Peabody, Massachusetts: Hendrickson Publishers Inc.

Du Preez, Max, 2003. *Pale Native: Memories of a Renegade Reporter.* Cape Town: Zebra Press

Genovese, Eugene, 1997. 'Marxism, Christianity and Bias in the Study of Slave Society', in Bruce Kuklick and D.G. Hart (eds.), *Religious Advocacy and American History.* Grand Rapids: Eerdmans, pp. 83–95.

Giliomee, Herman and Mbenga, Bernard, (eds.), 2007. *A New History of South Africa*. Cape Town: Tafelberg.

Graybill, Lyn S., 2002. *Truth and Reconciliation in South Africa*. Boulder, CO: Lynner Rennier Publishers.

Hayner, Priscilla, 2002. *Unspeakable Truths: Facing the Challenge of Truth Commissions*. London: Routledge.

L'Ange, Gerald, 2005. *The White Africans: From Colonisation to Liberation*. Cape Town: Jonathan Ball.

Lodge, Tom, 1990. *Black Politics in South Africa*. Johannesburg: Ravan Press.

Lodge, Tom, and Nasson, Bill, 1991. *All, Here and Now: Black Politics in South Africa in the 1980s*. Ford Foundation & David Philip.

Luthuli, Albert, 2006. *Let My People Go*. Cape Town: Tafelberg & Mafube.

Makgoba, Malegapuru William (ed.), 1999. *African Renaissance: The New Struggle*. Cape Town: Tafelberg & Mafube.

Marx, Anthony W., 1992. *Lessons of Struggle: South African Internal Opposition 1960–1990*. Cape Town: Oxford University Press.

Mbeki, Thabo, 1998. *Africa, the Time has Come*. Cape Town: Tafelberg.

Moyers, Bill, 2008. *Moyers on Democracy*. New York: Doubleday.

Ramphele, Mamphela, 2008. *Laying Ghosts to Rest: Dilemmas of the Transformation in South Africa*. Cape Town: Tafelberg.

Sacks, Jonathan, 2006 (2002). *The Dignity of Difference: How to Avoid the Clash of Civilizations*. New York: Continuum.

Slabbert, Frederick van Zyl, 2006. *Duskant die Geskiedenis: 'n persoonlike terugblik op die oorgang in Suid Afrika*. Cape Town: Tafelberg.

Terreblanche, Sampie, 2002. *A History of Inequality in South Africa 1652–2002*. Pietermaritzburg: University of Natal Press.

Villa-Vicencio, Charles, and Verwoerd, Wilhelm (eds.), 2000. *Looking Back, Reaching Forward*. Cape Town: UCT Press; London: Zed Books.

Tutu, Desmond, 1994. *The Rainbow People of God*. New York: Doubleday.

Tutu, Desmond, 1999. *No Future Without Forgiveness*. London & Johannesburg: Rider.

Van Kessel, Ineke, 1999. *Beyond Our Wildest Dreams: The United Democratic Front and the Transformation of South Africa*. Charlottesville: University of Virginia Press.

Wallis, Jim, 1994. *The Soul of Politics*. New York: The New Press; Maryknoll, N. Y.: Orbis Books.

Wolterstorff, Nicholas, 2008. *Justice: Rights and Wrongs*. Princeton: Princeton University Press.

INDeX

ph. on Boesen in WG.